Voluntary Organisations and Social Policy in Britain

D0413605

Voluntary Organisations and Social Policy in Britain

Perspectives on Change and Choice

Edited by

Margaret Harris

and

Colin Rochester

palgrave

First published 2001 by
PALGRAVE
Houndmills, Basingstoke, Hampshire RG21 6X5 and
175 Fifth Avenue, New York, N.Y. 10010
Companies and representatives throughout the world

PALGRAVE is the new global academic imprint of St. Martin's Press LLC Scholarly and Reference Division and Palgrave Publishers Ltd (formerly Macmillan Press Ltd).

ISBN 0-333-79313-7 hardback
ISBN 0-333-79314-5 paperback

This book is printed on paper suitable for recycling and made from fully managed and sustained forest sources.

A catalogue record for this book is available from the British Library.

Library of Congress Cataloging-in-Publication Data
Voluntary organisations and social policy in Britain: perspectives on change and choice
/edited by Margaret Harris and Colin Rochester.
    p.cm.
Includes bibliographical references and index.
ISBN 0–333–79313–7 (cloth)
    1. Volunteers—Great Britain. 2. Associations, institutions, etc.—Great Britain. 3.Great Britain—Social policy. I. Harris, Margaret, 1945– II. Rochester, Colin,

HN400.V64. V63 2000
361.3'7'0941—dc21   00–033360

10 9 8 7 6 5 4 3 2 1
10 09 08 07 06 05 04 03 02 01
Printed in China

Contents

v

Acknowledgements

This book rests on foundations laid by many hands.

We are especially grateful to our colleagues and students at the LSE's Centre for Voluntary Organisation. Their discussions with us about the complex relationship between social policy change and organisational issues in voluntary agencies stimulated and informed our approach to the present volume.

The individual chapters began life as papers presented to the Centre's twentieth anniversary symposium held in September 1998. They represent, however, only a small selection from a total of thirty papers given at that meeting by scholars from many countries. Our collegiate debates over those two memorable days helped the contributors to this particular book to revise their contributions for publication.

Finally, we wish to thank Irene Rochester, whose painstaking and patient labours enabled us to present a finished typescript to the publishers in timely fashion.

MARGARET HARRIS
COLIN ROCHESTER

Notes on the Contributors

David Billis is Visiting Professor at Imperial College. In 1987 he founded PORTVAC, the first university-based programme working with voluntary agencies and in 1987 he became Director of the Centre for Voluntary Organisation at LSE, which built on and incorporated the work of PORTVAC. He co-founded the journal Nonprofit Management and Leadership. He has extensive research and consultancy experience in the public, private and voluntary sectors in several continents and is author or co-author of a number of books, including *Welfare Bureaucracies* (1984), *Organising Public and Voluntary Agencies* (1995) and (edited with Margaret Harris) *Voluntary Agencies; Challenges of Organisation and Management* (1996).

Justin Davis Smith is Director of the Institute for Volunteering Research, a joint initiative of the National Centre for Volunteering and the Centre for Institutional Studies at the University of East London. His extensive research includes a 10 nation European study of volunteering and recent commissions for the Home Office and the United Nations. Publications include *Volunteering and Society* (1992) and (as co-editor) *An Introduction to The Voluntary Sector* (1995). He is editor of the journal *Voluntary Action* and co-founder and Honorary Secretary of the Voluntary Action History Society.

Nicholas Deakin holds a Leverhulme Fellowship at the Local Government Centre at Warwick University. Until 1998 he was Professor of Social Policy and Administration at Birmingham University, a post he had held since 1980. Previously he worked in central and local government and at an independent research institute. He has held numerous research grants and has written widely on urban policy, race relations and the voluntary sector. He was Chair of the Commission on the Future of the Voluntary Sector 1994–96. Recent publications include *The Enterprise Culture and the Inner City* (with John Edwards, 1993); a new edition of his text *The Politics of Welfare* (1994), *Contracting for Change* (with Birmingham colleagues, 1997) and *The Treasury and Social Policy* (with Richard Parry, 2000).

Peter Halfpenny is Professor of Sociology and Director of the Centre for Applied Social Research at the University of Manchester. His main interests in the voluntary sector revolve around resourcing issues. He was responsible for the design and analysis of the Charities Aid Foundation's individual giving survey, which ran for seven years in the late 1980s and early 1990s. Since then, he has undertaken a series of studies of the determinants of individual giving, giving by small companies, the income of the UK Jewish voluntary sector, and the impact of funding changes on the voluntary sector.

Margaret Harris is Professor of Voluntary Sector Organisation at Aston University Business School and was formerly Assistant Director of the Centre for Voluntary Organisation at the London School of Economics. Before moving into academia she worked in local government administration and research, and as a volunteer adviser and trainer for the Citizens Advice Bureau Service. She has researched and published numerous articles on voluntary sector management, governing bodies and congregations and other faith-based organisations. She edited (with David Billis) *Voluntary Agencies: Challenges of Organisation and Management* (1996) and is the author of *Organising God's Work* (1998). She is International Editor of the journal *Nonprofit Management and Leadership*.

Steven Howlett is Senior Research Fellow at the Institute for Volunteering Research. He was previously Research Fellow at the Centre for Institutional Studies at the University of East London where he worked on a project to evaluate urban regeneration programmes in East London. Other research interests have included the changing roles of voluntary organisations in local service delivery and its implications for stakeholder groups and for local governance. He has also worked in local government as an Economic Development Officer at Durham County Council where he was involved in developing and implementing projects to regenerate the East Durham coal field area.

Jeremy Kendall is Research Fellow at the Personal Social Services Research Unit and the Centre for Civil Society at the London School of Economics and Political Science. His research interests include the development of the mixed economy of social care in the UK; the social, political and economic contributions of the voluntary sector internationally; and the voluntary sector in the UK in general. He has published (with Martin Knapp) *The Voluntary Sector in the UK* (1996) and co-edited (with Perri 6) *The Contract Culture in Public Services: Studies from Britain, Europe and the US* (1997). Recent journal articles include, with Helmut Anheier, 'The third sector and the European Union policy process: an initial evaluation', *Journal of European Public Policy* (1999). He is editor of *Voluntas*, the international journal of voluntary and non-profit organizations.

Martin Knapp is Professor of Social Policy and Director of the Personal Social Services Research Unit at the London School of Economics and Political Science. He is also Professor of Health Economics, and Director of the Centre for the Economics of Mental Health at the Institute of Psychiatry. His current research is mainly concentrated on mental health services, the developing mixed economies of health and social care (particularly in relation to community care), child social care and the voluntary (non-profit) sector.

Diana Leat is Visiting Professor at VOLPROF, City University Business School. She has held research and teaching posts in a number of Universities and national voluntary organisations and has written extensively on the voluntary sector and on social policy. During 1999–2000 Diana held a fellowship in philanthropy with Philanthropy Australia.

David Lewis is Lecturer in Non-Governmental Organisations at the LSE's Centre for Civil Society and convenor of the MSc in the Management of NGOs. He has written extensively on NGOs and development issues and is author (with K. Gardner) of *Anthropology, Development and the Postmodern Challenge* (1996), co-editor of *NGOs and the State in Asia* (1993) and editor of *Voluntary Action in North and South: Reshaping the Third Sector* (1998). He has a range of consultancy experience with non-governmental and governmental development organisations (including Oxfam, Save the Children Fund, Concern Worldwide, UNDP, ODA/DFID and Sida) mainly in South Asia.

Michael Locke is Reader in the Centre for Institutional Studies at the University of East London. He has undertaken research and consultancy projects for central and local government and for a range of voluntary organisations and associations, mostly concerned with policy review or with professional or organisation development. He leads UEL's programme for the MA or Postgraduate Diploma/Certificate in Voluntary Sector Studies. He is involved (with Paul Robson and Nasa Begum) in an action research programme on user involvement in the governance and management of voluntary organisations (funded by the Joseph Rowntree Foundation). He is currently developing research on voluntary action with the Institute for Volunteering Research; on funding and capacity-building of women's organisations; and on social enterprise.

David Mullins is Senior Lecturer in Housing Studies at the Centre for Urban and Regional Studies, University of Birmingham. He previously followed a career in housing and not-for-profits before becoming an academic in 1990. He is a housing association board member.

Stephen P. Osborne is Reader in Management Research and Director of the Voluntary and Non-profit Research Unit at Aston University Business School. He is currently editor both of a major book series on voluntary and non-profit sector management, and of the journal *Public Management*. He edited the text book *Managing in the Voluntary Sector* and has written extensively on the topic of the management of non-profit organisations.

Moyra Riseborough is Lecturer in Housing Studies at the Centre for Urban and Regional Studies, University of Birmingham.

She followed a career in housing and not-for-profits before becoming an academic in 1991. She is a housing association board member.

Paul Robson is Principal Research Fellow at the Centre for Institutional Studies, University of East London. He also undertakes consultancy in a freelance capacity. At present he is leading a programme of action research to develop user involvement in the governance and management of voluntary organisations (funded by the Joseph Rowntree Foundation). The dissemination of findings from this programme includes publications, short courses, seminars and in-house assistance to individual organisations. He teaches on the governance and policy modules of the MA in Voluntary Sector Studies at UEL.

Colin Rochester is Consultancy Leader and Principal Lecturer, Nonprofit and Voluntary Sector Management, at the University of Surrey, Roehampton. From 1988 to 1999 he was Research and Dissemination Officer and part-time Lecturer at the LSE's Centre for Voluntary Organisation. He has more than thirty years' experience of working in and with the voluntary and community sectors as practitioner, manager, consultant and researcher. He has published widely on sector issues and devised and co-edited *An Introduction to the Voluntary Sector* (1995). His most recent publication is *Juggling on a Unicycle: A Handbook for Small Voluntary Agencies* (1999).

Kathleen Ross is Lecturer in local government management at the University of Birmingham. She has previously worked as a consultant with public agencies and NGOs in southern Africa, and was Lecturer in Public Management in the Department of Law and Public Administration at Glasgow Caledonian University. She is undertaking research in a number of areas including: public-private partnerships and the New Labour Government, public-private partnerships and Early Education policy; and the impact of the Voluntary Sector Compact on voluntary – statutory relationships in England and Scotland.

Lynne Russell has been Research Associate in the Department of Social Policy and Social Work at the University of Manchester since 1992. She has worked with Duncan Scott on a number of different studies concerning changing funding patterns, the impact of the contract culture, the changing role of volunteers and responses to exclusion in rural areas.

Duncan W. Scott is Senior Lecturer in Social Policy, University of Manchester. He is a part-time activist at neighbourhood level; consultant to urban and rural voluntary agencies; former chair of national committees concerned with the education and training of part-time/voluntary youth and community workers; and co-author of numerous publications on the impact of state funding on voluntary organisations.

Marilyn Taylor is Professor of Social Policy at the University of Brighton. Before taking up her first academic post at the School of Advanced Urban Studies at the University of Bristol in 1990 she worked for twenty-one years in the voluntary and community sectors, including four years as Head of Policy Analysis at the National Council for Voluntary Organisations. She has written widely on community development and voluntary sector issues. Recent publications include *Unleashing the Potential: Bringing Residents to the Centre of Regeneration* (1995) and *The Best of Both Worlds: voluntary organisations and local government* (1997).

List of Abbreviations

ACF	Association of Charitable Foundations
ATP	Aid and Trade Provision
BME	Black and minority ethnic
CAF	Charities Aid Foundation
CASE	Centre for Analysis of Social Exclusion
CCT	Compulsory competitive tendering
CVO	Centre for Voluntary Organisation
CVS	Council for Voluntary Service
DETR	Department of Environment, Transport and the Regions
DFID	Department for International Development
DSS	Department of Social Security
FID	Foreign income dividend
IMF	International Monetary Fund
LDA	Local Development Agency
LGMB	Local Government Management Board
LOVAS	Local Voluntary Activity Surveys
LSE	London School of Economics
LVDA	Local volunteer development agency
LVSC	London Voluntary Service Council
NCVO	National Council for Voluntary Organisations
NGO	Non-governmental organisation
NHF	National Housing Federation
NLCB	National Lottery Charities Board
NNGO	Northern non-governmental organisation
NSPCC	National Society for the Prevention of Cruelty to Children
OECD	Organisation for Economic Co-operation and Development
PONPO	Program on Nonprofit Organisation

1

Voluntary Organisations and Social Policy: Twenty Years of Change

Margaret Harris, Colin Rochester and
Peter Halfpenny[1]

The immediate origin of this collection of essays was the twentieth anniversary symposium held at the Centre for Voluntary Organisation of the London School of Economics in September 1998. More than thirty voluntary sector researchers from many countries came together over two days to examine the links between third sector organisations and the public policy contexts within which they operate. This volume brings together just a small proportion of the many stimulating papers prepared especially for that event. The papers here have been selected for the perspectives they provide on our theme of 'change and choice'.

The policy, intellectual and academic origins of this book, however, are older than that memorable symposium. They lie in three events which took place in the UK twenty years before, in the late 1970s. One of these was the publication of the Wolfenden Committee's report on *The Future of Voluntary Organisations* (Wolfenden Committee, 1978). Another was the General Election of 1979 which brought to power the radical Conservative government led by Margaret Thatcher. The third was the establishment in 1978 at Brunel University of the UK's first university-based programme focusing on voluntary organisations. This, the Programme of Research and Training in Voluntary Action (PORTVAC), was to become the LSE's Centre for Voluntary Organisation in 1987 and to celebrate its 20th birthday in 1998.

Enter the voluntary sector

At the heart of the Wolfenden Report was the idea of the *voluntary sector* as one of the four sets of institutions through which social needs could be addressed. The report conceptualised the voluntary sector as taking its place in welfare service provision alongside the state or public sector (where services were provided by governmental agencies); the informal sector (where need was met by households, families, friends and neighbours); and the market or private sector (where services could be purchased from commercial suppliers). The importance of *voluntary action* had long been acknowledged – not least by Beveridge (1948). And, despite the dominance of the state in welfare provision in the period following the Second World War, *voluntary organisations* were enduring features of the British social policy landscape, especially the larger national ones such as the NSPCC and the Citizens' Advice Bureaux. But the idea of a voluntary *sector* was new and was to be a powerful influence on the development of policy, practice and academic endeavour over the following two decades.

In the first place it provided a number of diverse organisations (ranging from the large service providers with their roots in Victorian philanthropy to small self-help groups inspired by the spirit of the 1960s) with a sense of common identity. It also spurred a growing consciousness of their distinctive characteristics and problems. This in turn created the conditions in which the sector developed its own infrastructure institutions and a more powerful voice in public and social policy debates. The National Council of Social Service signalled a major shift in its role and function by changing its name to the National Council for Voluntary Organisations in 1980. Instead of focusing its work on substantive social concerns like the welfare of older people or the needs of tenants on new housing estates, the renamed body increasingly concentrated on relations between the voluntary sector and government on the one hand and on ways of improving the effectiveness and capacity of voluntary organisations on the other. Councils of Social Service at local level followed this lead.

The 'invention' of the voluntary sector in the late 1970s also provided one of the intellectual segues into the radical social welfare reforms seen in the UK in the 1980s and 1990s. Once welfare services were conceptualised as occurring in different 'sectors' and once it became clear that the voluntary sector was a sturdy survivor of the postwar welfare state era with plenty of potential for further expansion, the way was open to propose a 'mixed economy of welfare'. Viable alternatives to the provision of welfare by governmental agencies could be envisaged in both policy and practice. 'Welfare pluralism' could replace 'welfare statism' as a central plank of social policy.

A changing social policy context for the sector

The idea of mixed economy of welfare was a key plank in the Thatcherite project of rolling back the frontiers of the state: an attempt to reduce the scale of governmental activity and to change its role from the direct provision of services to the planning, monitoring and regulating of services provided by other 'sectors'. There were two immediate, but somewhat contradictory, impacts on the voluntary sector and its constituent organisations.

On the one hand, voluntary organisations were propelled into the centre of the social policy stage with an expanded role in welfare provision. Instead of meeting social needs in ways which complemented, supplemented or provided an alternative to the state, voluntary organisations increasingly took responsibility for delivering 'mainstream' services which were previously provided by statutory bodies (Billis and Harris, 1986; Billis and Harris, 1992). Their importance and status were dramatically enhanced. Governmental agencies, particularly local authority departments, now *needed* voluntary organisations in order to plan and implement their social policies (Kramer, 1981).

On the other hand, although the voluntary sector's status was enhanced by the pluralist trends in social policy, other concurrent new themes in social policy in the Thatcher period were increasingly leading voluntary sector managers to feel that they were at best 'junior partners' in the new era of welfare pluralism and at worst helpless supplicants (Deakin, 1995; Harris, 1998a). The market became the dominant model for understanding the relationship between governmental organisations and agencies in other sectors. Thus voluntary organisations became 'providers' and 'contractors', competing to sell their services to government

'purchasers' and increasingly guided by agreements which specified expected performance levels in some detail. At the same
time, commercial business practices became the preferred model
for managing all organisations, irrespective of sector, and voluntary
organisations were expected to demonstrate that they were
'business-like' if they wanted to participate in the social policy
market-place.

These seismic shifts, with their challenging new demands on
voluntary sector organisations, transformed the British social policy
landscape during the 1980s and early 1990s. At the time of writing,
as the 1990s decade draws to its close, the new landscape appears
to be settling down and is not likely to be subject to any further
major shifts in the near future. Like its immediate Conservative
predecessors, the Blair government sees the private and voluntary sectors as key instruments for the delivery of its policies. It
has also continued in the Thatcherite tradition of expecting the
voluntary sector to demonstrate its efficiency and effectiveness
and to submit itself to close monitoring and regulation. True,
the language and style of policy discourse are softer and generally more empathetic to the sector: the talk is of 'partnership',
'compacts' and a 'Third Way' conducive to a flourishing 'third
sector'. There is also an acknowledgement of the distinctive
features of the voluntary sector and the contribution it can
make to 'civil society' and new forms of governance (Giddens,
1998). But it remains the case that the social policy expectations
of voluntary organisations and the voluntary sector have undergone a dramatic transformation in the twenty or so years since
the Wolfenden Committee reported and Mrs Thatcher entered
10 Downing Street.

An academic response

In that same twenty-year period in which the social policy landscape underwent dramatic change and the concept of a voluntary
sector gained currency, the Centre for Voluntary Organisation
developed from its modest and tentative beginnings (Billis and
Harris, 1996a) into one of the world's leading centres for the
study of third sector organisations. Research projects, workshops
and consultancies and a steady stream of books, articles and

working papers contributed to the development of a theory of the voluntary sector and underpinned a substantial programme of postgraduate teaching. A growing number of PhD candidates were attracted to the Centre and well over two hundred students graduated from the pioneering MSc in Voluntary Sector Organisation which was established in 1984. A second Masters programme for people working in non-governmental organisations in developing countries was launched in 1995.

The Centre's development in its first twenty years reflected the growing importance of the voluntary organisations which were the focus of its work: a focus which was appreciated not only by students, researchers, policy analysts and practitioners but also by a small group of charitable funders who provided crucial support.[2] It also reflected the enduring relevance of the Centre's two key founding principles. The first of these principles was a recognition of the need to bridge the traditional gap between 'practice' and 'theory': between, on the one hand, the day-to-day challenges which face those who manage and lead voluntary agencies and, on the other, what academics choose to study and write about. From the outset, the PORTVAC/CVO research agenda was set by voluntary sector practitioners who took part in collaborative projects and workshops with Centre staff. Emerging research findings were fed back and tested against practitioner experience.

Theories were developed but they were 'usable' theories (Billis, 1984) providing explanations which helped practitioners to understand why things happened in their organisations the way they did and which suggested appropriate responses to practical problems of organisation and management. Postgraduate students were encouraged to take a similar approach so that they completed their studies with a collection of theoretical tools to apply to the challenges they would face in the future.

Reflecting this founding principle of linking theory to practice, the 15th anniversary celebration of the CVO in 1994 took the form of a symposium in which voluntary sector managers and researchers participated. The researchers used their own research and the work of others to throw light on some of the key practical challenges of organisation and management in voluntary agencies at that time. Their papers – edited in the light of comments by the practitioners – were subsequently published in book form as *Voluntary Agencies: Challenges of Organisation and Management* (Billis and Harris, 1996b).

The present book can be seen as a companion to this earlier work. The occasion for its development was the 20th anniversary of the establishment of the Centre. The theme for the symposium organised to mark this event was the second key founding principle of the programme: the need to explore the link between public and social policy on the one hand and voluntary sector organisational issues on the other. As David Billis, the founding Director of PORTVAC/CVO, has argued, 'models of organisation can help to shed light on public policy and, conversely . . . public policy must take account of the fundamental structural characteristics of different organisations (Billis, 1993, p. 16).

The CVO celebration in 1998 thus marked twenty years of the Centre's own growth and achievement by looking at the fundamental change in social policy that had taken place during its lifetime and the new opportunities and challenges it had created for voluntary organisations. In tackling this task, members of the Centre and their guests were able to draw on the parallel development of research interest in the voluntary sector over the same twenty-year period.

Twenty years of voluntary sector research

At the time of the establishment of PORTVAC in 1978, there was a mere handful of researchers in the UK who had demonstrated any kind of ongoing interest in volunteering and/or voluntary organisations. Even in the United States, the non-profit sector was only just starting to emerge as a topic for serious academic attention, boosted by the establishment of PONPO (Program on Nonprofit Organizations) at Yale University in 1976. But during the 1980s and 1990s, academics played an important role in securing visibility for the voluntary sector in policy debates and in securing respect for its distinguishing characteristics. This expanding body of voluntary sector research can be grouped roughly under five themes. These are sketched out in the following subsections along with some observations about the ways in which the research was influenced by, and itself influenced, public and social policy debates over the same period.

How do voluntary organisations differ from other organisations?

Many of the policy arguments for a mixed economy of welfare are founded on claims that voluntary sector organisations differ from those in the private and public sectors. Numerous studies have sought to identify and describe these differences. For example, the Wolfenden Committee (1978) sponsored research which maintained that voluntary organisations were cost-effective, innovative, flexible and pioneering. Welfare pluralists have argued that voluntary organisations are responsive, close to needs, participative and empowering, especially in contrast with their local authority service provider partners (Hadley and Hatch, 1982).

Knapp and his colleagues (1990) subjected a list of the supposedly distinctive features of voluntary organisations to scrutiny in the course of investigating whether they provide an adequate rationale for government support of the sector. They examined the provision of different services; the provision of specialised services; cost-effective provision of services; flexibility in responding to differences and changes in need; innovation; advocacy; and citizen participation through the voluntary contribution of money and time. They concluded that some claimed advantages were untestable and that for others the empirical evidence was inconsistent. Similarly, after reviewing six broad groups of purported differences between for-profit and non-profit organisations – their goals, values, financial strategy, structure, staffing and skills, and stakeholders – Leat (1995) concluded that the two types of organisation could not be differentiated on these dimensions.

However Billis and Harris (1996c) found that voluntary organisations do share common features and challenges which are distinctive, if not necessarily unique to the sector, and Billis and Glennerster (1998) have argued that voluntary sector organisations have *comparative* advantages in relation to other sectors in certain kinds of policy environments. Harris (1998b) further notes that voluntary *associations*, such as self-help groups, neighbourhood associations, leisure groups and professional and trade associations, face distinctive organisational challenges that may not occur in larger, bureaucratic voluntary organisations, especially those that employ staff. This is a useful reminder of the diversity of the voluntary sector, some parts of which might have distinguishing features not shared by others.

Many commentators have noted that whatever differences there may have been in the past between the more formal voluntary sector organisations and those in other sectors, these are in danger of being eroded as voluntary agencies become more dependent upon the state for resources and more engaged in the market. DiMaggio and Powell (1983) used the term 'isomorphism' to describe the processes through which organisations operating in the same field take on the same characteristics. The policy relevance of such processes is that government and industry can shape voluntary organisations in their own image by requiring conformity to certain standards as a condition for supporting them and engaging them in partnerships.

What organisations comprise the sector?

Building on early research conducted for the Wolfenden Committee (Hatch, 1980), considerable progress has been made in the 1980s and 1990s in classifying voluntary organisations according to several different criteria, and in operationalising these distinctions for application across the UK (Kendall and Knapp, 1995; Marshall, 1997; Paton, 1991). The criteria invoked include the organisations' human and financial resources; their functions or outputs; their beneficiaries; their internal structures of management and control; their external relations with the other three sectors; their legal status; their values; and their fields of activity. Despite the successes of this work, however, it has proved difficult to achieve definitions fitted for their varied specific purposes which nevertheless retain sufficient commonality to allow comparability across studies. Different definitions have provided widely different estimates of the number of voluntary organisations in the UK.

Irrespective of the definition used, the voluntary sector is diverse. In fact, the diversity is so great and operates on so many dimensions that any claim to be researching the voluntary sector *per se* is as improbable as any similar claim to be researching the public, corporate or informal sectors as a whole. In practice, it is specific aspects of particular areas within each sector that engage the attention of policy-makers and that come under academic scrutiny. But faced with diversity within the sector and overlap between it and the other sectors, there is a temptation to impose definitions that 'create' a more homogeneous and discrete sector for research and analysis than really exists. There is also a tendency to develop and apply definitions which give weight to the larger and more structured voluntary organisations (which are easier to identify, count and describe) at the expense of more informal voluntary activities.

Once a definition has been selected, counting can begin. In the case of registered charities the task has been made easier by the computerisation of the Charity Commission's register and recent efforts, prompted by surveys conducted for the Office of National Statistics (Hems and Passey, 1996), to remove moribund organisations. The structural/operational definition developed by the Johns Hopkins Comparative Nonprofit Sector Project, which takes in a wider range of voluntary organisations than registered charities, enabled Kendall and Knapp (1996) and Kendall and Almond (1998) to provide estimates of the size of the voluntary sector in 1991 and 1995. And smaller, less formal organisations which might fall outside the net of the Johns Hopkins trawl have been located by other methods developed by Marshall (1997) for the Local Voluntary Activity Surveys (LOVAS) project.

How is the sector resourced?

As well as refining their definitions of the sector, academic researchers have made substantial advances in measuring the resources it commands – its finances and its paid and volunteer workforce. It is easy to forget how little was known about these resources twenty years ago.

In the absence of any reliable official statistics, researchers have pursued information from two sources. One is from the voluntary organisations themselves, beginning with Posnett's (1987) pioneering work on estimating the income of registered charities by examining a sample of the accounts submitted to the Charity Commission. The income of the biggest charities is now well documented on an annual basis (CAF, 1998; Rattigan, 1997).

The other source of data is donors and volunteers who can supply information about the amounts of money and time that they give. We have had surveys of individual donations of money (Halfpenny and Lowe, 1994), local authority grants (Mocroft, 1998), the largest corporate donors (Brown and Smyth, 1997;

Pharoah, 1998), small company donations (Halfpenny, Hudson and Jones, 1998), and volunteering (Davis Smith, 1998). In addition, there has been some useful work on estimating the financial value of volunteering, allowing both forms of voluntary input – time and money – to be scaled on a single dimension (Gaskin, 1997). Attempts have also been made to estimate the value of the tax reliefs that charitable organisations receive, which can be seen as, in effect, grants by the government (Williams, 1998).

A corollary of the selective attention devoted to the relatively small number of larger voluntary organisations has been the neglect of the majority of agencies, the tens of thousands with modest incomes and very few, if any, paid staff. Yet these are probably proportionately more 'voluntaristic' than their larger relations and their operation is more dependent on volunteer labour. For a better understanding of the fortunes of this vital part of the voluntary sector, more case study work of the type undertaken by Scott and his colleagues is needed (Russell *et al.*, 1995). This not only attends in fine detail to how local, small voluntary agencies go about securing and deploying their resources, but also traces changes over time.

It is easy to understand the policy preoccupation with academic research on definitional and resourcing issues. If the voluntary sector is to play a part in providing goods and services that would otherwise be the responsibility of the state, then it is important to know the extent of the sector's capacity to undertake this role. British conservative governments were keen that the sector should not rely too much on the state for its income but that it should increase the amount raised from private sources, both individuals and companies. To encourage this, they promoted the notion of social responsibility to accompany the rights (or consumer choice) that were being extended by 'rolling back the state' or clarified through citizen's charters. The pressure group 'Business in the Community' was set up to encourage socially responsible business. The slogan 'Active Citizenship' was coined to encourage individuals to invest volunteer time in their communities. Alongside such exhortations, tax incentives were introduced to encourage donations: extension of the types of companies that could set gifts against tax, the payroll deduction scheme and Gift Aid. Similarly, the National Lottery was intended to attract further funding for 'good causes'.

Why do voluntary organisations exist?

Why are certain goods and services provided by voluntary sector suppliers rather than private or public or informal sector providers? This question takes on added force given the gradual establishment of the welfare state from the beginning of the twentieth century and its consolidation after 1945. In the light of 'voluntary failure' (the term used by Salamon, 1987 to describe the weaknesses of the voluntary sector such as its amateurism, patchiness, paternalism and insufficiency), why did the universal provisions of the British welfare state not displace the haphazard and particularistic grants and services offered by voluntary agencies? Conventional economic theory predicts that private provision of public goods will be crowded out by state supply (Halfpenny, 1999) but clearly this did not happen in the UK.

The report of the Wolfenden Committee argued that the sector exists because it fills gaps, provides alternatives and identifies new needs and new means of service delivery. It also has a campaigning role, critically evaluating state goods and services and championing cases that state provision fails to meet. This explanation is compatible with the accounts presented by neo-classical economists in the USA about market and government failures (for example, Weisbrod, 1988). Their argument is that private sector provision of public goods fails because of free-riding: that is, consumption without contributing to the cost. Such goods are therefore provided by the state, which extracts payment for them coercively through taxation. However, the government in turn fails, deliberately or accidentally, to meet the full demand for public goods, and therefore voluntary organisations spring up (or are subsidised by the state) to fill the gaps.

As the policies of the Thatcher administration moved the British voluntary sector into the role of mainstream service provider and exposed it to market-like forces, the research focus shifted from questioning why voluntary organisations were not subjugated to the welfare state to asking why they were not subjugated to the private commercial sector. One answer is that they can compete effectively in the market because they have lower costs due, for example, to the tax concessions gained from charitable status, the use of volunteers, paying their employees lower wages than in the private sector, internal cross-subsidies from one group of users to another, external subsidies from their other sources of income and freedom from regulations that govern other sectors. A second answer, again offered primarily by US writers (Hansmann, 1980; Weisbrod, 1988), is the 'contract failure' one that hinges on trust. Voluntary organisations, it is argued, typically operate in markets where outputs are difficult to measure. In such markets, normal contract mechanisms fail to provide consumers with adequate information to differentiate between producers and they seek to remedy this by preferring providers which inspire trust. This favours voluntary organisations which, because they do not distribute profits, have little incentive to maximise profits at the expense of their customers: they can be trusted to deliver better quality services than their private sector rivals.

A problem for researchers is that different combinations of explanatory factors are responsible for the establishment and continued existence of different kinds of agencies in different kinds of policy environments. Moreover, despite the proliferation of explanatory theories, it is possible that there is a cruder explanation for the continued existence of parts of the voluntary sector – political expediency. Some parts are tolerated or promoted by the government of the day because they are seen as useful in covering policy deficiencies or in contributing to the achievement of high-profile policy initiatives.

What is the voluntary sector's relationship with other sectors?

'Partnerships' with the state and the possibility that these result in constraints on voluntary agencies' autonomy have frequently been the focus of research attention in the 1980s and 1990s. The term 'partnership' is invoked to describe a wide variety of different relationships between the voluntary and the statutory and/or private sectors (Billis, 1993; Wilson and Charlton, 1997), and the formation of partnerships in some form is increasingly a prerequisite for bidding for EU or central government funding programmes in the UK (Williamson *et al.*, 2000).

Shifts from local authority funding to central government funding have caused concern about the autonomy of the sector (Taylor and Bassi, 1998). Over the 1980s and 1990s, major central government initiatives, such as the Department of Environment's Urban

Programme, the Manpower Services Commission's Youth Training Scheme, the Housing Corporation's subsidisation of housing associations and the implementation of the 1990 NHS and Community Care Act, injected enormous amounts of money into the voluntary sector over a short period. This heavily influenced the shape and operation of the sector (Kendall and 6, 1994) both when the funds arrived and in some cases when they were abruptly withdrawn. Recent increases in funding from fees and charges for services may well be changing the relationship between voluntary organisations and their clients. And researchers have yet to tease out the implications for the sector of the availability of National Lottery grants. They appear to affect not only the overall funding of the sector but also the distribution of funds across the sector (Unwin and Westland, 1997).

In parallel with research questions raised by the changing inputs to the sector are issues about outputs, with accountability being the key term. Accountability takes several different forms (Leat, 1990; Rochester, 1995) and disentangling its features becomes more urgent as the voluntary sector moves increasingly into contracting or forming compacts with other sectors (Lewis, 1996; Kumar, 1997). For some, accountability is seen as the mechanism for disciplining the voluntary sector, just as profit operates in the private sector and votes in the public sector. Attention then turns to accountability measures, either in terms of outputs (Dobson *et al.*, 1997; Pearce *et al.*, 1998) or of benchmarking (Paton and Payne, 1997).

The stress placed by both policy analysts and researchers on partnerships and on input and output measures again gives prominence to those voluntary organisations that are structured, formalised and professionalised, and therefore capable of cooperating or competing with public and private sector organisations. This 'professional turn' diminishes the attention given to the messy and muddled yet vibrant sorts of voluntarism that often spring up as collective expressions of opposition to state and private sector policies and practices. Examples include direct action to protect jobs or to prevent degradation of the environment: the sorts of activities captured by the term 'social movements'. Public policy is the poorer for the emphasis on the professionalised sector, as is research. Hedley (1995) ends a wide-ranging review of the local and national voluntary sector in the UK by stating that 'the real strength of the voluntary sector is its actual diversity, and its role must be one of dissent'. He echoes the views of others suspicious that the professionalised voluntary organisations coopted into partnerships with the public and private sectors displace or control dissent (Beckford, 1991; Brenton, 1985; Gladstone, 1982; Knight, 1993).

Voluntary organisations and social policy – this book

Since 1978, then, researchers have built up an unprecedented body of knowledge about the characteristics of voluntary sector organisations, their numbers and the resources they deploy. They have suggested explanations for the existence of the sector and attempted to identify the features that differentiate voluntary organisations from for-profit companies and public sector bodies. They have also explored the relationship between voluntary agencies and the institutions of the other sectors.

The accumulation of these specialist research studies has made this book possible. The changed social policy landscape described earlier in this chapter has made this book necessary. It draws on two decades of research at the Centre for Voluntary Organisation and elsewhere in the UK to focus on the new challenges and opportunities that face voluntary sector organisations as we enter a new millennium.[3] It provides a variety of perspectives on change and choice which illuminate key aspects of social policy implementation. Three distinct but overlapping questions are explored.

- How are different aspects of social policy playing out from a voluntary sector viewpoint?
- How are social policies affecting particular kinds of voluntary organisation?
- How are social policies affecting key groupings within voluntary organisations?

In Chapter 2 Nicholas Deakin provides a broad overview of recent changes in the social policy environment and the ways in which the voluntary sector, which he argues is far more than a passive spectator of the process, has responded to them.

The next five contributions (Chapters 3 to 7) focus on the ways in which specific aspects of policy are being experienced by voluntary sector organisations. David Billis examines the new high-profile 'policy current' of social exclusion and discusses the kinds of contributions the sector can make to attempts to tackle it. Duncan Scott and Lynne Russell look at the consequences for voluntary agencies of the introduction of contracting as the result of the NHS and Community Care Act 1990, focusing on issues of money, organisation and volunteers. Colin Rochester examines the impact of regulation on the activities and organisation of local voluntary groups and suggests that policies aimed at minimising risk are at odds with social policy goals of encouraging voluntary action and citizen involvement. Policies for area regeneration are the focus of Stephen Osborne and Kathleen Ross's chapter which looks at the response of voluntary organisations, in particular local development agencies, to the evolution of public–private partnerships as a means of economic and social revitalisation. Finally in this section, Marilyn Taylor discusses the growing emphasis on 'partnership' and the new opportunities this brings for voluntary organisations to contribute to the development, as well as the implementation, of policy as 'insiders' rather than 'outsiders'.

Chapters 8 to 11 tackle our second question: how are social policies affecting particular kinds of voluntary organisation? Martin Knapp and Jeremy Kendall discuss the impact of community care on voluntary sector providers of care to older people. They compare and contrast voluntary sector responses with those of counterparts in the for-profit sector. Diana Leat considers the effects of recent social policy trends on the practices of grant-making trusts and foundations and suggests that many of them have had to review their purposes and practices in a radical fashion. David Lewis looks at the changing relationship between UK-based international aid agencies (such as Oxfam and Save the Children) and government development policy and considers the implications for other areas of social policy analysis. And in the final chapter in this section David Mullins and Moyra Riseborough challenge the view that housing associations are mere agents of government provision and discuss how they have developed the capacity to influence the policy agenda.

Our third question – how are social policies affecting key

groupings within voluntary organisations? – is the theme of Chapters 12 to 14. First, Margaret Harris looks at the impact of recent changes in social policy such as the moves towards contracting, competition and community care on the governing bodies, or boards, of voluntary organisations. She suggests that the processes of implementing social policy changes are seen as problematic when they threaten the voluntary and independent nature of the board role. Next, Justin Davis Smith assesses the extent to which government policies in general and the Major administration's Make A Difference programme in particular succeeded in promoting and encouraging volunteering. Michael Locke, Paul Robson and Steven Howlett conclude this section with an account of the 'tide of change' affecting the relationship between voluntary organisations and the users of their services. They identify the principal obstacles to the greater involvement of users in decision-making and discuss some of the factors involved in selecting appropriate and effective approaches to overcoming them.

In the final chapter of the book Margaret Harris draws together the major themes underlying the individual contributions. She reframes the rich material provided by the authors of the individual chapters to address three key questions about the implications of social policy change for voluntary organisations.

- To what extent have they themselves changed in response to their changing environment?
- Have they been forced into change or have they exercised autonomy and choice?
- Have they themselves been able to play a role in the development of social policy?

Finally, the chapter and the book close with some final reflections on the extent to which the academic field of social policy has – and has not – been changed by the new role of voluntary organisations in the development and delivery of social policy.

Notes

1. Peter Halfpenny's paper for the CVO 20th anniversary symposium provided a comprehensive overview of social policy research on the voluntary sector in the preceding twenty years and this material forms the basis of the section on voluntary sector research in the middle of this chapter.

2. Over twenty years these included: Allied Dunbar, BP, the Charities Aid Foundation, Citibank, the City Parochial Foundation, Cope and Denning, the Heron Foundation, the Inform Group, the Lankelly Foundation, the Lloyds TSB Foundation for England and Wales, Marks and Spencer plc, the Save and Prosper Educational Trust, Williams Lea and an anonymous trust.

3. In this chapter we have used the terms 'voluntary organisations', 'voluntary agencies' and 'voluntary sector' to refer broadly and inclusively to non-governmental and not-for-profit organisations. We are all too aware, however, that there is no consensus among scholars, policy-makers and practitioners over this usage. There is a bewildering variety of terms in use and a lively and unresolved debate about which should be preferred. In the absence of a consensus and in what we think is an appropriate spirit of pluralism we have suggested to the contributors to this book that they should use the terms with which they are familiar and comfortable and to provide brief explanations of them where necessary.

References

Beckford, J.A. (1991) 'Great Britain: voluntarism and sectional interests', in R. Wuthnow (ed.) *Between States and Markets: The Voluntary Sector in Comparative Perspective*, Princeton University Press, Princeton, NJ.

Beveridge, W. (1948) *Voluntary Action*, Allen & Unwin, London.

Billis, D. (1984) *Welfare Bureaucracies*, Heinemann, London.

Billis, D. (1993) *Organising Public and Voluntary Agencies*, Routledge, London.

Billis, D. and H. Glennerster (1998) 'Human services and the voluntary sector: towards a theory of comparative advantage', *Journal of Social Policy*, 27(1): 79–98.

Billis, D. and M. Harris (1986) *An Extended Role for the Voluntary Sector: the Challenge of Implementation*, Working Paper 3, Centre for Voluntary Organisation, London School of Economics, London.

Billis, D. and M. Harris (1992) 'Taking the strain of change: UK local voluntary organisations enter the post-Thatcher period', *Nonprofit and Voluntary Sector Quarterly*, 21(3): 211–26.

Billis, D. and M. Harris (1996a) 'Introduction: enduring challenges of research and practice', in D. Billis and M. Harris (eds) *Voluntary Agencies: Challenges of Organisation and Management*, Macmillan, London.

Billis, D. and M. Harris (1996b) *Voluntary Agencies: Challenges of Organisation and Management*, Macmillan, London.

Billis, D. and M. Harris (1996c) 'Conclusion: emerging challenges for research and practice', in D. Billis and M. Harris (eds) *Voluntary Agencies: Challenges of Organisation and Management*, Macmillan, London.

Brenton, M. (1985) *The Voluntary Sector in British Social Services*, Longman, London.

Brown, P. and J. Smyth (1997) *A Guide to Company Giving*, 1997/98 edition, Directory of Social Change, London.

CAF (1998) 'CAF's top 500 fundraising charities', in C. Pharoah and M. Smerdon (eds) *Dimensions of the Voluntary Sector*, 1998 edition, Charities Aid Foundation, West Malling.

Davis Smith, J. (1998) *The 1997 National Survey of Volunteering*, Institute for Volunteering Research, London.

Deakin, N. (1995) 'The perils of partnership', in J. Davis Smith, C. Rochester and R. Hedley (eds) *An Introduction to the Voluntary Sector*, Routledge, London.

DiMaggio, P. and W.W. Powell (1983) 'The iron cage revisited: institutional isomorphism and collective rationality in organizational fields', *American Sociological Review*, 48: 147–60.

Dobson, S., E. Ozdemiroglu and D. Pearce (1997) 'Measuring the social value of charities', in C. Pharoah and M. Smerdon (eds) *Dimensions of the Voluntary Sector*, 1997 edition, Charities Aid Foundation, West Malling.

Gaskin, K. (1997) *The Economic Equation of Volunteering: A Pilot Study*, CRSP, Department of Social Sciences, Loughborough University, Loughborough.

Giddens, A. (1998) *The Third Way: The Renewal of Social Democracy*, Polity Press, Cambridge.

Gladstone, F. (1982) *Charity Law and Social Justice*, Bedford Square Press, London.

Hadley, R. and S. Hatch (1982) *Social Welfare and the Failure of the State*, Allen & Unwin, London.

Halfpenny, P. (1999) 'Economic and sociological theories of individual charitable giving: complementary or contradictory?', *Voluntas*, 10(3): 197–215.

Halfpenny, P. and D. Lowe (1994) *Individual Giving Survey 1993*, Charities Aid Foundation, London.

Halfpenny, P., S. Hudson and J. Jones (1998) *Small Companies' Charitable Giving*, University of Manchester Working Paper in Applied Social Research, Manchester.

Hansmann, H. (1980) 'The role of the nonprofit enterprise', *Yale Law Journal*, 89: 835–901.

Harris, M. (1998a) 'Instruments of government? Voluntary sector boards in a changing public policy environment', *Policy and Politics*, 26(2): 177–88.

Harris, M. (1998b) 'Doing it their way: organisational challenges for voluntary associations', *Nonprofit and Voluntary Sector Quarterly*, 27(2): 144–58.

Hatch, S. (1980) *Beyond the State*, Croom Helm, London.

Hedley, R. (1995) 'Inside the voluntary sector', in J. Davis Smith, C. Rochester and R. Hedley (eds) *An Introduction to the Voluntary Sector*, Routledge, London.

Hems, L. and A. Passey (1996) *The UK Voluntary Sector Statistical Almanac 1996*, National Council for Voluntary Organisations, London.

Kendall, J. and S. Almond (1998) *The UK Voluntary (Third) Sector in Comparative Perspective: Exceptional Growth and Transformation*, Personal Social Services Research Unit, Canterbury.

Kendall, J. and M. Knapp (1995) 'A loose and baggy monster', in J. Davis Smith, C. Rochester and R. Hedley (eds) *An Introduction to the Voluntary Sector*, Routledge, London.

Kendall, J. and M. Knapp (1996) *The Voluntary Sector in the UK*, Manchester University Press, Manchester.

Kendall, J. and P. 6 (1994) 'Government and the voluntary sector in the UK', in S.K.E. Saxon-Harrold and J. Kendall (eds) *Researching the Voluntary Sector*, Vol. 2, Charities Aid Foundation, Tonbridge.

Knapp, M., E. Robertson and C. Thomason (1990) 'Public money, voluntary action: whose welfare?', in H.K. Anheier and W. Seibel (eds) *The Third Sector: Comparative Studies of Nonprofit Organizations*, de Gruyter, Berlin.

Knight, B. (1993) *Voluntary Action*, Home Office, London.

Kramer, R. (1981) *Voluntary Agencies and the Welfare State*, University of California Press, Berkeley.

Kumar, S. (1997) *Accountability Relationships between Voluntary Sector 'Providers', Local Government 'Purchasers' and Service Users in the Contracting State*, York Publishing Services, York.

Leat, D. (1990) 'Voluntary organizations and accountability: theory and practice', in H.K. Anheier and W. Seibel (eds) *The Third Sector: Comparative Studies of Nonprofit Organizations*, de Gruyter, Berlin.

Leat, D. (1995) 'Theoretical differences between for-profit and non-profit organisations', Appendix One in D. Leat, *Challenging Management*, VOLPROF, City University Business School, London.

Lewis, J. (1996) 'What does contracting do to voluntary agencies?', in D. Billis and M. Harris (eds) *Voluntary Agencies: Challenges of Organisation and Management*, Macmillan, London.

Marshall, T. (1997) *Research Manual*, Local Voluntary Activity Surveys (LOVAS) Paper Number 1, Home Office Research and Statistics Directorate, London.

Mocroft, I. (1998) 'The survey of local authority payments to voluntary and charitable organisations for 1996–97', in C. Pharoah and M. Smerdon (eds) *Dimensions of the Voluntary Sector*, 1998 edition, Charities Aid Foundation, West Malling.

Paton, R. (1991) 'The emerging social economy', *Management Issues*, 3: 2–7.

Paton, R. and G. Payne (1997) 'Benchmarking – passing fad or probable future?', in C. Pharoah and M. Smerdon (eds) *Dimensions of the Voluntary Sector*, 1997 edition, Charities Aid Foundation, West Malling.

Pearce, D., V. Foster, S. Mourato, E. Ozdemiroglu and S. Dobson (1998) 'What is the economic value of the charitable sector?', in C. Pharoah and M. Smerdon (eds) *Dimensions of the Voluntary Sector*, 1998 edition, Charities Aid Foundation, West Malling.

Pharoah, C. (1998) 'CAF's top 500 corporate donors', in C. Pharoah and M. Smerdon (eds) *Dimensions of the Voluntary Sector*, 1998 edition, Charities Aid Foundation, West Malling.

Posnett, J. (1987) 'Trends in the income of registered charities', in *Charity Trends 1986/87*, Charities Aid Foundation, Tonbridge.

Rattigan, A. (ed.) (1997) *Baring Asset Management Top 3000 Charities*, Caritas, London.

Rochester, C. (1995) 'Voluntary agencies and accountability', in J. Davis Smith, C. Rochester and R. Hedley, *An Introduction to the Voluntary Sector*, Routledge, London.

Russell, L., D. Scott and P. Wilding (1995) *Mixed Fortunes: The Funding of the Voluntary Sector*, Department of Social Policy and Social Work, University of Manchester, Manchester.

Salamon, L.M. (1987) 'Partners in public service: toward a theory of government–nonprofit relations', in W.W. Powell (ed.) *The Nonprofit Sector: A Research Handbook*, Yale University Press, New Haven, Conn.

Taylor, M. and A. Bassi (1998) 'Unpacking the state: the implications for the third sector of changing relationships between national and local government', *Voluntas*, 9: 113–36.

Unwin, J. and P. Westland (1997) *Local Funding: The Impact of the National Lottery Charities Board*, Association of Charitable Foundations, London.

Weisbrod, B.A. (1988) *The Nonprofit Economy*, Harvard University Press, Cambridge, Mass.

Williams, S. (1998) 'The cost of UK tax reliefs relating to charities', in C. Pharoah and M. Smerdon (eds) *Dimensions of the Voluntary Sector*, 1998 edition, Charities Aid Foundation, West Malling.

Williamson, A., D. Scott and P. Halfpenny (2000) 'Rebuilding civil society in Northern Ireland: the community and voluntary sector's contribution to the European Union's Peace and Reconciliation District Partnerships Programme', *Policy and Politics*, 28: 49–66.

Wilson, A. and K. Charlton (1997) *Making Partnerships Work*, Joseph Rowntree Foundation, York.

Wolfenden Committee (1978) *The Future of Voluntary Organisations*, Croom Helm, London.

2

Public Policy, Social Policy and Voluntary Organisations

Nicholas Deakin

Introduction

In this chapter, I want to address some of the main implications for voluntary organisations of the changes in public policy now taking place across the developed world. One of the most significant trends in voluntary action in the UK over the 1990s has been the closer relations that have been developing between voluntary agencies and the state, both locally and nationally (Kendall and Knapp, 1996). These developing relationships have taken a variety of different forms, ranging from new funding arrangements to active institutional partnerships.

The process of convergence has been the subject of much comment and some criticism (for example, Whelan, 1996). However, the debate around these closer relations often seems to be conducted without any awareness of the truly dramatic changes that have been taking place within the public sector which have fundamentally changed the role of the state both as an actor in its own right and as a potential partner. One result has been that the arena in which social policy is devised, its objectives defined and articulated and its implementation developed, has been transformed. In the discussion that follows I therefore begin by tracing the process through which change has taken place before setting out some of the main implications for voluntary organisations.

The end of an era

The process of change in the public sector has been an international one, although it has been led by politicians in the 'Anglo-Saxon' countries: the United States, the United Kingdom, Australia, and particularly New Zealand, where these developments have been pushed furthest of all. The basic message has been spread, in what has been aptly termed a 'missionary' process (6, 1995): partly by the action of international agencies like the World Bank and the Organisation for Economic Co-operation and Development (OECD, 1996), whose public management project, known as known as PUMA, has been particularly influential; partly by independent 'think tanks' which have spread the gospel during their periods of maximum political influence; and latterly by consultants. These consultants, sometimes facilitated by national governments and usually employed by large international firms or the commercial arms of academic institutions, have been particularly assiduous in marketing change in government, especially in the so-called 'transition' countries emerging from almost half a century of state socialism.

In essence, the product has been presented as business-*like* government, in which market values and procedures have primacy. Such procedures, reinforced by techniques drawn from the new technology, are employed to make the processes of government approximate as closely as possible to market transactions. In this approach, privatisation is the highest form of development because it tips ownership as well as the operating processes wholly into the private sector, allowing former state bodies not merely to mimic commercial organisations in their operations but also to become fully fledged companies. But the business-based approach has also generated a variety of intermediate bodies: agencies, quangos and arm's-length subsidiaries in which a simulacrum of market procedures (competition, greater managerial freedom to hire, fire and innovate) has been developed. The objective is to create an environment in which the machinery of government is 'reengineered' so as to bring market disciplines to bear on all the traditional functions of the public sector.

Change has not stopped with internal reforms. The ways in which the public sector conducts its relationships with other agencies have also been profoundly affected by the desire to be as 'business-like' as possible in the way in which transactions are undertaken. The clearest example of this type of change can be seen in the subcontracting of a whole series of traditional government functions, which has had the effect of exporting the new values of the transformed state to the other organisations and agencies with whom they contract. This process has affected many of the mainstream areas of social policy (health, housing education, social services). It is a change of fundamental significance for many voluntary organisations that provide services in these areas. They have found it necessary to adapt to the new imperatives of the 'contract culture' and, in so doing, to reformulate their style and approach to the content of their work.

The origins of the changes

The impetus for change in government sprang from a number of different developments, often operating in parallel. One of the most important of these was the so-called 'crisis' of welfare, which arose in most developed countries during the course of the 1970s. But criticisms of the postwar welfare settlement – by no means all of which came from advocates of market-based solutions – fed into an altogether more radical approach which took the view that the public sector, in welfare as elsewhere, is essentially beyond redemption, since it is by definition chronically inefficient. Because it operates according to fixed bureaucratic rules and procedures and is not subject to market disciplines, it is inherently unresponsive to the needs and wishes of its users. This is not surprising, because large bureaucracies are dominated by professional interest and therefore subject to producer capture, most notoriously by public sector unions but also and more insidiously by senior managers who have a vested interest in expanding the operation to meet their own interests.

This view was propagated at the academic level by economists of the public choice school (Dunleavy, 1991), at the level of political debate by right-wing 'think tanks' on both sides of the Atlantic, and in popular discourse through persistent ridicule in the media of the excesses of public bureaucracies and their operating style. That their critique touched a nerve is hardly to be denied. Users of public services undoubtedly did feel excluded and patronised by the way in which the large state bureaucracies treated them: rules were over-elaborate and insufficiently clearly explained; staff were not trained to communicate effectively either in person or by telephone; buildings were inaccessible and their public spaces unfriendly; opening hours were inconvenient; and the needs of groups with special circumstances (disabled people, mothers with small children) were not adequately met (Donnison, 1982).

But the neo-liberal approach did more than provide a critique: it offered an alternative. In place of the state-run bureaucracies, a market-based approach would create an environment that would be consumer-friendly. Empowering the customers of welfare by equipping them with cash and giving them choice in a market would increase efficiency, through promoting competition, and diminish the power of professional interests. This process would in turn make individuals responsible for reaching their own decisions, enabling costs to be reduced and ending the culture of dependency which was seen as one of the main adverse consequences of the previous system (Ridley, 1988).

Organisations seeking to operate in this new environment would need to be leaner and more enterprising in what they had to offer and closer to their customers in the way in which it was provided. In order to achieve this, they would need to encourage managerial enterprise and motivate staff through incentives and by equipping them with access to new technology. The ideal model (explicitly) was the modern supermarket (Green, 1993). This model also requires there to be sufficient real competition to facilitate consumer choice, with consequent pressure on providers to perform at a level that will satisfy their customers. Among the providers whose participation in the supply of services has been actively encouraged are voluntary sector organisations.

The implementation of this agenda, with its seductive overall motif of 'shrinking the state', became politically feasible in the UK after the election of the Conservative government under Margaret Thatcher in 1979.

What has actually been attempted?

The product of the changes that have taken place since 1979, in the UK and elsewhere, is usually labelled the 'New Public Management' but this term can be deceptive. It lumps together under a single heading a variety of different approaches which have been introduced at different times in different services and different locations (Ferlie *et al.*, 1996). However, all the currents of reform have three features in common: they are focused on management issues; they require the recipients of services to be seen as customers; and they have been implemented 'top down' from the centre.

The managerial emphasis is crucial: whatever the structural changes, the motivation of those with executive responsibility for service delivery has been seen as central to the project. It is best achieved through changing the culture of the organisation and the inculcation of alternative key values expressed in slogans, acronyms and mission statements. The stress on the user of services as a consumer is also vital: it draws on market experience in conceiving the self-interest of the individual purchaser of welfare as the key motivation and the relationship to the provider of services as one in which they seek to obtain maximum advantage from each separate transaction.

Finally, despite the emphasis on responsiveness to consumer preferences, the reforms of the public sector have been imposed from above, not negotiated or developed through experiment or local case studies. Furthermore, though often associated with individual politicians, they are presented, in rhetoric at least, as 'non-political' – reforms that are self-evidently rational because based on our common experience in the market-place. There has been little place for traditional politics in their implementation. Nevertheless, they carry a strong ideological charge – so much so that one recent critical account suggests that the movement as a whole is best seen simply as the material expression of an ideology and analysed in those terms (Clarke and Newman, 1997).

The process of change

The trajectory of the public sector reforms in the UK has been thoroughly traced by other commentators (especially Foster and Plowden, 1996) and for present purposes I need only highlight a few key developments. The early stages of the process were driven by ministers' desire to bring the public sector unions to heel (a long and bitter civil service strike was broken in 1991) and by the introduction of a series of operational reforms designed to introduce business-like procedures into the public sector. At the national level, the most important subsequent development was the 'Next Steps' programme, breaking the civil service down into operational units with slimmed-down central departments responsible for policy development and semi-independent agencies charged with implementation and service delivery. By the early 1990s the Department of Social Security, once one of the UK's major employers of clerical labour in its benefits 'factories', had shed 95 per cent of its staff to agencies.

At the local level, resistance to the government was stiffer (Stoker, 1988). The changes that were imposed took three forms: the super-imposition of new external mechanisms for quality control, in the shape of the Audit Commission; strict regulation of expenditure through restrictions on local spending ('ratecapping'); and, in extreme cases, abolition of recalcitrant authorities like the Greater London Council or imposition of non-elected bodies to take over many of their functions (Urban Development Corporations).

By the end of the 1980s, a new environment had been created in which fundamental reform of major areas of social policy (health, education and social services) could be imposed (Timmins, 1996). The key feature of this new environment was the attempt to replicate market conditions through the creation of a competitive environment, the introduction of performance measures and quality control and the use of market devices, principally the use of tendering and contracts. All of these were designed to slim down the size of the public sector and change its culture to an emphasis on enabling rather than providing.

Although these changes were imposed on the public sector, not chosen, they quickly found 'product champions' in those individual senior managers who were stimulated by the opportunities for increased pay and responsibility and not deterred by the end of lifetime job security, which was especially traumatic for the civil service. The impact was not only internal. New models of inter-organisational relationships emerged from the change of culture, with typical managerial careers taking practitioners through a sequence of posts across the private and public sectors and, latterly, the third sector as well. The premium is on generic skills seen to be transferable – enabling the individual manager to develop a 'portfolio' career. In this, there is no longer any place for traditional trade unionism, once so strongly entrenched in the public sector. The reform process in the UK reached its apogee at the end of the 1980s. Intoxicated by their successes, ministers and neoliberal think tanks toyed with apocalyptic visions of a future without a public sector in any form that would have been recognised a decade earlier (Ridley, 1988). Not merely had public utilities been decanted into the private sector, but core state functions like prisons were now regarded as legitimate candidates for privatisation. The outright abolition of local government was seriously canvassed, reinforced by suggestions that voluntary action would provide an acceptable substitute for the local activities of the state. But the attempt to settle the troublesome issue of locally-determined public expenditure by harnessing consumer self-interest in order to bring it under control failed. The poll tax was the first serious setback for the reform process and contributed significantly to Margaret Thatcher's downfall in 1991 (Jenkins, 1995).

A change of direction

The reaction against the more extreme forms of public sector reform was prompted in part by the economic recession of 1990–2 and the change of prime minister. The shift of direction was based in part on experience in the 1980s which suggested that the need for the state was greater than the extreme vision of restricted functions had implied. Rather, it showed that local elected government, in particular, could play a significant role in the new reformed universe – if efficiently managed. It could secure best value for the community as a whole as well as for individual service users: acting as the representative of the collective citizen interest; mediating between competing claims on the basis of local knowledge and experience; and maintaining where necessary a stake in service delivery.

Conversely, it became clear that the positive contribution of the market needed to be weighed against a number of unwelcome consequences of the wholesale introduction of market procedures.

These included slippage in standards both in performance and behaviour. Below senior management level, many staff lost security, status or often their actual jobs – a ritual slaughter of middle managers has been a regular feature of the reform process and huge losses in manual staff numbers became so common as to be barely even remarked upon.

Most important, some reforms did not deliver to customers the improvements in service quality that the rhetoric of the 1970s had held out as one of the chief justifications for change. Devolution of executive responsibility had its successes but also its spectacular failures: in the health service (blood transfusion, breast cancer) and among the 'Next Steps' agencies (the Child Support Agency[1]). Some regulators (rail, lottery) proved to be ineffective. The introduction of new technology also produced more than its fair share of waste and even corruption (Public Accounts Committee, 1994).

Attempts to address these issues took a variety of different forms. The Citizen's Charter, John Major's own 'big idea', was much mocked domestically but received with greater sympathy abroad, where it was paid the compliment of repeated imitation. Although still resolutely individualistic (note the placing of the apostrophe), the attempt to set performance standards and reward institutions as well as individuals for success in achieving them ('Chartermarks') and the attempt to provide the citizen with some form of remedy for failure to achieve them opened up a new front. The Charter approach, despite some weaknesses, did recognise the legitimacy of the public sector's contribution. The emphasis is on improving the quality of existing services, not on privatisation or abolition.

So, by the end of the Conservatives' period in government, the outline of a synthesis was beginning to appear. Some of the functions no longer undertaken by the state were seen as legitimate candidates for discharge by voluntary agencies but there was now recognition that these bodies could not simply substitute for statutory ones: their organisational form, financial regimes, internal procedures and cultures were often dissimilar in ways that might crucially affect their capacity to undertake new tasks. This has led in turn to a much closer interest in the efficient management of voluntary organisations concerned with service delivery and in the principles to be observed when such organisations are in receipt of public money (Nolan Committee, 1995). A greater awareness has also emerged of the importance of devising proper means of ensuring accountability, not just to funders of services but also to users. This has stemmed in part from a recognition that the market model of accountability through satisfying the consumer does not fit those situations where there is a collective as well as an individual interest. This in turn involves 'bringing the politics back in'.

The election in May 1997 of a Labour government did not put the whole process of reform into reverse, as at one stage might have seemed likely. Rather, the change of government reinforced it by demonstrating that changes in the public sector were no longer a matter of partisan politics but an irreversible transformation. Even the Citizen's Charter survived the departure of John Major, to be reborn under New Labour with the anodyne new title of 'Service First'. Only in the area of local government has there been a significant deviation from the path mapped out by Labour's Conservative predecessors. Here, the vesting of significant new responsibilities in local authorities, under the rubric of 'community governance', reverses the trend towards loss of political power of elected bodies: a development certain to affect their relationships with other agencies at local level, chief among them voluntary bodies.

The impact on the third sector

The voluntary and community sector is not simply a spectator of this process of change. At the centre, the spectacular break-up of the Whitehall monolith has created a new web of relationships, linking third sector organisations with agencies and quangos of a whole range of different sizes and operating styles. But the major differences produced by recent changes have been at the local government level, where voluntary bodies involved in service delivery have traditionally formed working relationships with the local authority operating in their area. True, these relationships have often been superficial and based on misleading stereotypes, on both sides. Sometimes they have been excessively cosy. At other times they have been confrontational (the activities of some environmental groups being the obvious case). But the unspoken assumption has been that local voluntary bodies, both individually and through the umbrella groups whose very existence depends upon them, will always have to deal with elected local government in one fashion or another. Now many of these past relationships are being overtaken by different linkages based on different priorities. These latter are often imposed as a result of developments that have taken place nationally and which have impacted in local situations – both on the local statutory sector and on the users of their services. The most dramatic example has been the Community Care legislation of 1991 which mandated the allocation of 85 per cent of the transitional funds to providers outside the statutory sector and by so doing promoted the rapid development of the 'contract culture' (Walsh *et al.*, 1997, and see also Chapters 4 and 8 of this volume).

Attempts to generate enthusiasm among voluntary bodies about the new opportunities being created by the reform of public administration were made nationally in the same style, but on a smaller scale, as the promotion of the changes in the public sector described earlier. A succession of reviews of policy and practice promoted by national coordinating bodies such as the Charities Aid Foundation and the National Council for Voluntary Organisations (NCVO) sought to equip the third sector with the capacity to cope successfully with the new environment.

External relations, with both state and market, were a main focus of the two major Commissions of inquiry on the future of the voluntary sector in England and Scotland, from which stemmed the notion of a compact to formalise relationships and safeguard the independence of the sector (Commission on the Future of the Voluntary Sector in England, 1996; Commission on the Future of the Voluntary Sector in Scotland, 1997). Internal cultural change, involving staff, management committees and volunteers, has also been promoted. Consultants have been active at all levels in spreading the word; training programmes have been developed and good-practice 'cookbooks' published (Wilson and Charlton, 1997). In the attempts to 'refocus' work to cope with the new situation, the special difficulties of specific groups like membership organisations, user groups, campaigning groups or generic bodies dealing with the needs of specific minorities have received particular attention (Harris, 1998).

Seen from the national level, the transformation in the voluntary sector, though perhaps not so great as that in the statutory sector, appears impressive. But at the ground level, with both parties passing through a process of change simultaneously, the impact of new developments has been more problematic. Recent research conducted for the Local Government Management Board (LGMB) in five case study areas shows that the attitudes and objectives that the different partners bring to the relationship and their different agendas produce a variety of quite complex patterns.

Relationships can be both formal and informal. History and personalities as well as the general operating style of each sector can be important influences. The study did not turn up much evidence of participation at the top end of the scale, of voluntary organisations being involved in corporate strategic policy developments, but it found much activity around the theme of funding – the form that it was taking and the preconditions for receiving it. Here, there has been a perceptible shift in the direction of negotiation and away from imposition by the statutory sector.

Both sides stand to benefit from this change. The credibility of the voluntary sector is enhanced by local government support when making approaches to other organisations, while councils have come to realise that the voluntary sector can open up an important new route for new funds to come into their area. The creation of specific structures to underpin new relationships can provide important opportunities for better understanding and closer relationships. But they can also lead to resentment on the part of groups that are seen as marginal to the process of joint planning and therefore excluded, or to 'consultation fatigue' in the case of those who are continually involved (Gaster *et al.*, 1999).

However, these findings are not necessarily typical of the whole range of relationships between state and third sector. Partnership between local authorities and local voluntary groups in service delivery is only a part of a larger picture. Third sector bodies have other relationships that may be equally significant: with health authorities, Training and Employment Councils and with government offices in the regions, especially in the context of Single Regeneration Budget activities. Relationships with other funding bodies such as the corporate sector, trusts and foundations, the National Lottery's Boards and Commissions may be equally or more important for some third sector organisations.

Third sector bodies that are not directly involved with service delivery will have different dealings with the state, ranging from campaigns against particular policies to outright opposition. They will have different experiences of the outcomes of these encounters, which in turn will generate different perspectives on government and the internal changes that have taken place within it. For example, viewed through the lens of third world organisations, relations with government and participation in its activities are likely to appear in a very different light to the 'partnerships' of some developed countries. Even here, there will always be those who regard any relationship as tainted, either for ideological reasons (Whelan, 1996) or on the strictly pragmatic grounds that there is never enough gained to justify the expenditure of time and good will.

Taking relationships forward in a changing environment

Most organisations will have to relate to the state, in some form, however remotely, at some time or another. What sort of rules of engagement should they now adopt? The terms of this debate have been significantly affected by the National Compact between government (in England) and the voluntary sector, signed by the Home Secretary and representatives of the sector in November 1998 (Home Office, 1998). This document, which is subject to a process of annual review, is intended to set new parameters for the relationship nationally, accepting the importance of independence of the sector and the legitimacy of campaigning and advocacy, and setting down new principles for funding procedures and involvement in policy-making.

The continued dominance of the financial environment in circumstances where more is constantly being expected of the voluntary and community sector means that there will be continuous pressure for longer-term security for organisations which deliver services. In such circumstances, the attractions of local compacts between the two parties along the lines of the one that has been introduced nationally must be considerable: a trade-off could be acceptable for voluntary bodies if it covered both funding and monitoring arrangements (Craig *et al.*, 1998). Such local compacts might form part of the community plans that local authorities are now being required to draw up. This approach has the merit of rationality. But the environment in which voluntary and community groups operate is not always a rational one. Indeed, there is a case for arguing that the unique selling proposition of the voluntary and community sector is its very unpredictability; that there should be space for chaos in a universe in which too much is already being pinned down for evaluation and measurement. One objection to compacts is that they over-formalise relationships that are necessarily fluid. Another is that the respective positions of the two parties may be about to diverge again. The Labour government's White Paper (DETR, 1998) makes it very clear that local government will be placed at the centre of the local scene: it will not be *primus inter pares*, as their Conservative predecessors preferred to see it, but equipped with the authority to impose its version of community government. The asymmetry of power which has always been a feature of the relationship with the local voluntary sector is likely to become even greater.

One can envisage a situation developing in which local voluntary organisations will continue to need local government's resources; but local government can find other ways of getting the services it needs to support its enabling role. A 'holistic' local authority will have less time for potentially messy – even chaotic – local partnership arrangements and may prefer to go in for 'smart' purchasing deals which would pay off in the short term rather than engage in a slow and frustrating process of building up social capital for the long haul (6, 1995). And if building social capital is to become an important objective for local government it may prefer to take the lead in its own manner rather than entrust it to unstable coalitions of voluntary organisations, often operating under disputed leadership and frequently accused of excluding smaller community and ethnic minority groups from the real action.

These are speculations, but they suggest another argument for local compacts, as seen from the voluntary organisation perspective. Maybe they would provide an opportunity to gain a foothold in the local policy process before it is too late. The legitimacy of their role in this context as policy entrepreneurs is a matter of particular importance at a time when a series of new programmes designed to revitalise local communities (the 'New Deal for Communities') has been launched by government: access to debates on the ends as well as the means of revitalisation could be of particular significance.

Conclusions

The full effects of the reforms in the public sector that began after 1979 have still not fully worked themselves through. But there is now sufficient evidence to show that the form which any future partnerships between state and voluntary sector may take is likely to be very different from the collaborations of previous epochs. Ambitious advocates of closer relations look hopefully towards the emergence of a third sector with sufficient authority and resources to form relations with its partners, in the market as well as the statutory sector, on a basis not of dependency but of near equality. (This is some way off still, even on the most optimistic estimate. But there is certainly an increasing awareness that the voluntary and community sector has qualities of its own that are both distinctive and valuable to bring to the party.)

Citizen and advocacy groups have a particularly important function to perform. Recent experience has shown how fallible the 'democracy of the market-place' can be. Changes were executed without reference to any sense of a need for the custodianship of the common good. For the individual's rights to be protected, it seemed sufficient to vest them with the same status in the public arena that they had always enjoyed in the private – that of customer. But recent events in the countries of East and Central Europe, the laboratories of the transformation from state- to market-dominated polities, show vividly the weakness of the sovereign consumer in adversity. A favourite cliché of the New Right in the 1970s was that democracy and the free market go hand in hand – no functioning democracy anywhere in the world is without a market. But the opposite is not the case: the existence of markets does not guarantee democracy. Rather, as we have been able to observe, the importation of capitalism to the transition countries in its ultimate high-octane free market form has been highly damaging, perhaps even fatal, to the attempts to reconstruct (or rather construct) democratic institutions there. In the extreme case, the former Soviet Union, it also emptied the supermarkets, the exemplars of benign change. In such circumstances, citizens cannot stand alone – the promotion of individual self-interest is not sufficient safeguard. They need the support of both strong democratic institutions and the informal resources that only civil society organisations can supply.

Note

1. The Child Support Agency was established by the Child Support Act, 1991, and given the responsibility of collecting financial contributions from absent parents. It was set ambitious targets which it has been unable to meet.

References

Clarke, J. and J. Newman (1997) *The Managerial State*, Sage, London.
Commission on the Future of the Voluntary Sector in England (1996) *Meeting the Challenge of Change: Voluntary Action into the 21st Century* (The 'Deakin Commission'), NCVO Publications, London.
Commission on the Future of the Voluntary Sector in Scotland (1997), *Heart and Hand* (The 'Kemp Commission'), SCVO publications, Edinburgh.
Craig, G., M. Taylor, C. Szanto and M. Wilkinson (1998) *Developing Local Compacts: Relationships Between Local Public Sector Bodies and the Voluntary and Community Sector*, Joseph Rowntree Foundation, York.
Department of Environment, Transport and the Regions (1998) *Modern Local Government: In Touch with the People*, (The Local Government White Paper 1998) HMSO, London.
Donnison, D. (1982) *The Politics of Poverty*, Martin Robertson, London.
Dunleavy, P. (1991) *Democracy, Bureaucracy and Public Choice*, Harvester Wheatsheaf, Hemel Hempstead.
Ferlie, E., A. Pettigrew, L. Ashburner and L. Fitzgerald (1996) *The New Public Management in Action*, Oxford University Press, Oxford.
Foster, C. and F. Plowden (1996) *The State under Stress*, Open University Press, Buckingham.
Gaster, L. *et al.* (1999) *History, Strategy or Lottery? Local government and the Voluntary Sector*, Local Government Management Board, London.

Green, D. (1993) *Reinventing Civil Society: The Rediscovery of Welfare without Politics*, Institute of Economic Affairs, London.

Harris, M. (1998) 'Doing it their way: organisational challenge for voluntary associations', *Nonprofit and Voluntary Sector Quarterly*, 27(2): 144–58.

Home Office (1998) *Getting it Right Together: Compact on Relations Between Government and the Voluntary and Conmmunity Sector in England*, Cm 4100, The Stationery Office, London.

Jenkins, S. (1995) *Accountable to None: The Tory Nationalisation of Britain*, Penguin Books, Harmondsworth.

Kendall, J. and M. Knapp (1996) *The Voluntary Sector in the UK*, Manchester University Press, Manchester.

Nolan Committee (1995) *Report on Standards of Behaviour in Public Life*, HMSO, London.

OECD (1996) *Governance in Transition: Public Management in OECD Countries*, OECD, Paris.

Public Accounts Committee, House of Commons (1994) Eighth report, session 1993/4: *The Proper Conduct of Public Business*, HMSO, London.

Ridley, N. (1988) *The Local Right*, Centre for Policy Studies, London.

6, Perri (1995) *Governing by Cultures*, Demos Quarterly, 7: 2–9.

Stoker, G. (1988) *The Politics of Local Government*, Macmillan, Basingstoke.

Timmins, N. (1996) *The Five Giants*, HarperCollins, London.

Walsh K., N. Deakin, P. Smith, P. Spurgeon and N. Thomas (1997) *Contracting for Change: Contracts in Health, Social Care and Other Local Government Services*, Oxford University Press, Oxford.

Whelan, R. (1996) *The Corrosion of Charity*, Institute of Economic Affairs, London.

Wilson, A. and K. Charlton (1997) *Making Partnerships Work*, Joseph Rowntree Foundation, York.

3

Tackling Social Exclusion: The Contribution of Voluntary Organisations

David Billis

Introduction

This chapter can be seen as a bridge between the broad social policy themes discussed in the first two chapters and the more specific studies of policy implementation that follow later in this volume. Thus the chapter has two objectives. First, it examines social exclusion, which is a major theme, or 'current', of the new policy agenda. Second, it speculates about the possible implications of the rise of this new 'policy current' for different types of voluntary organisations.

The opening section provides a brief overview of social exclusion as a rather unusual social policy theme. Then, building on earlier work by Billis and Glennerster (1998), four states of disadvantage are proposed as a more manageable way of approaching social exclusion and of exploring the area between policy context and organisational implementation. These sections lay the foundations to approach central questions for voluntary sector policy-makers and practitioners. For what sorts of agencies will social exclusion be of particular interest? And why? What might lie ahead?

Social exclusion: just another confused term?

Social exclusion is a new and unusual term that has crept on to the public policy agenda. It is unusual for a number of reasons.

First, it is a negative term. Unlike prevention or community care it does not conjure up a positive image. Neither, like contracting or GP fund-holding, does it point to a change in practical public policy. If anything the term sounds like some unwelcome social disease – if not quite the bubonic plague then certainly a severe and chronic state of influenza. It is the diminution, or avoidance, of social exclusion that is the policy objective.

Second, it seems to be neither of British origin nor an American import. Its origins appear to be Continental, and few such terms have successfully made the short trip across the Channel and taken root in the pragmatic British environment. The policy journey across the Atlantic and back to the UK has been much easier.

A third reason is that it is what might be called a 'policy current' – a guiding, fluid policy that moves across the boundaries of many government departments. 'Policy currents' are powerful terms that flow through all aspects of official policy. They can serve as rallying calls, as directional pointers and as broad benchmarks against which policies can be 'measured', not in a precise way but in terms of their political 'correctness'. They may act as what Lewis and Glennerster (1996) call 'policy threads'. Most policies can be measured by their contribution to reducing social exclusion.

Finally, the concept has been backed by the personal authority of (at the time of writing) an extremely popular and powerful Prime Minister. A special Unit forms part of the PM's staff. Those involved in social welfare would be ill-advised to ignore a policy current which is the Gulf Stream of New Labour social policies.

In attempting to get to grips with this term we can turn to the most comprehensive review of the literature to date. This begins unpromisingly. Entitled *The Concept of Social Exclusion*, the report immediately lowers expectations. The opening paragraph reveals that having made a 'sweep of the different uses and users . . . there is no one exact definition of social exclusion' (CASE, 1998, p. 8). The authors suggest that for national governments, social exclusion (rupture of the social tie) is similar to the concept of relative deprivation and is in effect a notion of relative poverty. It is primarily perceived as a threat to cohesion which results from poverty and as a threat to state budgets (p. 9).

Not only are governments confused but 'there is little more coherence in the perspectives of academics than there is amongst governments and inter-governmental organisations' (p.13). The report variously describes the term as a 'convenient label' or 'portmanteau'.

This chapter does not attempt to update the comprehensive review by the Centre for Analysis of Social Exclusion (CASE). It 'reviews the review' and adds some later academic and policy literature. For our purposes it is helpful to consider this literature as falling within three broad groupings. The groups overlap and interact and these comments are brief and necessarily broadbrush.

In the first place there is that large body of writing which is primarily concerned with poverty (a British intellectual tradition) and in particular the links with unemployment (CASE, 1998; Walker, 1995; Walker and Walker, 1997). Typical of this approach is the argument that shifts in the nature of employment together with unemployment have increased income inequalities and as a result 'certain social groups have become increasingly excluded from the mainstream of economic and social life' (Lawless, Martin and Hardy, 1998, p. 9). More emphatically it is suggested that 'unemployment cannot be equated with social exclusion – but it can act as a useful surrogate' (Lawless and Smith, 1998, p. 201). This may be regarded as a 'narrow' approach to exclusion. A 'narrow' approach may nevertheless lead to an argument for a broad response from government. Thus a focus on inequality, unemployment and multiple deprivation concludes with demands for a clutch of policy currents: 'It is essential that strategic issues are adopted which involve a holistic, multi-disciplinary, cross-departmental and partnership approach' (Lee *et al.*, 1995, p. 45).

The narrow poverty approach to social exclusion may be contrasted with the broader 'fabric of society' approach. As Room (1995) points out, this is a Continental tradition in which society is seen as a status hierarchy or as a number of collectivities, bound together by sets of mutual rights and obligations which are rooted in some broader moral order. Work on 'networks' can be included in this group (Demos, 1997). The demands on government can be essentially the same as those emerging from the narrower poverty emphasis. Thus it is argued that a different model of government is needed which is 'more holistic, more preventive, and more personal' (6, 1997, p. 5). This has been expressed more simply and clearly by the politicians: 'Joined-up problems demand joined-up solutions' (Blair, 1997).

Some authors attempt to break out of what has been called the 'colonization' of poverty by the economists, and the sociologists' concern with accounting for the disadvantaged (CASE, 1998, p. 14). Thus Jordan (1996, p. 118) attempts to explain 'poverty-related social exclusion in terms of the economics of collective action in groups of all kinds'. The British Prime Minister takes a similar approach when he argues that social exclusion is about a bit more than poverty – 'it is about prospects and networks and life-chances' (Blair, 1997).

A third emerging approach to social exclusion can be described as 'organisational'. Here the focus is on specific institutions or groups of institutions – often part of the welfare state – and why citizens are excluded (or sometimes exclude themselves). Typical examples of this growing body of literature are studies that look at schools (Ball, 1998) and social housing (Butler, 1998). It is also the territory most easily encompassed by politicians and the PM's Social Exclusion Unit (SEU). Thus one of the first priorities of this Unit was to examine 'rough sleeping' and the recommendations of its report (July 1998) are entirely organisational in nature.

So far, we have argued in this section that social exclusion is yet another imprecise or confused concept. Although this may seem neither original nor particularly helpful, clarity is not necessarily the overriding prerequisite of a policy current. Indeed a recent paper began a discussion on 'The definition of social exclusion' by suggesting that not only is its meaning 'not always clear', but that 'it seems to have gained currency in part *because* it has no precise definition and means all things to all people' (Atkinson, 1998, p. 6).

Lack of clarity is a feature shared with social exclusion's policy relative – 'the underclass' (Murray, 1984, 1990). 'The principal problem one encounters in writing about the underclass is that it is never entirely clear what one is writing about' (Devine and Wright, 1993, p. xxi). A comparison of two terms from the social policy family, both distinguished by their ambiguity, is well outside the possibilities of this chapter but a superficial examination indicates that the underclass concept has most affinity with the narrow poverty approach to social exclusion. Social exclusion, however, does not suggest permanence in the social structure of the underclass.

Probably more important, social exclusion is capable of translation through its organisational dimension into distinct groups of people (rough sleepers, truants and so on). In turn this makes it possible to tackle identified problems. Lack of clarity as a source of strength is a not unfamiliar refrain in the literature. However we suggest here that the strength of policy currents emanates from other sources. For example the concept must reflect what might be called 'enlightened perceived wisdom'. It is not sufficient just to reflect on the accepted wisdom of the day; it must look a little ahead, to offer challenges and to hold out the expectation of a better state of affairs. It must provide a banner behind which the social policy troops from most corners of the political landscape can march. And the tunes that emerge must be in harmony with the ideological aspirations of the politicians in power.

Social exclusion and comparative advantage

Social exclusion as a policy current – however defined – must have a particular resonance for the UK voluntary sector, or at least that substantial part of the sector which is in the field of social welfare. The sector's central claims to legitimacy can be said to respond to all the main interpretations of the policy current.

At the heart of the narrow definition is the concern for poverty. And in the heartland of the voluntary sector are to be found the charities for which the 'relief of poverty' remains one of the four categories of purpose which the law recognises. The second, broad fabric of society approach echoes an equally powerful legitimising theme which is that the sector organisations are 'facilitators of social and political integration' (Ware, 1989, p. 19). The third – organisational – approach to social exclusion resonates in an equally powerful fashion since it can be argued that voluntary organisations' core strength is that they deal with those that have fallen through the net of the welfare state – the most excluded of all.

But the argument so far remains at a broad level. Are there more specific implications for particular types of voluntary organisations? To approach this question we draw on earlier research (Billis and Glennerster, 1998) and relate this to ideas about social exclusion. This research proposed that voluntary organisations have comparative advantages over public and for-profit organisations with respect to certain types of users. The essence of the argument is that:

(a)   there are inherent structural characteristics (ownership, stakeholders and resources) of organisations in each sector;
(b)   this predisposes them to respond more or less sensitively to different states of 'disadvantage' experienced by their users; and
(c)   voluntary organisations have a comparative advantage over agencies in other sectors in *some* areas of disadvantage because of their ambiguous structures.

The approach adopted in that earlier research was 'to group the various states of severe welfare problems that might beset citizens and lead them to be incapable of benefiting from traditional supply mechanisms' (Billis and Glennerster, 1998, p. 87). These states of disadvantage are:

- financial disadvantage – individuals who lack the purchasing power to seek solutions in the market;
- personal disadvantage – potential users who cannot articulate a coherent preference from the organisation in question;
- societal disadvantage – individuals and groups who are blamed or stigmatised;
- community disadvantage – people who suffer primarily from the fact that they live in a particular community and face the absence of the usual institutions of civil society.

Although our research was undertaken before the arrival of the New Labour government and the rise of social exclusion as a policy current, there are clear similarities between the two approaches. For example, the various approaches to exclusion (narrow, broad and organisational) appear to have an affinity with the different states of disadvantage. Thus the poverty-focused narrow approach may be close to the analysis of those who are financially disadvantaged. The broad fabric of society approach to exclusion has many themes in common with community disadvantage and deprived areas. There are some links also between this broad approach to exclusion and societal disadvantage which is concerned with groups such as drug addicts, alcoholics, people with HIV/Aids – groups to whom society has chosen not to listen. The emerging organisational approach to exclusion with its focus on specific institutions is more difficult to pin down to a particular state of disadvantage although there are already indications that it will align most closely to those who are to some degree blamed or stigmatised (the societally disadvantaged). The group of disadvantaged that seem to be excluded from the debate about social exclusion are those we have called personally disadvantaged – such as people with learning difficulties and mental health problems, young children and confused elderly people.

We have so far suggested in this section that (a) social exclusion is a policy current that should be of particular interest to the voluntary sector and that (b) by considering states of user disadvantage we can begin to link the policy current with the position of users and voluntary organisations. In other words the 'disadvantage approach' is one way of closing the gap between broad currents and organisational responses.

Discussion: social exclusion and implications for the voluntary sector

What are the implications of our analysis for the voluntary sector? Some of the initial questions for this chapter were: for what sort of agencies is the concept likely to be of interest? What might lie ahead? We might have added a further question which is: to what extent will the UK academic and governmental components of the policy current move in a similar direction?

A preliminary response might be that academic endeavour is likely to stay rooted within the traditional boundaries, with the social policy economists and poverty interests making a particularly strong showing. The old social administration approach, focused on policy *implementation* and organisational issues, seems to be absent from the current study of social exclusion.

Turning to the governmental approach to social exclusion, it is in the work of the SEU where the most obvious manifestation of the possible policy directions is likely to be found. We have already noted the organisational focus of the Unit in its 'street living' or 'rough sleeping' report (SEU, 1998). The other two priorities for 1998 were even more focused on organisational aspects: truancy and school exclusion, and 'worst housing estates' (SEU, 1997). It is likely that future priorities will also be organisational – by this we mean not necessarily that their focus is on institutions as 'owners of the problem' but, as in the case of rough sleeping, that new institutions may be sought to resolve the problems. The possible solutions to government's priorities are limited, and in the main will require setting up new institutions, changing the boundaries of existing organisations, encouraging them to be drawn into the provision of services, or persuading organisations to work together. Alternatively, there may be the familiar clarion call for 'more volunteers'. All these approaches can be found in the *Rough Sleeping* report.

The first conclusion or implication must therefore be that the new policy current will continue the move to overlapping boundaries between the state and the voluntary sector (Billis, 1993). The role of the sector is still seen as central; the new approach depends 'above all [on] the voluntary sector on whom any approach depends for success' (SEU, 1998, p. 18). But, if anything, the internal agonising about the independence of the sector will increase since the new current emphasises integration and coordination far more than previously. The inelegant but telling expression 'joined-up solutions' will inevitably draw the voluntary sector as a perceived key player in the response even closer into the ambit of government. It is again the service-providing voluntary agencies that are likely to be in demand.

The second implication emerges when we turn to examine the various states of disadvantage. Some groups are likely to receive less attention. As we noted, those who are *personally disadvantaged* – who cannot articulate a coherent preference from the organisation – do not loom large in the academic debate. Interestingly, they do not even appear on an otherwise huge agenda of issues which the London Voluntary Service Council raises in its 'anti-exclusion agenda' (LVSC, 1998). The absence of the personally disadvantaged from both the academic and policy debates is perhaps not surprising. If, as was suggested, social exclusion is the great Gulf Stream of present policy, practical implementation demands a narrower focus and a choice of priorities. It is natural – from the very title of the policy current itself – that the focus and choice of priorities will be on problems that are seemingly 'social' in both origin and potential solution. Therefore, according to this analysis, problems often with an apparently daunting or intractable individual medical dimension (mental illness and handicap, the confused elderly, for example) are unlikely to appear on early policy agendas.

A third implication which flows from the above is that there is room for voluntary agencies working, for example, in the fields of learning disability, mental health and with elderly confused people to begin to influence the policy agenda. This is particularly important since it has been argued that it is precisely in this area that voluntary agencies, because of their distinctive ambiguous structures, have a competitive advantage over other sectors since their structures produce incentives for more sensitive service (Billis and Glennerster, 1998).

The fourth implication is that those dealing with *societally disadvantaged* or stigmatised people are unlikely to be high on the priority list. An important practical factor here appears to be whether in any period politicians are likely to lose votes by supporting their cause. Many of those in this category such as alcoholics and drug users represent unattractive potential recipients of public money for voters – and therefore for politicians too.

A fuller discussion of social disadvantage and social exclusion would necessitate both an examination of the nature of stigma and a deeper exploration of the meanings of exclusion. However recent definitional work undertaken by CASE (Le Grand, 1998) provides additional reasons why socially disadvantaged people are likely to remain in the backwaters rather than the mainstream. It is suggested that: 'an individual is socially excluded if' (a) he or she is geographically resident in a society but (b) for reasons beyond his or her control he or she cannot participate in the normal activities of citizens in that society and (c) he or she would like to so participate' (Le Grand, 1998).

The critical phrase here is 'beyond his or her control'. If this definition is held in general currency then there will be those who will undoubtedly argue that many of the socially disadvantaged could solve their problems if they so wished. (Of course this line of argument could be extended to other groups of disadvantaged people but it is has most power when applied to the stigmatised groups.)

It has been suggested that the state can resolve many of the problems of those who are *financially disadvantaged* and that voluntary agencies have no particular comparative advantage over other sectors (Billis and Glennerster, 1998). Our fifth conclusion is that although the new current policy places a heavy emphasis on poverty, the voluntary sector can play only a minor role. The exception to this is the extent to which the sector can provide employment, a hope expressed in many government publications. Should pressure be put on the sector in this area, questions about its legitimacy would inevitably be raised.

Those who have been described as *community disadvantaged* are probably most aligned to the new policy current. 'Worst estates' are already high on the government's agenda. In this area of disadvantage it has been argued that the local churches of all denominations have a special role to play: 'they provide formal services in an individualised and sensitive way to socially marginalised users' (Cameron, 1998, p. 342). Thus our sixth implication is that churches and other religious organisations, could, if they so wished, find themselves more centre stage than hitherto. However as Harris (1995) has earlier pointed out, limited resources may restrict the role of congregations in formal care and they are more likely to sustain 'quiet care; the less "organised" types of welfare such as mutual aid, social integration and various kinds of informal care' (p. 69).

Finally, the search for 'joined-up' solutions may have implications above and beyond our first conclusion regarding the extension of the ambiguous boundaries of the formal welfare state. It may bring back on to the agenda the issue of competition and cooperation between voluntary agencies themselves. It is unlikely that a government so heavily committed to integration, coordination and cooperation will fail to point to failures in these areas amongst voluntary agencies. We may yet witness an increase in the pressure for mergers.

This chapter has argued that social exclusion – with all its confusion – is here to stay for a while and can be thought of as a new policy 'current' which is likely to serve as an increasingly powerful rallying call. Indications of its increasing usage can be observed by the growing number of studies and reports that have 'exclusion' or less frequently 'inclusion' in their title. By introducing the notion of different states of disadvantage links have been made between social exclusion on the one side and the organisational characteristics of voluntary agencies on the other side. Seven possible implications for voluntary organisations have been identified. Since policy currents may have a powerful impact on future official policies, an analysis of them may enable voluntary agencies to reexamine their position in relation to potential policy changes – to 'stay ahead of the game'. This chapter has tried to demonstrate how an analysis of social exclusion and disadvantage may contribute to that objective and to the wider analysis of public policy.

References

Atkinson, A. (1998) 'Social exclusion, poverty and unemployment', in CASE, *Exclusion, Employment and Opportunity*, Centre for Analysis of Social Exclusion, London School of Economics, London.
Ball, M. (1998) *School Inclusion: The School, the Family and the Community*, Joseph Rowntree Foundation, York and London.
Billis, D. (1993) *Organising Public and Voluntary Agencies*, Routledge, London.
Billis, D. and H. Glennerster (1998) 'Human services and the voluntary sector: towards a theory of comparative advantage', *Journal of Social Policy*, 27(1): 79–98.
Blair, T. (1997) 'Bringing Britain Together', speech at the launch of the SEU, 8 December, mimeo, Social Exclusion Unit, London.
Butler, S. (1998) *Access Denied: The Exclusion of People in Need from Social Housing*, Shelter, London.
Cameron, H. (1998) 'The social action of the local church', PhD thesis, London School of Economics, London.
CASE (1998) *Exclusion, Employment and Opportunity*, Centre for Analysis of Social Exclusion, London School of Economics, London.
Demos (1997) *The Wealth and Poverty of Networks: Tackling Social Exclusion*, Demos Collection Issue 12, Demos, London.
Devine, J. and J. Wright (1993) *The Greatest of Evils: Urban Poverty and the American Underclass*, de Gruyter, New York.

Harris, M. (1995) 'Quiet care: welfare work and religious congregations', *Journal of Social Policy*, 24(1): 53–71.

Jordan, B. (1996) *A Theory of Poverty and Social Exclusion*, Polity Press, Cambridge.

Lawless, P., R. Martin and S. Hardy (eds) (1998) *Unemployment and Social Exclusion: Landscapes of Labour Inequality*, Jessica Kingsley Publishers, London.

Lawless, P. and Y. Smith (1998) 'Poverty, inequality and exclusion in the contemporary city', in P. Lawless, R. Martin and S. Hardy (eds) *Unemployment and Social Exclusion: Landscapes of Labour Inequality*, Jessica Kingsley Publishers, London.

Lee, P., A. Murie, A. Marsh and M. Riseborough (1995) *The Price of Social Exclusion*, National Federation of Housing Associations, London.

Le Grand, J. (1998) 'Social exclusion in Britain today', paper presented to conference '*Counting me in: Pathways to an Inclusive Society*', held at Church House Conference Centre, Westminster, London on 3 December 1998.

Lewis, J. and H. Glennerster (1996) *Implementing the New Community Care*, Open University Press, Buckingham.

LVSC (1998) *Barriers: Social and Economic Exclusion in London*, London Voluntary Service Council, London.

Murray, C. (1984) *American Social Policy 1950–1980*, Basic Books, New York.

Murray, C. (1990) *The Emerging British Underclass*, IEA Health and Welfare Unit, London.

Room, G. (1995) 'Poverty in Europe: competing paradigms of analysis', *Policy and Politics*, 23(2): 103–13.

6, Perri (1997) 'Social exclusion: time to be optimistic', in Demos, *The Wealth and Poverty of Networks: Tackling Social Exclusion*, Demos Collection Issue 12, Demos, London.

Social Exclusion Unit (1997) *Social Exclusion Unit: Purpose, Work Priorities and Working Methods*, Cabinet Office, London.

Social Exclusion Unit (1998) *Rough Sleeping*, Cm 4008, HMSO, London.

Walker, R. (1995) 'The dynamics of poverty and social exclusion', in G. Room (ed.) *Beyond the Threshold: The Measurement and Analysis of Social Exclusion*, Policy Press, University of Bristol.

Walker, A. and C. Walker (eds) (1997) *Britain Divided – The Growth of Social Exclusion in the 1980s and 1990s*, Child Poverty Action Group, London.

Ware, A. (1989) *Between Profit and the State*, Polity Press, Cambridge.

4

Contracting: The Experience of Service Delivery Agencies

Duncan W. Scott and Lynne Russell

Introduction

In this chapter we turn from consideration of the broad social policy context and a major theme or 'current' of the contemporary policy agenda to the first of a series of studies of specific areas of policy implementation. Its focus is one of the most significant changes of the 1990s for organisations involved in the delivery of welfare services in the UK, the implementation in 1993 of the NHS and Community Care Act 1990. The chapter draws on the findings from three separate but interlinked studies[1] to highlight significant impacts of the contract culture on the finances and management of these organisations and on the ways in which volunteers were involved in their work.

The NHS and Community Care Act 1990

Commentators on the 1990 NHS and Community Care Act distinguish four key aspects (for further discussion see also Chapter 8 of this volume):

- a shift from institutional to community (a mix of day and domiciliary) care;
- an emphasis on needs-led (user/carer preferences) services rather than supply-led ones;

- a decentralisation of strategic responsibilities from central to local government; and
- the development of a mixed economy of care with independent for-profit and non-profit providers alongside, or instead of, state provision.

The greater prominence given to voluntary and private sector providers by these changes was accompanied by the development of contracts for the purchase of community care services and a growing and more widespread formalisation of the relationship between the statutory and voluntary sectors. Statutory funders, concerned to target support of the voluntary sector towards their own priorities and to ensure accountability and value for money at a time of financial constraint, were increasingly replacing arm's-length grant aid with contracts and service agreements. By 1994/5 fees, as opposed to grants, comprised almost three-quarters of social services expenditure in the voluntary sector (Mocroft, 1996).

It was some time, however, before the implications for the voluntary sector became clear. The Act did not become fully operational until April 1993 and even then many local authorities were not ready to implement it. We read of an 'immature' care market (Walsh *et al.*, 1997, p. 152) in which ' . . . funders were not quite sure what they really wanted' (Davis Smith, 1997, p. 62).

Furthermore, funders' strategic knowledge, and understanding, of local service delivery voluntary organisations was incomplete and there were grave shortfalls in local authority funding at exactly the moment when implementation began (Hudson, 1992: Leat, 1994). But after several years of full implementation of the Act, local authority social services departments were reported as being more positive about the idea of care markets and the potential contributions of both commercial and non-profit service providers (Kendall and Knapp, 1996). We also learn that 'an information gap' (about non-residential, non-statutory services) had been 'largely removed', although there remained ' . . . little development of strategic frameworks for considering the appropriate organisation, regulation and control of the social care system' (May, 1999, pp. 2, 4). In the meantime, in the first years following implementation of the legislation, purchasing agreements tended to take the form of 'sweetheart deals' with established providers, these contracts often replacing existing grant aid.

It is difficult to identify the specific impacts of contracts as a result of the complexity, first, of the wider legislative environment and, second, of related organisational structures and processes. It has also been suggested that many of the changes alleged to have been caused by contracting in fact pre-date 1993; that existing regulatory and bureaucratic trends as well as processes of professionalisation were already having an impact (Taylor and Lewis, 1997).

The studies

The findings reported in this chapter were largely obtained from detailed case study research in four different locations in the north of England. Since 1991 relationships have been developed with 27 service delivery voluntary organisations which work primarily with older people, children and families. Almost all these agencies are locally based and are small to medium in size, with incomes which ranged in 1989/90 from around £7,000 to £309,000. The research process was intensive and time-consuming, and required: 'a recurring pattern of preparation [of the respondents], face to face interviews, long telephone conversations, feedback and group workshops' (Russell *et al.*, 1996, pp. 339–400).

The three studies were:

- 1993: a study of the total income and funding profile of 21 organisations since 1989;
- 1995: a continuation of this work but with a particular focus on statutory funding in 1993/4 and 1994/5. The research mapped the income of 17 organisations and also included a study of the perspectives of local statutory funders;
- 1997: an exploration of the impact of the contract culture on the role and relevance of volunteers in 15 agencies. As before there were detailed interviews with chief officers, but the research also included a postal survey of 275 volunteers; and individual interviews with 70 volunteers; a postal survey of member branches of a voluntary organisation

providing services for older people in England and Wales;
and interviews and a workshop with a sample of senior
managers in statutory agencies.

Financial impacts

At the point at which the community care legislation was about
to be implemented, our 1993 study of financial trends since 1989
within 21 locally based service delivery voluntary organisations
provides the context for these agencies' response to changing
political and statutory agendas in general, and for their response
to contracts and the community care legislation in particular.

Between 1989/90 and 1992/3 the total income of our sample
had grown significantly to £1.8 million, a 40 per cent increase in
real terms. In particular, statutory funding had almost doubled,
and comprised 50 per cent of total income in 1992/3. This reflected the emphasis within the sample on organisations working
with older people and with children and families. The pattern
of overall growth, however, concealed a more complex reality,
which was characterised by financial uncertainty, volatility and
constraint. The income of the majority of these organisations
was a precarious patchwork of short-term funding, likened by
one worker to 'preparing a meal for 50 people on a Baby Bell-
ing – constantly having to warm up lots of small pots'. Thus
even among those organisations which had experienced net growth,
14 had seen their annual income decline at some point during
this period.

Almost every organisation told a story of financial constraint
and uncertainty. Very often growth was achieved against a back-
cloth of underfunding and one-third of the sample had in fact
seen a net decline in statutory support. Where Section 11[2] funding and the Urban Programme were significant, organisations
were facing a particularly uncertain future as these began to be
phased out. When funding for new areas of work *had* been obtained, it did not reflect the total cost of providing that service:
the development of new projects relied on piecing together a
package of supplementary funding. This uncertainty was experienced against a background in which two-fifths of the sample
had no reserves or contingency funds.

The uncertainty experienced by these organisations was destabilising and inhibited strategic planning. Funding was a constant preoccupation, which for some organisations consumed 30–40 per cent of individual worker hours. It was against this background, and the particular vulnerability of these organisations to changes in statutory priorities and funding streams, that the community care legislation was implemented and the 'contract culture' developed.

The second phase of our work considered the emerging impact of the community care legislation and the development of contracts. In 1993/4, sample agencies saw a sharp rise in total revenue income – a 23 per cent increase to £2.1 million in just one year. Statutory funding increased to £1.2 million and comprised almost 60 per cent of total funding.

Until 1992/3 there had been no discernible pattern to success in attracting statutory funding. Now, however, there was a sharp divide between agencies working with children and families and those working predominantly with older people. Statutory funding to the latter almost doubled between 1992/3 and 1994/5 compared with a 21 per cent increase for those organisations working with children and families. Over half of the total growth of statutory funding identified in these two years came from the Special Transitional Grant (STG) for the implementation of the community care legislation,[3] while only a quarter came from within existing mainstream or grant aid budgets.

The picture of 'winners' and 'losers' was more complex, however, than simply the divide between organisations working with older people and those working with children (a trend which may since have been reversed, particularly by more recent changes in the political agenda and the emphasis of the present administration on the family and early years). Within the framework set by purchasers' policies, priorities and preferences, those organisations which were most successful or confident in their negotiations (at least in this initial stage of implementing the community care legislation) were:

- organisations which dominated a particular market niche in terms of service, client group or geographic location;
- organisations which were influential in political and professional networks; and, most importantly

- organisations which were *relatively* large, where size was a proxy for level of resources, perceived management skills, capacity to network and a known track record.

Organisational impacts

Implementation of the community care legislation and the requirement that 85 per cent of STG be spent in the independent sector had a dramatic impact on the income and activities of some organisations. In the 1997 survey, 60 per cent of contracts led to a significant increase in service levels – either because the contract represented funding for the development of new areas of work or because it involved an increased level of funding for existing services. This experience was echoed in the 1997 case study agencies. For example, within one year, 'Support' (which together with the other organisations identified has been given an alias) saw a 44 per cent increase in its total revenue budget as a result of funding to develop a new day centre. Another local organisation, 'Ethnic Support Services; experienced a 28 per cent increase as a result of a £250,000 contract to provide domiciliary care.

Financial success, however, was a mixed blessing. Those organisations which had attracted new funding for the development of community care services now faced a dual challenge – managing the rapid development of new services while simultaneously managing continuing financial constraints on their other activities. Funding for Support's new day centre, for example, increased the annual revenue budget for day care from £15,000 to £150,000 – but support for its core activity, its management and infrastructure remained unchanged and dependent on subsidy from voluntary income. Similarly, while Ethnic Support Services began the process of appointing 17 workers to deliver the domicilary care service, redundancies were having to be made in response to shortfalls in funding for its work with children and families.

The windfall represented by community care contracts presented familiar dilemmas to many organisations in our sample. Should they pursue the opportunity to expand and develop services, although their core activity was under-resourced and their physical and management infrastructure was inadequate? And should they pursue new funding for areas of work which were not necessarily a priority within the organisation's existing objectives?

> When we get these bulletins [from social services] how much do we shape our work in response to them when our own internal monitoring might tell us there are more pressing needs – and given that we are physically limited in terms of space and workers? . . . The contract culture may present difficult choices. It may be possible to articulate internal justifications for taking on certain areas of work – if they enable resources to be released for other aspects for example. We may indeed have to diversify. (Voluntary agency manager)

Often the response was opportunistic in practice. Within the context of financial volatility, insecurity and constraint, one explanation offered was that this new cash would help sustain the organisation and might even cross-subsidise elements of its infrastructure. The £250,000 contract for domiciliary care mentioned above, for example, specifically included a 10 per cent management fee to the organisation, over and above the cost of the three core workers appointed to manage and administer the service. The reality, however, was that the development of contract services was often subsidised by an increased voluntary input from paid workers, and that contracts continued the pattern of underfunding typical of vaguer grant regimes.

Thus the national survey of 1997 which identified a total of 199 contracts found that in many cases the fee did not reflect the full cost of the service. Nevertheless, new funding opportunities proved seductive for organisations with low cash reserves, accustomed to living from hand to mouth, and at a time when the narrower focus of funding to voluntary sector welfare agencies increasingly reflected statutory sector purchasing requirements, at the expense of other activities and core funding.

The development of a market in care services as a result of the 1990 legislation accelerated an already existing move towards more formal funding agreements between statutory funders and voluntary agencies – the replacement of 'arm's length' grant aid with contracts or service-level agreements. The 1997 national survey, for example, found that a quarter of the contracts identified had first been negotiated prior to 1993. There was then a rapid increase in the negotiation of contracts in 1993 and 1994 and, of these, almost half replaced existing grant aid. By 1995/6 contract fees represented 60 per cent of the income of these 75 organisations, and were expected to rise a further 12 per cent in the following year.

By 1995, 14 of our 17 case study agencies had experience of negotiating contracts for all or part of their statutory funding. Immediate impacts of negotiating contracts were twofold. First, voluntary agencies had to develop specific operational policies (Equal Opportunities, Health and Safety, for example). They also had to develop systems and processes for contract compliance and for facilitating monitoring and evaluation – changes which were often found to be beneficial:

> Contract compliance has forced us to be more efficient in creating internal systems for recording information and has refined our skills. If I am honest I have to admit that our systems were woolly. (Voluntary agency manager)

Second, appreciable amounts of time had to be given to negotiations – with a consequent distraction of energy in relatively small organisations. Describing the process of negotiating a contract to provide day care in 1994, one chief officer commented, 'We went through agony to get £3,000.' Organisations involved in contracting continue, even now, to go through unwieldy and difficult procedures disproportionate to their organisational capacities and the level of funding sought. One of the case study agencies which secured its first contract in 1998 had to spend a considerable amount of time and energy in drawing up a three-year business plan and financial profile for a one-year contract worth £9,500. This is an organisation with only two part-time workers and a shared office in a church hall.

More strategic impacts which were anticipated were that contracts would give rise to longer-term funding agreements, greater clarity, increased stability and continuity on the one hand, but a possible loss of autonomy and distraction of mission and ethos on the other. In practice, three years after the implementation of the legislation and the rapid growth of contracting, the anticipated gains had not been fully realised. Two-fifths of contracts identified by the national survey of 1997, for example, were still for only one year. Even where longer-term contracts were secured, the potential impact of a developing market in care services and the growth of competitive tendering was becoming evident. Voluntary organisations described themselves as being 'pinned down' in 'more ferocious [and unrealistic] price negotiations'. A focus on unit cost rather than the concept of 'best value' had undermined both organisational stability and continuity for users in a project which had provided family-based respite care for children and young people with disabilities since the early 1980s. In 1999 it lost its contract to a partnership of two large national voluntary agencies, which have absorbed the service into their existing provision. This resulted in redundancies and the transfer of users and volunteer carers to the new providers with little consultation or explanation, and despite their vociferous and public objections.

The case study research also highlighted a number of examples of contract specifications and relationships with purchasers which potentially undermined the autonomy of voluntary sector providers and the wider ethos, values and constraints which determined their internal policies and practice (Russell *et al.*, 1995; see also Chapter 12 of this book). One example was a purchaser's insistence that an organisation employ full-time rather than part-time workers. This was unacceptable, as one of its non-service aims was to provide opportunities for women to develop new skills and return to work. Very often such differences reflect purchasers' lack of knowledge and understanding of local voluntary organisations and their wider mission.

The impact on volunteers

In 1994, there was little recognition by the senior managers we interviewed in social services and the health service that the contract culture might have wider implications for voluntary organisations:

> The voluntary sector is being moved into a business culture and the financial relationship is commissioner driven, but there is no reason why these organisations should not retain their values and culture in terms of how they deal with clients, how

they use volunteers and in terms of their style and presenta-
tion. (Social Services Department Officer)

By 1996, however, there appeared to be a growing, if uneven,
awareness of the impacts on both individual agencies and on
the sector as a whole. A continuing blind spot, however, remained
the implications for volunteer activity, beyond a limited recognition of the increasing demands now made on management
committee members and the skills which contracting demanded
of them. In practice, purchasers were often unaware of the role
played, if any, by volunteers in the delivery and support of contracted services and were concerned with outputs rather than
the detailed specification of inputs. Few contracts made more
than a passing reference to volunteers; half did not mention them
at all. It is hardly surprising then that, in half the cases where
the delivery of contracts had increased the cost of training and
support of volunteers, these increased costs were not fully reflected in the contract fee which was therefore subsidised by the
voluntary agency.

The reality suggested by our research is that, although many
organisations heavily involved in contracting may be moving increasingly towards a growing reliance on paid workers, volunteers
remain significant in contract delivery and support, while the
trustees' role is one of the sector's defining characteristics. In
the 75 contracting agencies which responded to our postal survey,
the human resources consisted of:

- Full-time paid staff   378
- Part-time paid staff   1,000
- Management committee volunteers   969
- Volunteers in service delivery and support   10,263

Respondents in both the national survey and the postal survey
of volunteers in case study agencies in 1997 echoed the findings
reported by Harris in Chapter 12 that the workload and level of
responsibility of management committee members have increased
significantly as a result of contracts, and this is particularly true
for those with key roles – the chairperson, treasurer and secretary. Around 80 per cent of chief officers in the national survey
felt that contracting had changed the role of committee mem-

bers and demanded increased skills – in financial management, business planning, service monitoring and evaluation, personnel management and legal expertise. One response to this in 80 per cent of organisations has been to headhunt new members with specific skills, a process of professionalisation which clearly raises questions about future patterns of volunteering and the role of the voluntary sector in facilitating the participation and personal development of a wider spectrum of people.

Another consequence of the technical demands made by contracting was that 75 per cent of contracting organisations were increasingly led by their senior paid workers rather than by the management committee. The strategic invisibility of volunteers was also found in respect of service volunteers who, in the majority of case study agencies, had not been involved in any discussions about the development of contracts and were often unaware that their organisation was involved in contracting.

Volunteers who continued to play a key role generally saw their workload and level of responsibility increased. For some this was welcome and, in our study, they reported increased satisfaction. A second impact was that many agencies moved to a greater use of, and dependence on, paid workers while others tended to formalise the roles of their volunteers. This included tighter specification of tasks, increased supervision and performance review. In both the latter cases the rationale for these changes was reported as guaranteeing service levels and ensuring contract compliance.

Recruitment of volunteers to both management and service delivery roles was reported by chief officers to have become more difficult as a result of contracts – exacerbating the problems experienced as a result of ageing local constituencies, changing patterns of economic activity and the increasing demand for volunteers by local clusters of organisations. Turnover of existing volunteers had also increased. One in six chief officers reported the resignation of some trustees as a response to contracting.

These responses by volunteers to a changing environment may be relatively short-lived. The processes of professionalisation – through the substitution of paid workers and the selective recruitment of volunteers – and formalisation, however, deny the important developmental and social significance of voluntary activity. If the contract culture prevents an inclusive approach to volunteering, and funding regimes inhibit the sector's developmental capacity, this will have longer-term implications for active citizenship and a qualitative impact on the delivery of some services.

Conclusion

An 'aerial view' reveals the patchwork quilt of sectoral responses to contracting. The global picture appears to be more bureaucracy, greater financial dependence of voluntary agencies on the local state, improved administrative and legal skills and mission-drift (if not shift). Some agencies have greater financial security, others less; the up-skilling of one category of volunteers is paralleled by the exclusion of those traditional volunteers who brought social rather than technical knowledge. At close quarters it is possible to discern how large and small agencies depend to a considerable extent upon often fragile internal and external relationships.

Successive governments in the 1990s have harnessed the energies of voluntary organisations. Policy-makers were committed to a mixed economy of welfare which would be efficient, innovative, accountable and distributive. But, at a strategic and an instrumental level, there has been only a confused and limited understanding of the voluntary sector as a whole, of its functional parts and its local ecologies. As a result, we have seen how the contract culture may erode the distinctive characteristics of service delivery voluntary organisations and even undermine other political objectives, such as the development of active citizenship through voluntary activity.

The research described here has shown that the first phase of contracting was a mixed blessing for voluntary organisations. Many, of all shapes and sizes, experienced growth and positive change. Many, likewise, struggled with the impact of contracting on their wider objectives and ethos, and the resultant disruptions to their internal and external networks. In the late 1990s, as the 'sweetheart deals' came up for review in the context of a more developed market and more price-competitive purchasing criteria, we began to see the more profound impacts which the contract culture had on the sector, on the pattern of service delivery and on attention to user preferences. Within our study area, there is evidence of a review by parts of the voluntary sector of its participation in contracting, and the development of alternative strategies. The success of these will depend on the restructuring of income streams, increasing the level of non-statutory income, mergers and the development of partnership working.

Certainly it will be important that voluntary organisations reevaluate whether the contract culture is compatible with social values, public service, flexibility and reciprocity; and whether it is possible to reconcile the managerialist approaches associated with contracting with broad-based governance and community participation. The chief officer of one voluntary organisation summed up their early experience of contracting as follows:

> Yes there are lessons to be learnt – particularly since many organisations do not have the necessary expertise to negotiate a contract on an equal footing. There is a danger of being seduced as we were by the apparent financial security a contract offers; a danger of failing to cost the service properly so that it becomes necessary to subsidise a statutory service with volunteer labour; a danger of losing sight of one's development plan and sense of priorities and simply responding to a market opportunity; a danger of alienating volunteers because we are seen to be no different to the private sector. (Russell and Scott, 1997, p. 68)

However, the greatest legacy from the contract culture may be the more differentiated understanding of voluntary organisations which has emerged because of their increased policy significance over the 1990s. We have discovered imperfect understandings of voluntary action not just in the town hall but also in the voluntary agencies themselves.

Perhaps the most effective response would be to encourage a greater academic, policy and practice commitment to the interdependencies between and within organisations, to individual and institutional exchanges – rather than to over-dichotomised sectoral frameworks. Thus the most useful and enduring legacy of contracting may not be a legal and rational one, nor an acceptance of the primacy of market forces in the delivery of social welfare, but a renewed attention to the *social* contract. To achieve a sustainable voluntary sector, purchasers and providers alike will need to generate more grounded, yet more dynamic, knowledge and understanding of their local interdependencies. Their mutual struggles in the contracting process may yet bring them closer together.

Notes

1. The findings of these studies have been reported in Russell, Scott and Wilding (1993 and 1995) and Russell and Scott (1997). Case study work is continuing with a sample of these and other organisations and the findings will be published in collaboration with Pete Alcock and Rob MacMillan in 2000.
2. Section 11 of the Local Government Act 1969, empowered the Home Office to provide funding for local projects and programmes that benefited black and minority ethnic communities.
3. In order to facilitate the transfer of responsibility for funding social care to social services departments, local authorities were provided by the Department of Health with substantial additional resources taken from the Social Security budget and 'ring-fenced' for the purpose.

References

Davis Smith, J. (1997) 'Expansion or withdrawal? The implications of contracting for volunteering', in Perri 6 and J. Kendall (eds) *The Contract Culture in Public Services: Studies from Britain, Europe and the USA*, Arena, Aldershot.

Hudson, B. (1992) 'Quasi markets in health and social care in Britain: can the public sector respond?', *Policy and Politics*, 20(2): 131–42.

Kendall, J. and M. Knapp (1996) *The Voluntary Sector in the UK*, Manchester University Press, Manchester.

Leat, D. (1994) 'Caring for people who care at home: ways forward', in I. Allen *et al. Stimulating Provision by the Independent Sector*, Policy Studies Institute, London.

May, A. (ed.) (1999) 'Managing social care: charting the cultural changes in local authorities', *'Evidence': Briefing Paper 3*, Nuffield Institute for Health (Leeds University)/PSSRU (London School of Economics), Leeds.

Mocroft, I. (1996) 'The survey of local authority payments to voluntary and charitable organisations for 1994–95', in C. Pharoah (ed.)

Dimensions of the Voluntary Sector, 1996 edition, Charities Aid Foundation, Tonbridge.

Russell, L. and D. Scott (1997) *Very Active Citizens? The Impact of Contracts on Volunteers*, University of Manchester, Manchester.

Russell, L., D. Scott and P. Wilding, (1993) *Funding the Voluntary Sector: A Case Study from the North of England*, University of Manchester, Manchester.

Russell, L., D. Scott, and P. Wilding (1995) *Mixed Fortunes: The Funding of the Voluntary Sector*, University of Manchester, Manchester.

Russell, L., D. Scott, and P. Wilding (1996) 'The Funding of the Local Voluntary Sector', *Policy and Politics*, 24(4): 399–407.

Taylor, M. and J. Lewis (1997) 'Contracting: what does it do to voluntary and nonprofit organizations?', in Perri 6 and J. Kendall (eds) *The Contract Culture in Public Services: Studies from Britain, Europe and the USA*, Arena, Aldershot, pp. 27–45.

Walsh, K., N. Deakin, P. Smith, P. Spurgeon and N. Thomas (1997) *Contracting for Change: Contracts in Health, Social Care and Other Local Government*, Oxford Unversity Press, Oxford.

5

Regulation: The Impact on Local Voluntary Action

Colin Rochester

Social policy and regulation

This chapter looks at the way in which the changing social policy environment in the UK has been accompanied by increasingly stringent measures to regulate the activities of voluntary organisations in order to minimise the risks inherent in using private bodies, rather than the institutions of the state, to meet social need. It examines the impact of regulation, registration and inspection on the activities and organisation of the many thousands of small local organisations which make up the great majority of the population of the voluntary and community sectors.[1] And it shows how the burdensome nature of risk-minimisation measures can be at odds with the encouragement of voluntary action and community involvement which has been a social policy goal for successive administrations and which is an important component of the Blair government's 'Third Way' project.

There have been two major consequences for the voluntary sector of the radical rethink of the nature and extent of the state's contribution to social welfare that is at the heart of the social policy revolution of the 1980s and 1990s. The first of these – and the one that has received by far the greater degree of attention – is the creation of the 'mixed economy of welfare' and the transfer of responsibility for the provision of many services from the government to independent agencies. Further discussion of this major development may be found, among other places, in Chapters 4 and 8 of this book.

Less attention has been paid to the second major element in the social policy changes of the last two decades of the twentieth century, a renewed interest in voluntary action and community involvement. The 'mixed economy of welfare' redefined the *nature* of the governmental role but another strand in the attempt to roll back the frontiers of the state was concerned to limit the *extent* to which it was expected to meet the full range of social need. Outside certain boundaries those in need would have to seek help from family and friends, purchase it from commercial enterprises or rely on voluntary action. From the vantage point of the Voluntary Services Unit at the Home Office in the 1980s it was suggested that there would be 'society benefits if all those who can play some active part in responding to common needs, or the needs of those disadvantaged or less fortunate, are encouraged or enabled and are not prevented from doing so' (Griffiths, 1986, p. 5).

Regulation

The attempt to roll back the frontiers of the state was not restricted to the field of social welfare. Enhancing the role of the voluntary sector can be seen as part of a wider programme of privatisation carried out by successive British Conservative administrations. The flagships of this project were the transfer of the utilities out of public ownership and the establishment of a national lottery administered by a private company. In all these fields loss of public control was tempered by the introduction of some form of regulation. Unlike the other areas of privatisation, however, the voluntary sector and the social need 'industry' did not find themselves subject to a single regulator. Instead they became subject to a bewildering variety of requirements for regulation, registration and inspection.

In the first place those who have become contractors to local authorities are regulated by the terms of the contracts as well as subject to inspection. One commentator has suggested that the 'contract state' has led to the 'regulatory state' (Kumar, 1996). Second, those which are registered charities are subject to the jurisdiction of the Charity Commission. The ability of the Commission to carry out its regulatory functions has been strengthened as the responsibilities of the organisations it supervises have grown. Its powers have been increased by the Charities Act 1993 and its ability to use them enhanced by more resources – in particular by the computerisation of the Register of Charities. Since 1996 charities have been required to meet compulsory standards for accounting and audit as well as to provide an annual report to the Commission (Framjee, 1998). A third set of regulations has been introduced in order to protect users of services. The requirements of registration and inspection for organisations providing services for young people under the Children Act 1989 is a prime example.

These measures can be seen as responses to the privatisation of welfare provision and the growing significance of the contribution made by voluntary organisations to meeting social need. They can also be viewed as symptoms of a wider set of social concerns. During the last twenty years of the twentieth century there was a growing conviction that the world in which we live is beset by danger and that it is a major responsibility of government to reduce to a minimum the many risks to which the population is exposed (Giddens, 1990; Beck, 1992). As well as the passage of primary legislation (like the Children Act 1989 and the Charities Act 1993) and the introduction of more rigorous rules under existing statutes or European law, this increasing consciousness of risk is also linked to more energetic approaches to implementation and enforcement. In this environment, too, regulations devised to deal with very different concerns may be extended to even the smallest of voluntary organisations. They find themselves caught up in the provision of measures including the Food Safety Act 1990, the Health and Safety at Work Act 1974 and its subsequent regulations, and the administration of public entertainment and other licences.

The promotion of voluntary action

In 1980 the Home Secretary launched the Development of Local Voluntary Action programme as a direct response by the Voluntary Services Unit to the report of the Wolfenden Committee (Wolfenden Committee, 1978). The programme was a blend of innovative projects, evaluative research studies and conferences. Based on the perception that the vitality of voluntary action in Britain varied from locality to locality it sought to develop ideas and actions which would assist the development of new forms of voluntary activity in different local areas. The rationale for the government's interest in promoting voluntary action, according to one of the architects of the programme, combined concern for the individual who could be enabled to play an active part in society with the need to address the inability and disinclination of the state to meet the full range of social need (Griffiths, 1986).

A similar mixture of motives underpinned the Make a Difference programme through which the Major administration sought to give some substance to earlier rhetoric about the 'Active Citizen'. The programme was based on a vision 'of a society in which the right of all citizens to engage in voluntary or community action is unequivocally recognised' (Make A Difference Team, 1995, p. 3). It was also, however, the product of a government which saw voluntary action as filling the gap between 'those areas which are the responsibility of individuals and those which are the responsibility of the government' (Home Office, 1992, p. 1). (A full account of the Make a Difference programme can be found in Chapter 13 of this book.)

The New Labour government was elected in May 1997 on a platform which included the pledge to 'put voluntary action at the heart of restoring civic society' (Labour Party, 1997, p. 6). In the speech in which he announced the formation of a high-profile Active Community Unit (on the lines of the Social Exclusion Unit referred to in Chapter 3) to 'raise the profile of the sector within government', Tony Blair suggested that his government's biggest challenge would be 'to ignite a new spirit of involvement in the community' (Blair, 1999, p. 5).

The promotion of voluntary action has thus been a social policy goal for successive governments through the 1980s and 1990s. Yet the evidence from the Home Office Local Voluntary Activity Surveys (LOVAS) and research undertaken by the author suggest that the local organisations which are the focus for much voluntary action are finding it increasingly difficult to maintain current levels of voluntary effort (Jermyn *et al.*, 1997a, 1997b; Marshall and Haggett, 1997; Woodburn *et al.*, 1997; Rochester, 1999).

Explanations for this apparent decline in the voluntary impulse are legion. They range from the economic – the opening of the labour market to women has left huge gaps in the ranks of those who traditionally played a major role in voluntary action (Hedley and Davis Smith, 1992; Hancock and Jarvis, 1997) – to the spiritual – a decline in the numbers adhering to the religious and ethical norms of altruism and philanthropy. There is, however, considerable support for the view that the increasing burden of regulation has had an important impact on the willingness and ability of people to engage in voluntary action at the local level. The changing social policy environment of the 1980s and 1990s has thus emphasised the importance of the contribution that voluntary action has to make while at the same time giving rise to circumstances which seriously inhibit its development.

Local voluntary action

By no means all voluntary action takes place at local level and not all local action is undertaken through voluntary organisations. But local voluntary organisations provide the setting for a very substantial amount of activity of the kind that successive governments have sought to promote. While no one can say with any certainty exactly how many bodies of this kind are active across the country, it is clear that they form the great majority of the constituents of a sector which, according to one recent estimate, is made up of 'far more than a million voluntary organisations of all kinds in the United Kingdom' (Elsdon, 1995, p. 3).

The range and variety of their activities cover the full gamut of human needs and interests. An attempt to classify these by the Home Office Local Voluntary Activity Surveys produced no fewer than 69 categories (Marshall, 1997). A less comprehensive list would include playgroups, nurseries and parent and toddler groups; associations for sports, recreation, hobbies and leisure; youth groups; cultural and arts bodies; reform and campaigning organisations; tenants' and residents' associations; groups concerned with health and disability issues; women's groups; and organisations based on ethnicity, culture or religion. The resources of the local voluntary organisations identified in the LOVAS study are modest. Few of them employ paid staff and their median annual income ranges from less than £1,000 to just over £5,000 (Jermyn *et al.*, 1997a, 1997b; Marshall and Haggett, 1997; Woodburn *et al.*, 1997).

Another important and often overlooked type of local voluntary organisation is made up of those who manage more than 18,000 village halls, community centres and other community buildings which play host to many, if not all, of the kinds of activities listed here. Their resources are also limited – an average annual turnover of £14,000 means that the only paid staff commonly employed are part-time cleaners and caretakers (Marriott, 1997).

The impact of regulation

The following discussion of the impact of regulation on local voluntary action draws on two research projects undertaken by the author with colleagues at the LSE's Centre for Voluntary Organisation. The first of these – the small agencies project – was concerned with identifying the distinctive organisational characteristics of very small voluntary agencies (those with no more than the equivalent of four full-time staff) in order to help them to improve their effectiveness. It involved interviews and group discussions with committee members and staff from a variety of organisations in two areas of England. The second – the community sector study – took as its focus organisations which were wholly dependent on voluntary action and aimed to develop new and more helpful ways of measuring the value of their activities. This involved working with groups of volunteers in three areas of the country as well as gathering information from national organisations with wholly voluntary-run local branches or affiliates.

Weight and complexity

While none of those involved in these two studies doubted the need for the regulation of their activities in order to protect their users and participants and the public at large, they felt very strongly indeed that the burden that regulation imposed on them was out of proportion to the benefits it provided. It is clear that the increased demands of a tighter and more complex regulatory framework and the greater rigour with which legal requirements have been enforced by statutory bodies have imposed a heavy additional workload on small voluntary organisations.

More of the energies of staff and volunteers have been devoted
to meeting the demands for accountability and dealing with a
growing mountain of paperwork (see also Chapter 12).
For small organisations, moreover, the sheer complexity of the
regulatory environment represents a major challenge. One honorary officer spoke of the difficulty of negotiating a 'minefield of
laws' and her anxiety that 'the whole charity is vulnerable if we
don't get it right'. People managing village halls and other community buildings have to cope with the greatest complexity;
Community Matters has calculated that they needed to be familiar
with no fewer than sixty pieces of legislation. More generally,
lay officers and paid staff alike feel ill-equipped to meet the
increasing demands from a growing number of bodies. Unlike
some larger organisations they lack expertise and specialist knowledge and rarely have the resources to obtain professional help
from outside their ranks. The result is often high levels of anxiety
and stress.

Costs

Regulation imposes costs on local voluntary organisations which
may make a significant impact on their limited finances. The
cost to local authorities of administering the Children Act, for
example, is recouped in part by registration and inspection fees.
Many community organisations run after-school clubs and holi-
day play schemes with minimal resources apart from the time
freely given by volunteers. The Charities and Voluntary Organisations Deregulation Task Force expressed the view that a uniform
registration fee that did not acknowledge the circumstances under
which this provision was made 'disadvantages small groups and
temporary or short term schemes, and can inhibit much needed
local initiatives' (1994, p. 51).
    If the costs of participating in the regulatory system can be
significant items in a local voluntary organisation's budget the
expenses involved in conforming to the requirements of the regulators can be very high indeed. The Children Act's safety and good
practice recommendations may demand improved lavatories and
fencing and ramps for wheelchair access. Organisations which
employ a handful of sessional staff for a few hours a week have
been required by health and safety at work regulations to com-

mission regular inspections of electrical wiring and other installations and undertake improvements to alarm systems and other fire precaution measures. Another possible cause of significant capital expenditure is the Food Safety Act 1990 under which organisations might be required to tile kitchens and install stainless steel work surfaces in halls or centres where users are provided with refreshments.

A further cost imposed on local organisations by the legislative and regulatory environment is that of training staff and volunteers. One local community care project in the small agencies study had to find the funds to pay a private training provider to ensure that everyone working in the kitchen was able to obtain a health and hygiene certificate, as well as the costs of training a health and safety officer and two first aiders. Other projects working with older people and people with disabilities had to invest in training volunteers in manual handling and lifting people to meet European Commission directives.

But perhaps the heaviest 'cost' imposed by the requirements of the regulators is the demand on administrative and managerial time. A study of managers of after-school clubs highlighted the volume of preparation needed for local authority inspections: 'there's a lot of paperwork and stuff that I've got to dig out and prepare . . . because there's things they need to see . . . incident books, risk assessment sheets' (Martin, 1998, p. 20). And after the inspection they were expected to 'produce written action plans addressing requirements and good practice recommendations' arising from the inspector's visit. This contributed to a heavy administrative burden; one manager said 'I work seventeen and a half hours a week but with the children it's fifteen hours, so two and a half hours are left for the admin work and it's not enough' (ibid., p. 26).

It is a similar story for those managing community buildings. They are open to inspection by a number of enforcement agencies and are required under both the health and safety and food hygiene regulations to undertake risk assessments, to develop safety policies and to keep detailed records of any incidents that occur or maintenance that is carried out. Paul Marriott's study of community buildings (1997) drew a distinction between managers who saw their role purely in terms of maintaining a physical resource for local groups, those who extended their aims to the provision of events for the whole community in the building and those who used the building as a base from which to promote the development of the local community. The pressures of the regulatory environment inhibit the pursuit of the more expansive views of the management committee's role by requiring them to concentrate their attention on the building itself.

Volunteers

The requirements of regulators also impact on the way volunteers are recruited and their work is organised. Interested members of the local community find it increasingly difficult to 'drop in for a chat' and 'generally lend a hand' as a means of becoming involved in the work of an organisation (Rochester, 1992). Instead the 'workplace model' of volunteering (Davis Smith, 1996) has increasingly become the norm. People who are going to work with children and vulnerable adults, in particular, need to be interviewed, provide references and undergo police checks. And, even when accepted, they will be subject to closer supervision than before the Children Act set new standards of care. The coordinator of a volunteer bureau summed up these and related changes pithily. She felt that volunteering had generally become too bureaucratic: 'good turns are too much clouded in policies, codes of practice, insurance, etc.'

The activities of local voluntary organisations

There is some evidence that the scale and nature of the activities undertaken by local voluntary organisations have been affected by the increasing number of regulations and the more zealous implementation of existing measures. This has been especially true of provision for children and young people. The volunteer bureau in the small agencies study, for example, decided that, as a result of the new regulatory regime associated with the Children Act, they no longer felt competent to place volunteers with children. There have also been significant changes in the conduct of summer play schemes and other out-of-school activities. The adoption of clearly defined staff–children ratios has not only restricted the number of children taking part but also changed the nature of what is being provided. There can be no question of running the facility on a 'drop-in' basis when numbers are crucial.

The implications of these changes are significant. Whatever might have been gained in risk reduction has to be balanced against the loss of the inclusive approach characteristic of schemes of this kind in the past when all the local children were welcome and adults were encouraged to 'drop in and help'. The informality and flexibility for which voluntary and community sector organisations have been valued are under serious threat. And there are other changes to the kind of provision made for young people. The new emphasis on safety has eliminated unsafe practices like transporting children without providing them with individual seats and seat-belts but it has also reduced the variety and changed the nature of out-of-school activities. The managers of after-school clubs interviewed by Martin (1998) felt that the attempt to eliminate risk struck at a key element in the nature of children's play. 'Play', they suggested, was 'about risk-taking to a certain extent' and 'the need to take risks hasn't changed; it is important in the development of the child' (Martin, 1998, p. 23). The emphasis on safety can curtail the range of activities and destroy the capacity to try out new things. And, in some cases, it may involve a qualitative change in the nature of the activity – a shift from offering opportunities for play and development for children to the provision of a child-care facility for their parents. What is taking place in this area is more than the move to a formal, professionalised model of care noted elsewhere (Billis and Harris, 1992) for it also involves a change in the original purpose of the provision as well as in the identity of its primary beneficiary.

The overzealous or inappropriate enforcement of other regulations may prevent local voluntary organisations from running certain kinds of activities. A village hall, for example, found the organisation of a disco for local children subject to the same licensing requirements as a large-scale, commercially run nightclub. These included checking the identity and age of everyone entering the premises; keeping a register of attendance; providing uniforms for those supervising the event; and maintaining a first-aid kit which included two hundred pairs of rubber gloves.

Is it worth the hassle?

Research suggests, then, that the growing complexity of the regulatory environment has had a significant impact on local voluntary agencies. It is a source of stress for those who lead and manage them. The costs involved are a major burden on their modest funds and their limited human resources. There is a major impact on the ways in which people become involved with them as volunteers. And the regulatory regime can shape the nature of the activities in which they engage. This is in line with the view of Tessa Baring, who chaired the Charities and Voluntary Organisations Task Force, that:

> The effect of numerous regulations coming from different sources, and often not designed with the voluntary sector in mind, is particularly damaging, acting as a marked disincentive to thousands of small groups . . . The danger is that volunteers are beginning to say 'It's not worth the hassle' – a phrase that could be the death-knell of voluntary activity in this country. (Charities and Voluntary Organisations Task Force, 1994, p. ii)

Deregulation and better regulation

The Charities and Voluntary Organisations Task Force was set up by the Department of Trade and Industry as an afterthought to the seven similar groups looking at the effect of regulation on different for-profit industries. In 1994, when the various task forces were wound up and replaced by a single body, the Charities and Voluntary Organisations Task Force issued its report. This lists '189 proposals for reducing the burden of regulation' put forward by its members and the response they had received at that point from fifteen government departments or agencies – '72 have been accepted in whole, in part or in principle; 60 are under review, and 57 have been rejected' (Charities and Voluntary Organisations Task Force, 1994, p. i).

The Task Force claimed two major successes. The first of these was the acceptance by the Charity Commission that registered charities with an annual income of less than £10,000 (the great majority of them) should be subject to a much lighter regulatory regime than their larger counterparts. The second was the extension of the 'Small Business Litmus Test' to voluntary organisations and community groups. Government departments were already required to conduct Compliance Costs Assessments of the effects of new regulations on business in general – and small businesses in particular – before bringing them into force. It was now accepted that, where appropriate, 'Departments should identify two or three typical small voluntary organisations or community groups as representative as possible of the sector to which the regulations will apply and discuss with them the impact the regulation will have on them' (1994, p. 1). While this was accepted in principle, however, there has been little evidence that this has led to a change in practice.

The general issue of the place of regulation in British society and the part it plays in the achievement of government policy objectives remained on the agenda of the incoming Labour administration. In September 1997 a new Better Regulation Task Force was established in line with the Labour Party's 'manifesto commitment to give small businesses and others affected by regulation a greater voice in ensuring that regulations are simple helpful and fair'. The aim was no longer 'deregulation' but 'better regulation' which meant 'cutting unnecessary red tape and making sure that regulation provides proper protection without meddling unnecessarily in people's lives' (Cabinet Office, 1997, p. 1).

The Task Force's published statement of the *Principles of Good Regulation* (Better Regulation Task Force, 1998a) included a section on proportionality which is of particular relevance to small voluntary organisations. It suggests that there should be 'no unnecessary demands on those being regulated – think small first'; that full consideration should be given to alternatives to regulation; and 'any enforcement action (i.e. inspection, sanctions etc.)' should be 'in proportion to the seriousness of the offence'. The Charities Working Group established by the Task Force at its first meeting in September 1997, however, has made little impact on the issues facing many small voluntary organisations. Its first priority was a review of the regulatory framework for government funding – an important issue but one which affected few of the local organisations which are the focus for this chapter.

The evidence suggests then that, in the case of local voluntary action, there is a long way to go before the balance between 'proper protection' and unnecessary 'meddling' can be established. Part of the problem – the Small Business Litmus Test notwithstanding – is the 'one size fits all' basis of much regulation. This is exacerbated by the unsympathetic and overzealous approach to the implementation of a range of regulations by many of those charged with their enforcement. Another set of problems has arisen from the way in which regulations have been developed. The piecemeal introduction of regulations in response to perceived issues of safety has created a 'complex patchwork' of requirements which create difficulties in understanding the rules not only for businesses and consumers but also for the enforcers (Better Regulation Task Force, 1998b, p. 5). And the implications for local voluntary action were not anticipated. In several areas of voluntary organisations' activities regulations appear to have been designed for private individuals or for business. Because the restrictive impact they have on voluntary effort was not foreseen at the time of drafting, no consultation took place with the sector (Charities and Voluntary Organisations Task Force, 1994).

The establishment of successive Task Forces has done little so far to change the circumstances under which local voluntary organisations and community groups operate. Their main function may have been to highlight problems rather than deliver solutions. Tessa Baring points to the limitations of the Task Force approach: 'at the very point at which we were getting to the heart of the problem, we came up against the frontier between deregulation and the "forbidden territory" of policy, in which the roots of the problem seemed to lie' (ibid., p. i). Another member of the first Task Force noted the contrast between the approach to the problem adopted by 'departments who deal directly with the issues of the Charity and Voluntary Sector, i.e. VSU/Home Office and Charity Commission' and other 'departments such as Inland Revenue and Customs and Excise'. The former were able to understand that the activities of small voluntary organisations could easily be stifled by inappropriate regulation while the latter were unable to look further than the need to apply the rules already in place (Howell, 1994, p. 4).

Conclusions

The problems associated with the excessive or inappropriate regulation of local voluntary action are thus not susceptible to technical solutions alone. There are more fundamental issues to be addressed. Where is the balance to be struck between the encouragement of spontaneous and freely undertaken informal voluntary action in local communities and the need to ensure that those involved are accountable for their actions? To what extent should small voluntary agencies and community groups be seen as public bodies or private organisations? Is it possible to reconcile the drive to reduce risk in many areas of our collective life with the promotion of spontaneous and informal voluntary action?

The present Labour government ought to be better placed than its recent predecessors to address these issues. In opposition the Labour Party took pains to consult the voluntary and community sectors and it has delivered on its promise to enter into a 'compact' which provides a framework for relations between the government and the sectors. Tony Blair has made it clear that voluntary action will play a central role in the implementation of the principles at the centre of his social policy – the Third Way (Blair, 1999). At the same time the reduction of risk remains an important current in the government's social policy.

For the future, much will depend on the relative weight that will be attached to two policy objectives that appear difficult to reconcile – the drive to reduce risk in many areas of our collective life through regulation and its handmaidens of registration and inspection, as against the encouragement of spontaneous and freely undertaken voluntary activity in local communities. A second important consideration is the nature of the institutional arrangements within which the two policy directions will be contested. Supporters of voluntary action are looking to the new Active Community Unit with its 'brief to work across the government to co-ordinate the work of departments' in pursuit of 'joined-up policies' (Blair, 1999, p. 8) to promote their interests in the corridors of Whitehall.

Only time will tell, however, if these commitments and arrangements will be sufficient to give priority to voluntary action and to overcome both the bureaucratic inertia of government departments and the deep divisions between them. This appears to be an essential precondition for a better appreciation of the nature and value of local voluntary action. Without that, the burdens of inappropriate regulation will continue to stifle initiative, reduce flexibility, restrict opportunities and divert time and energy from operational activities. The result, as David Howell (1994, p. 5) summed it up, will be 'reduced voluntary social welfare provision – reduced voluntary action'. And the current administration's pledge to put voluntary action at the heart of restoring civic society will remain a largely unfulfilled aspiration.

Note

1. The term 'community sector' was coined by a group of national organisations with local branches or affiliates which are small, very modestly funded, entirely or almost entirely dependent on voluntary effort and active at a local or community level to describe these kinds of organisations. The term distinguished them from larger, professionally staffed voluntary agencies whose interests and needs, it was argued, dominated discourse about the voluntary sector to the extent that their smaller counterparts were invisible to academics, policy-makers and funding bodies alike and their needs and concerns disregarded. Those who coined the term have seen it gain increasing currency; the Home Office Active Community Unit, for example, uses the formula 'voluntary and community sector'.

References

Beck, U. (1992) *Risk Society: Towards a New Modernity*, Sage, London.
Better Regulation Task Force (1998a) *Principles of Good Regulation*, Better Regulation Task Force, London.
Better Regulation Task Force (1998b) *Review: Consumer Affairs*, Central Office of Information, London.
Billis, D. and M. Harris (1992) 'Taking the strain of change: UK local voluntary agencies enter the post-Thatcher period', *Nonprofit and Voluntary Sector Quarterly*, 21(3): 211–25.
Blair, T. (1999) Speech to the NCVO Conference on the Third Sector, Third Way, 21 January 1999, 10 Downing Street Press Notice, London.
Cabinet Office (1997) *News Release: New Better Regulation Task Force Launched*, Cab 85/97, London.

Charities and Voluntary Organisations Task Force (1994) *Proposals for Reform: Deregulation Report with an introduction by Tessa Baring – Volume 2: Full Report*, Charities and Voluntary Organisations Task Force, London.

Davis Smith, J. (1996) 'Should volunteers be managed?', in D. Billis and M. Harris (eds) *Voluntary Agencies: Challenges of Organisation and Management*, Macmillan, London.

Elsdon, K. (1995) *Voluntary Organisations: Citizenship, Learning and Change*, NIACE, Leicester.

Framjee, P. (1998) 'Charity financial reporting, fiscal matters and governance', in D. Grimwood-Jones and S. Simmons (eds) *Information Management in the Voluntary Sector*, ASLIB, London.

Giddens, A. (1990) *The Consequences of Modernity*, Polity Press, London.

Griffiths, H. (1986) *Developing Local Voluntary Action*, Home Office, London.

Hancock, R. and C. Jarvis (1997) 'Trends in volunteering and implications for the future', in C. Pharoah (ed.) *Dimensions of the Voluntary Sector*, 1997 edition, Charities Aid Foundation, West Malling.

Hedley, R. and J. Davis Smith (1992) *Volunteering and Society: Principles and Practice*, National Council for Voluntary Organisations, London.

Home Office (1992) *The Individual and the Community: The Role of the Voluntary Sector*, HMSO, London.

Howell, D. (1994) *Defining Deregulation*, Community Matters, London.

Jermyn, H., C. Haggett, S. Woodburn and T.F. Marshall (1997a) *Creswell, Whitwell and Clowne, Derbyshire*, LOVAS Area Report 5, Home Office, London.

Jermyn, H., C. Haggett, S. Woodburn and T.F. Marshall (1997b) *Accrington, Lancashire*, LOVAS Area Report 1, Home Office, London.

Kumar, S. (1996) 'Accountability: what is it and do we need it?', in S. Osborne (ed.) *Managing in the Voluntary Sector*, International Thomson Business Press, London.

Labour Party (1997) *Building the Future Together: Labour's Policies for Partnership between Government and the Voluntary Sector*, Labour Party, London.

Make a Difference Team (1995) *Make A Difference: An Outline Volunteering Strategy for the UK*, Make A Difference Team, London.

Marriott, P. (1997) *Forgotten Resources? The Role of Community Buildings in Strengthening Local Communities*, Joseph Rowntree Foundation, York.

Marshall, T.F. (1997) *Research Manual*, LOVAS Paper 3, Home Office, London.

Marshall, T.F. and C. Haggett (1997) *Huddersfield, West Yorkshire*, LOVAS Area Report 9, Home Office, London.

Martin, G. (1998) 'Playing with a double-edged sword; a study of the effects of statutory influence on voluntary sector after-school clubs', MSc dissertation, Centre for Voluntary Organisation, London School of Economics, London.

Rochester, C. (1992) 'Community organisations and voluntary action', in R. Hedley and J. Davis Smith (eds) *Volunteering and Society: Principles and Practice*, National Council for Voluntary Organisations, London.

Rochester, C. (1999) *Juggling on a Unicycle: A Handbook for Small Voluntary Agencies*, Centre for Voluntary Organisation, London School of Economics, London.

Wolfenden Committee (1978) *The Future of Voluntary Organisations*, Croom Helm, London.

Woodburn, S., C. Haggett, H. Jermyn and T.F. Marshall (1997) *Billericay, Essex*, LOVAS Area Report 4, Home Office, London.

6

Regeneration: The Role and Impact of Local Development Agencies

Stephen P. Osborne and Kathleen Ross

Introduction

This chapter focuses on area regeneration policy and explores the implications for voluntary and non-profit organisations (VNPOs).[1] It argues, first, that over the 1990s such regeneration policies have shifted from being primarily economic towards being concerned with the holistic regeneration of local communities. That is, there have been moves to consider *together* the needs for social, economic and community regeneration. In this respect, social and economic *policies* have become increasingly integrated (Hall and Mawson, 1999). Second, the chapter emphasises the growing importance of public–private partnerships (PPPs) in such initiatives, both as a tool of policy implementation and as a means to promote social inclusion (Peck and Tickell, 1994; Jones, 1998; McQuaid, 1998). (This theme is explored in more depth by Marilyn Taylor in the following chapter and in Osborne and Ross, 1999.) Finally, the chapter focuses in particular on the role of Local Development Agencies (LDAs). These are VNPOs whose role is to support and foster voluntary and community action in their own communities and who operate at the interface between the voluntary sector and government (Osborne, 1999).

The chapter begins by outlining the changing policy context for area regeneration in the UK. It then explores the challenges that face VNPOs, and LDAs in particular, as a consequence of involvement in such policies. It concludes by highlighting the key issues for LDAs in promoting area regeneration in local communities. The empirical component of the chapter draws on studies conducted by the authors and colleagues. This includes research about the role of LDAs in promoting voluntary action in local communities (Osborne, 1999) as well as research on area regeneration programmes, including in rural areas (PSMRC, 1991; Hall and Mawson, 1999).

The evolving policy context of area regeneration in the UK

A key feature of area regeneration initiatives over the 1990s has been the centrality of PPPs within them. Diverse regeneration programmes in the UK, such as the Single Regeneration Budget (SRB) in urban areas and the Priority 5(b) Programme of the European Community in rural areas, are predicated upon belief in the significance of partnership with the voluntary sector for both local government and the business community. Indeed, partnership has fast become the 'buzz word' to sprinkle liberally through any funding application in order to improve its chances of success. Such applications can cover projects as diverse as local training initiatives, the redevelopment and utilisation of abandoned buildings, and promoting social inclusion.

An important point in this context is the extent to which regeneration has become a key component of social, and not just economic, policy. In the early 1980s, area regeneration was approached in primarily economic terms. However, the thrust of developments since then has emphasised the need for regeneration to be seen in a social as well as an economic context. Whilst this debate may have been stimulated by the European emphasis on social inclusion (Deakin *et al.*, 1995), it has now become a central component of the Labour government's drive to create what has been termed 'joined-up' government. This recognises the extent of the interrelationship, and interaction, between social, economic and community issues (Labour Party, 1997; see also Chapter 3 of this book).

Within this broad emphasis on partnerships for regeneration there has been an especial interest in partnerships with the voluntary and community sectors. They are perceived to offer benefits to all parties. For local government, they can offer a seductively easy route into local and community experience and views (and particularly those of disadvantaged sections of the community). At their best, VNPOs can offer an independent voice not linked to political or commercial ends and they can provide specialist expertise in areas ranging from community care through to conservation and the environment. For the local voluntary and community groups themselves, partnerships can offer a valuable source of funding, particularly of revenue costs, and over a longer term than has been available through the previous urban and rural programmes of central government. Finally, for local communities they can offer a chance to influence the shape of initiatives directed towards them (Osborne, 1998).

The extent to which these various aspirations can be achieved is dependent upon the interaction between the overarching national policy framework for regeneration and its actual implementation at the local level. It is this dynamic interaction that the remainder of this chapter seeks to explore.

The approach to area regeneration of the 1979–97 Conservative governments was strongly influenced by what has become known in recent years as the 'New Public Management' agenda (Hood, 1991; Ferlie *et al.*, 1996; and see also Chapter 2 of this book). In the early years, it introduced a complex armoury of market mechanisms and contracts to govern relationships between public sector organisations and their various partners in service provision (Stewart, 1996). Central to such partnerships was the contract – as the core governance mechanism.

This approach to area regeneration was maintained throughout the period of Conservative government despite shifts in emphasis. The top-down model of area regeneration promoted during the 1980s focused primarily on economic regeneration, for example, property and physical regeneration (Colenutt and Cutten, 1994). However, it failed to produce the hoped-for 'cascade' impact whereby economic benefits at the macro level cascaded down to local communities (Audit Commission, 1989). This ultimately led in the 1990s to a greater emphasis on 'community empowerment' as an essential tool of area regeneration – as in the City Challenge and SRB schemes, for example. These placed more emphasis both on local community initiatives and on VNPOs as key actors in them. Despite this shift of emphasis, however, the hegemony of government within these schemes remained. Colenutt and Cutten (1994) commented at the time that

community involvement in these initiatives is thus carefully circumscribed. Neither City Challenge nor SRB are designed to empower local communities to any significant extent but to keep local communities 'on side' as far as possible. Most community organizations take the pragmatic view that if they do not co-operate they will not get the money. (p. 138)

Other analysts have also questioned the degree to which the SRB actually enhanced voluntary and community participation. Instead it has been argued that the competitive bidding arrangements which characterised SRB were 'constructed with a view to getting one over the competition and, above all, getting the money' (Peck and Tickell, 1994, p. 253). Mawson (1995), National Council for Voluntary Organisations (NCVO) (1995) and Tilson *et al.* (1997) have all highlighted the low level of success of voluntary and community sector bids in the first round of the SRB Challenge Fund and the low level of participation in other bids compared with private and public sector partners.

Under Conservative leadership, therefore, area regeneration in the UK was associated with an inherently centralist agenda. The model emphasised the role of VNPOs in delivering government policies (policy agency) and allowed the separation of the policy-making process from the management of regeneration policies. The most negative view of this model of regeneration has argued both that it was concerned more with introducing market disciplines to the VNPO sector than with regeneration (Mackintosh, 1992) and that it conveniently deflected attention away from government underfunding of regeneration policies; and that it depoliticised the issue of area regeneration by requiring partners to demonstrate external compliance with 'effective partnership' as a condition of funding, thus engendering an uncritical consensus perspective on local problems (De Groot, 1992).

The election of the Labour government in 1997 undoubtedly led to a change of emphasis in the approach to area regeneration. A key theme has been the pursuit of 'joined-up' government, of the integration of social and economic priorities and of agencies, as a response to complex social and economic problems. VNPOs have been identified by this government as having an important contribution to make to this initiative because of their potential to focus on identifying unmet needs in a way which transcends the traditional departmental boundaries and professional specialisms of local and central government (Labour Party, 1997; DETR, 1998). The input of VNPOs is therefore being increasingly sought by central government to promote its agenda of cross-sectoral policy-making and implementation in response to social and economic issues and problems. Crucially, and in contrast with the previous administration, the Labour government emphasises their potential *formative* role in regeneration policy, rather than seeing them solely as agents of implementation. Within this policy formulation role, emphasis is placed upon the contribution that the voluntary and community sector can make to mobilising communities and giving voice to minority views (Labour Party, 1997; Working Commission on Government Relations, 1998). This raises core questions about the role of VNPOs in the local *implementation* of such regeneration strategies. These questions are considered in the next part of this chapter.

Managing the challenge of regeneration partnerships in local communities

As has been argued at several points above, the involvement of local voluntary and community groups has many advantages to offer to the process of area regeneration. Despite such advantages, however, the regeneration partnership process is also one fraught with challenges for all parties.

One issue which can make PPPs especially difficult to achieve for local government is the sheer diversity of the voluntary and community sector. Because of this, the role of local intermediary bodies in the voluntary and community sector (Local Development Agencies or LDAs) has become particularly important in area regeneration initiatives in the UK. LDAs are bodies whose mission is to serve the local voluntary and community sector within a defined geographic community. LDAs can be one of three types (Burridge, 1990). They can be generic, providing a range of services to the full range of voluntary and community groups in their locality (such as Councils for Voluntary Service (CVSs) and Rural Community Councils (RCCs)); they can be functional, providing a specific service to the full range of local groups (such as Volunteer Bureaux (VBx)); and they can be specialist, providing a full range of services to a specially identified subgroup of organisations (such as Play Associations). Dependent upon the nature of the local voluntary community, any particular locality might possess a single, usually generic, LDA or a number of differing LDAs, possibly overlapping with one another in their remits.

Their core mission, of supporting the voluntary and community sector in developing their role in local communities and of providing an interface with local government (Wolfenden Committee, 1978; Osborne and Tricker, 1994; Commission on the Future of the Voluntary Sector, 1996), inevitably places LDAs on the cusp between the local community, local government and the local voluntary and community sector. Because of this, they have been identified by many as key players in the development of local regeneration strategies. Potentially, LDAs can both link voluntary and community groups into regeneration partnerships and play a core role themselves.

Based on a major study of the work of LDAs by one of us (Osborne, 1999), we would highlight a number of challenges to be met if this potential is to be fulfilled. For *the local community*, a key challenge is that the continued organisational focus of many regeneration programmes may lead to the substitution of voluntary organisations for local more informal community activity. Whilst such effort may feed into the goals of these organisations themselves, there is a real concern that it will do so at the expense of local community activity and neighbourhood helping. Chanan (1991, 1996) has been particularly vociferous in raising this spectre of national voluntary organisations colonising local communities for their own ends and redirecting development funding away from community groups and towards themselves. It is important therefore that the voluntary sector, and LDAs in particular, engage in work which enhances the involvement of local communities rather than limiting it.[2]

For *the local VNPO sector*, we would highlight four concerns about the role of LDAs in regeneration policies. These are:

- that local authorities can use LDAs as a substitute for the wider involvement of VNPOs;
- that the LDAs can themselves become the puppets of the local authority and their area regeneration strategies, rather than the supporters of the local voluntary and community sector;
- that LDAs can abuse their privileged access to local government to ensure that a greater proportion of regeneration resources is directed to themselves, rather than to the broader voluntary and community sector; and
- that, even in ideal circumstances, LDAs cannot represent fully the diverse and pluralistic nature of local voluntary and community sectors (see also Lansley, 1997).

In our research many LDAs also identified such pressures from local authorities – whilst stressing that they themselves had resisted them strenuously! Indeed such a route must seem attractive to hard-pressed and overworked local government officers. Here, apparently, are bodies that they can access easily, which understand the way in which regeneration programmes work and which will undoubtedly enhance their claims to 'local partnership' with the national and European funders of their own programmes. Whilst attractive, however, such an approach risks both the alienation of local communities from regeneration programmes and the discrediting of the LDAs with their own constituencies.

For *Local Development Agencies* themselves, three challenges to successful involvement in regeneration partnerships emerge. The first is the lack of understanding, by many of the governmental agencies involved in area regeneration, about the core activity of LDAs in their local communities. There persists an understandable, if incorrect, perception within local authorities that regeneration partnership-oriented work is the sole purpose of LDAs.

A second, related, challenge for LDAs is to recognise that involvement in regeneration partnerships may further 'crowd out' or distort their work away from their mission-critical activity of supporting the local voluntary and community sector. A good example of this latter pressure was one Volunteer Bureau in our study that had become involved in an employment initiative, for good initial reasons, with the local Training and Enterprise Council. This had resulted in it spending more time on the administrative requirements of this scheme (such as achieving International Standards Organisation recognition for its quality assurance system) than on recruiting volunteers – and nearly led to its demise. This can happen as a result both of the sheer volume of potential regeneration projects that LDAs can become involved in and of the skewing effect that such funding can have, diverting LDAs away from their core objectives and towards those of the regeneration initiative itself (Pifer, 1967; Blackmore *et al*., 1997).

Finally, there is the overriding challenge for LDAs of avoiding twin dangers. These are

- *incorporatism*, whereby they become perceived as just another arm of the local state (Wilson and Butler, 1985), perhaps as a funding filter and conduit; and
- *isomorphism*, whereby they lose their distinctiveness and come to mirror the characteristics of other organisations with which they are working (DiMaggio and Powell, 1988).

Both these would spell disaster for the role of LDAs in their local communities and undermine their distinctive contribution to local economic development programmes. One CVS in this study became so much a part of the local government funding regime that it lost all credibility with its VNPO constituency and eventually collapsed. Such an end served the needs neither of the local voluntary and community groups nor of the local authority.

In conclusion, it is apparent that area regeneration partnerships at the local level offer important challenges for the voluntary and community sector in general and for LDAs in particular. Notwithstanding these, however, they do have significant benefits to offer to the regeneration process. In order to achieve these benefits, it is necessary for all the parties at the local level to be aware of the dangers and to work together to resolve, if not solve, these issues. In this context both Huxham and Vangen (1996) and Jones (1998) have offered invaluable guidance to all parties involved in local regeneration partnerships (see also Kickert *et al*., 1997). The concluding section of this chapter suggests ways in which LDAs can support both local VNPOs and the local community in engaging with the challenges of integrated area regeneration strategies.

The role of LDAs in supporting voluntary and community involvement in area regeneration

As has been suggested earlier in this chapter, LDAs have the potential to support the involvement of voluntary and community organisations in area regeneration initiatives. They can both promote the economic regeneration of local communities and build social inclusion within these communities. We conclude by highlighting six linked implications for LDAs if this potential is to be maximised.

First, LDAs need to adopt an orientation which is focused on the needs of the community rather than on those of the local authority. This may seem self-evident but has not always been the case in the past. As has been suggested earlier, regeneration programmes have been dogged by 'top-down' approaches which have minimised the opportunities for building sustainable development in local communities. LDAs need to be proactive in linking social and economic needs in their communities and in using approaches which help build the capacity of local communities to respond to emerging needs. Capacity-building can often be a vague 'buzz word' but in our research (Osborne, 1999) it was helpfully defined by one respondent as . . . 'skilling individuals to deliver services, to influence policy and to work inside organisations to meet the needs of their [communities]'.

Such 'capacity-building' is most effective when it combines the development of a specific service with work to develop skills within the community – sometimes called a *catalytic approach* (PSMRC, 1991; Osborne and Tricker, 1994). Again one respondent in our study gave a good summary of this approach:

> We learned a lot from [the RCC]. Before we had a private consultancy helping us. They did it for us and we learned nothing. With [the RCC] they helped us but we did it and we've learned. We now have the skills to do it ourselves, so we've started other projects . . . We've learned ever such a lot of things. We're afraid of no one now. It's brilliant!

Second, whilst this catalytic approach requires the active engagement with local voluntary and community groups, it is important also to recognise that many local communities rely upon a relatively small number of key activists. The challenge is therefore to support the work of these activists whilst also drawing other community members into the process. In this context the model of supporting local 'animateurs' in regeneration initiatives is important. These are individuals who are able to take a lead role in inclusive regeneration initiatives in local communities and who are also conscious of their role and can use it to develop social capacity and inclusion (Oakley, 1991; Bryden *et al.*, 1994).

Third, in promoting area regeneration, it is important that LDAs work through existing networks rather than replace or duplicate them. The latter is often more efficient in achieving concrete services but is highly counterproductive for building sustainable social capacity in local communities (Osborne, 1999). In this context the model of network support and network working offered by the Rural Action initiative is highly pertinent (Tricker and Osborne, 1999). This model offers a framework for such network support and highlights some of the challenges that it poses for LDAs – and for local government.

Fourth, at an organisational level, LDAs need to remain focused on their core mission of supporting and promoting local voluntary and community action, by providing the infrastructure that local groups need to achieve their own ends. This 'infrastructure' work includes the provision of training opportunities in organisational management and survival, facilitating communication within and across the voluntary and community sector and providing means for representing views of local groups to the local authority.

Fifth, it is important that VNPOs recognise that partnership is not only about formal relationships. Rather, as a range of studies have illustrated, it is a *process* of negotiation and of the building of trust between the various actors in any partnership (Davis and Walker, 1997; Falconer and Ross, 1998; Osborne and Murray, 1998; Craig *et al.*, 1999).

Finally, LDAs, and the broader voluntary and community sector, need to engage with local government (and other significant local actors) in establishing a role for the sector in policy formulation as well as implementation. Such an approach will best harness the local strengths and knowledge of the sector and move it away from being simply a tool for government-derived policy towards being a vehicle for genuinely inclusive policy-making – both across the social and economic fields and within local communities. This is an especially challenging role for LDAs. It requires them to see regeneration partnerships not as an outcome of their work but rather as part of a process of engagement with local government in the social and economic regeneration of their local communities.

Notes

1. Voluntary and non-profit organisations are defined as organisations which are formally structured; were founded independent of state control; are governed by an independent management committee; cannot distribute any surplus but must reinvest it; have voluntary income not raised through taxation; and hold some normative voluntary value.

2. Examples of such approaches in rural areas include the 'village appraisal' model (Osborne and Tricker, 1999) and the network-based approach of the Rural Action initiative (Tricker and Osborne, 1999). Both emphasise the significance of supporting local community action rather than replacing it (see also Oakley, 1991).

References

Audit Commission (1989) *Urban Regeneration and Economic Development: The Local Government Dimension* HMSO, London.

Blackmore, M., Y. Bradshaw, S. Jenkinson, N. Johnson and I. Kendal (1997) 'Intermediary organisations in the new welfare mix: a case study', *Non Profit Studies*, 1(2): 13–20.

Bryden, J., J. Black, E. Conway and D. Shucksmith (1994) *WISL LEADER Evaluation*, WISL LEADER Group, Stornaway.

Burridge, D. (1990) *What Local Groups Need*, NCVO, London.

Chanan, G. (1991) *Taken for Granted*, Community Development Foundation, London.

Chanan, G. (1996) 'Regeneration. Plugging gaps or pushing frontiers?', *Local Economy*, 11: 98–103.

Colenutt, B. and A. Cutten (1994) 'Community empowerment in vogue or vain', *Local Economy*, 9(3): 236–50.

Commission on the Future of the Voluntary Sector (1996) *Meeting the Challenge of Change*, NCVO, London.

Craig, G., M. Taylor, C. Szanto and M. Wilkinson (1999) *Developing Local Compacts*, York Publishing Services, York.

Davis, H. and B. Walker (1997) 'Trust based relationships in local government contracting', *Public Money and Management*, 17(4): 47–54.

Deakin, N., A. Davis and N. Thomas (1995) *Public Welfare Services and Social Exclusion*, IFILWC, Dublin.

De Groot, L. (1992) 'City Challenge: competing in the urban challenge game', in *Local Economy*, 7(3): 224–39.

Department of Environment, Transport and the Regions (DETR) (1998) *Community-Based Regeneration Initiatives: A Working Paper*, DETR, London.

DiMaggio, P. and W. Powell (1988) 'The iron cage revisited', in C. Milofsky (ed.) *Community Organisations*, Oxford University Press, New York.

Falconer, P. and K. Ross (1998) 'Public–Private Partnerships and the New Labour government in Britain', in L. Montanheiro, B. Haig, D. Morris and N. Horovatin (eds) *Public and Private Sector Partnerships: Fostering Enterprise*, Sheffield Hallam University Press, Sheffield.

Ferlie, E., L. Ashburner, L. Fitzgerald and A. Pettigrew (1996) *The New Public Management in Action*, Oxford University Press, Oxford.

Hall, S. and J. Mawson (1999) *Challenge Funding: Contracts and Area Regeneration*, York Publishing Services, York.

Hood, C. (1991) 'A public management for all seasons?', *Public Administration*, 69: 3–19.

Huxham, C. and S. Vangen (1996) 'Managing inter-organisational relationships', in S. Osborne (ed.) *Managing in the Voluntary Sector*, International Thomson Business Press, London.

Jones, R.A. (1998) 'The European Union as a promoter of public–private partnerships', in L. Montanheiro, B. Haig, D. Morris and N. Horovatin (eds) *Public and Private Sector Partnerships: Fostering Enterprise*, Sheffield Hallam University Press, Sheffield.

Kickert, W., E.-H. Klijn and J. Koppenjan (eds) (1997) *Managing Complex Networks. Strategies for the Public Sector*, Sage, London.

Labour Party (1997) *Building The Future Together: Labour's Policies for Partnership Between Government and the Voluntary Sector*, Labour Party, London.

Lansley, J. (1997) 'Intermediary bodies in the 1990s: new settings, old problems?', *Nonprofit Management & Leadership*, 7(2): 169–80.

Mackintosh, M. (1992) 'Partnership: issues of policy and negotiation', *Local Economy*, 7(3): 210–24.

McQuaid, R. (1998) 'The role of partnerships in urban economic regeneration', in L. Montanheiro, B. Haig, D. Morris and N. Hrovatin (eds) *Public and Private Sector Partnerships: Fostering Enterprise*, Sheffield Hallam University Press, Sheffield.

Mawson, J. (1995) *The Single Regeneration Budget: The Stock-Take*, University of Birmingham/Local Authority Association, Birmingham.

National Council for Voluntary Organisations (NCVO) (1995) *A Missed Opportunity: An Initial Assessment of the 1995 Single Regeneration Budget Approvals and its Impact on Voluntary and Community Organisations*, NCVO, London.

Oakley, P. (1991) *Projects with People: The Practice of Participation in Rural Development*, ILO, Geneva.

Osborne, S. (1998) 'Partnerships in local economic development? A bridge too far for the voluntary sector?', *Local Economy*, 12(4): 290–5.

Osborne, S. (1999) *Promoting Local Voluntary Action*, York Publishing Services, York.

Osborne, S. and V. Murray (1998) *Collaboration between Nonprofit Organisations in the Provision of Social Services in Canada: Working Together or Falling Apart?*, Aston Business School Research Institute Working Paper, Aston University, Birmingham.

Osborne, S. and K. Ross (1999) 'Service agent or community governance? The management of government–nonprofits partnerships for area regeneration in the UK' paper presented to the 1999 Conference of the American Academy of Management, Chicago, 7–11 August.

Osborne, S. and M. Tricker (1994) 'Local development agencies: supporting voluntary action', *Nonprofit Management & Leadership*, 5(1): 37–52.

Osborne, S. and M. Tricker (1999) *Village Appraisals: A Tool for Sustainable Community Development in Rural Areas in the UK?*, Aston Business School Research Institute Working Paper, Aston University, Birmingham.

Peck, J. and A. Tickell (1994) 'Too many partners . . . the future for regeneration partnerships', *Local Economy*, 9(3): 251–65.

Pifer, A. (1967) *Quasi Autonomous Non Governmental Organizations*, Carnegie Corporation, New York.

Public Services Management Research Centre (PSMRC) (1991) *Managing Social and Community Development Programmes in Rural Areas*, Aston University, Birmingham.

Stewart, J. (1996) 'A dogma of our times: the separation of policy-making and implementation', *Public Money and Management* (July–September): 23–30.

Tilson, B., J. Mawson, M. Beazely, A. Burfitt, C. Collinge, S. Hall, P. Loftman, B. Nevin and A. Srbljanin (1997) 'Partnerships for regeneration: the Single Regeneration Budget Challenge Fund Round One', *Local Government Studies*, 23(1): 1–15.

Tricker, M. and S. Osborne (1999) *Assessing the Contribution of Community Development and Community Organizations to Sustainable Development in Rural Areas. A Review of Recent UK Experience*, Aston Business School Research Institute Working Paper, Aston University, Birmingham.

Wilson, D. and R. Butler (1985) 'Corporatism in the British voluntary sector', W. Streeck and P. Schmitter (eds) *Private Interest Government. Beyond Market and State*, Sage, London.

Wolfenden Committee (1978) *The Future of Voluntary Organisations*, Croom Helm, London.

Working Commission on Government Relations (1998) *Consultative Document on the Development of a Compact between Government and the Voluntary and Community Sector*, NCVO, London.

7

Partnership: Insiders and Outsiders

Marilyn Taylor

Introduction

The UK voluntary sector has long seen itself as a watchdog on the state, exerting an influence on policy from outside the sphere of government, and it takes pride in its campaigning and lobbying role (Commission on the Future of the Voluntary Sector, 1996; Taylor, 1998). However, current policies are drawing many organisations into the policy process in another role – as 'partners'. For some, this offers the potential for new forms of governance for the twenty-first century. Others see it as a source of frustration and continued marginalisation, coopting voluntary and community organisations as 'peripheral insiders' (Maloney et al., 1994) to a government agenda.

It is now commonplace for voluntary sector scholars and other commentators to warn of the dangers of incorporation that follow from the voluntary sector's involvement in mainstream service delivery. Does a parallel involvement in policy development offer similar dangers? This chapter draws on four research studies in which the author has been involved to assess the implications for the voluntary sector of a move from the 'outside' to the 'inside' of the policy-making process. Two of the studies were concerned with voluntary and community sector involvement in area regeneration, the third was concerned with consultation more generally and the fourth with the development of local 'compacts'.[1]

The rise of partnership

In its manifesto before the 1997 general election, New Labour expressed its intention to move 'from a contract culture to a partnership culture' (Labour Party, 1997). The concept of partnership was not new – previous Conservative administrations had long since broken down the dominance of local government in local delivery and policy systems. But under the new Labour government, 'partnership' moved very much to centre stage, accompanied by a language of 'governance' rather than 'government'.

For voluntary and community organisations two factors in the transition to partnership have been particularly important. The first is the transfer of service delivery from the state to the independent sector. From a role in which voluntary and community organisations generally complemented and supplemented mainstream state services, voluntary organisations in the 1990s were increasingly called on to provide those services themselves, albeit with funding from the state and often under conditions specified by the state. The second important factor is the growing expectation that public sector bodies should consult with the voluntary and community sectors. The transition towards welfare markets under the Conservative administration in the 1980s and 1990s brought with it an increasing emphasis on consultation with the voluntary and community sectors. This was part of a growing concern with consumer feedback and the need to coordinate growing numbers of providers, especially in the fields of social care and housing provision. Community involvement was also required in regeneration and in environmental planning. Under Labour, the drive towards consultation has intensified, with the development of 'Best Value' across local government services likely to prove particularly significant for voluntary and community organisations as providers or as service user organisations.

In consultation and participation exercises, voluntary and community organisations were initially outsiders in a policy process dictated from the top down. The language of partnership apparently moves them to the inside. Partly inspired by Conservative governments' desire to reduce the powers of local government and to give business a greater role in local governance, partnership has since spread across the policy agenda under the Labour government, as part of its drive towards 'joined-up thinking'. It is seen as a critical tool in tackling the issues that fall outside the responsibility of any one public agency (such as regeneration, community safety, early years provision and social exclusion). It is also a theme in such fields as employment (as part of the New Deal) and in health and education (with the introduction of Action Zones).

The importance of voluntary and community organisations within this 'partnership culture' has been acknowledged in the launch of national 'compacts' between government and the voluntary sector in different parts of the UK. These recognise the role of voluntary and community organisations as both insiders and outsiders in the policy process. As well as making commitments to consult the sector, the English compact, for example, recognises and supports the right of the sector 'to campaign, to comment on Government policy and to challenge that policy' (Home Office, 1998, 9.1).

Voluntary organisations have been embedded in policy networks for years, through what Wistow *et al.* (1992, p. 33) call a 'complex interweaving of elected members and management boards', providing a recruiting ground (and sometimes a retirement home) for both officers and politicians in the public sector and involving officers and members in their management committees. But the engagement of the voluntary and community sectors in various forms of partnership is now much more explicit and more transparent. It can be seen as a consequence of the blurring of the boundaries between sectors in a mixed-welfare market. Some might argue that it is also the product of an increased realism within the sector, as organisations and social movements born in the heady days of the 1960s and 1970s move through an inevitable life cycle from protest to a more cooperative approach to policy influence (Fainstein and Hirst, 1995; Tarrow, 1994).

However, there is a fine line between realism and incorporation, as demonstrated, for example, by the study of Local Development Agencies reported in Chapter 6. For many voluntary organisations, the spread of partnership, with its implied shift from outsider to insider, entails considerable heart-searching (Hulme and Edwards, 1997). There is concern that involvement in partnerships will incorporate voluntary and community organisations into a government agenda, and thus neutralise their potential to make a distinctive contribution. And, although much has been made of differences within the sector between larger, incorporated institutions and small independent groups (see, for example, Knight, 1993), government's concern to reach excluded communities and service users means that community and user-led organisations are as likely as more 'professional' organisations to be faced with the choice between insider and outsider strategies. In response, some of these community organisations have chosen to pursue a consciously separatist agenda (Crook, 1995) because of their distrust of a mainstream policy process from which they continue to feel excluded. This has been the case, for example, with a number of minority ethnic, disability and gay and lesbian groups.

What then are the challenges that partnership as a policy has posed for the voluntary sector to date?

The experience of partnership

The incentives for public authorities to enter into partnership with voluntary and community organisations are greater now than ever before. This offers these organisations the opportunity to set agendas, to develop policy initiatives, to plan services and to implement these alongside statutory and other partners. But research suggests that, while there have been gains, voluntary and community organisations have, on balance, found partnership and consultation exercises an unsatisfactory experience, with statutory partners unwilling to share power in any meaningful way (Hastings *et al.*, 1996; Jeffrey, 1997; Taylor *et al.*, 1998). It also suggests that influence is most likely to be possible in policy *implementation*, with agendas and policy development still dominated by statutory partners.

Maloney *et al.* (1994) see the key boundaries to policy influence as lying not between insiders and outsiders but between outsiders, peripheral insiders and core insiders. There are few 'true' or 'core' insiders. However, becoming a peripheral insider is easy: 'In most cases, it would cause the official more problems to ignore the failed insiders than to accord them polite recognition' (p. 32). Achieving the status of 'peripheral insiders' still leaves voluntary organisations relatively marginalised.

'Power', argues Clegg, 'will always be inscribed within contextual "rules of the game" which both enable and constrain action ... with some players having not only play-moves but also the refereeing of these as power resources' (1989, pp. 200–1). This creates a number of problems for voluntary and community organisations who find that they do not determine the rules of play; that they do not have the resources to play on equal terms; that their right to play is frequently questioned; and that the cards are stacked in favour of more powerful players (Taylor, 1998). The rules are appropriate neither to the complexity of the policy environment nor to the demands of partnerships involving very different organisational cultures.

The rules of play

Central government and other external actors have been significant in promoting partnership. But they have also imposed demands that set partnership up to fail. Chief amongst these is a preoccupation with structure and regulatory requirements (see also Chapter 5). Thus, while the money involved in regeneration initiatives can provide the incentive for partnership arrangements, it also constrains them – swamping agendas and timetables with procedural and (upward) accountability issues and alienating potential participants. In these circumstances, the need to get the systems right often takes precedence over the need to establish a common vision and policy is made by default. The prospect of funding may keep the more persistent on board, but prospects for a wider understanding of partnership are damaged.

Partnerships tend to be framed in the language, structures and cultures of statutory agencies and rarely subjected to any scrutiny. Ways of working that are inimical to partnership are entrenched in local authority systems: departmentalism works against holistic community definitions of issues and problems; incentive and performance-monitoring systems reward inputs and outputs rather than outcomes. Several authors have questioned the dependency of consultations and partnerships on the traditional committee meeting (see, for example, Jeffrey, 1997). There is little consideration of alternative forms of operation and there is also an assumption that voluntary and community sector participants can operate within these systems with no induction or training.

Hastings *et al.* (1996) identify a consensus culture as another obstacle to voluntary and community sector participation. Any failure by residents to 'deliver their communities' by bringing a united view to the table is treated with impatience and any resistance to suggestions by other partners as obstruction. This failure to accept and work with difference can feel very disempowering to voluntary and community organisations, especially when they are trying to reflect the views of very diverse constituencies.

Again, official concepts of representation may differ from those of many in the community. The need on the part of community representatives to check back with their constituencies can be seen as obstructive by public authorities and by business partners who do not have similar constraints. This is exacerbated in regeneration partnerships which are often constituted as private companies, where there may well be a tension between the transparency that voluntary and community sector representatives require, the interests of the company and cultures of commercial secrecy imported by business representatives (Atkinson, 1999).

Paradoxically, the nature of many partnerships can contribute to conflict. Although the promise of funding is a spur to organisations to engage in partnership, it can also drive a wedge between them. Jeffrey (1997) reports that systems which generally worked well 'broke down when groups were in competition for grants' (p. 26) and that even 'those "good" democrats, who truly endeavoured to make themselves accountable confessed that they behaved differently when grants were to be prioritized' (p. 28).

The imbalance of time and resources

For many voluntary and community organisations, the opportunity to influence decisions comes too late. Official partners frequently criticise consultation because of the time it takes. But for voluntary and community sector respondents the real problem is the reluctance of authorities to go out to consultation until they have dotted all the i's and crossed all the t's. By the time they let voluntary and community sector participants into the process, vested interests have been established, time has run out and it is too late to admit new definitions of the issue or new ideas from the outside (Craig *et al.*, 1999).

If time-scales weight partnerships against the voluntary and community sectors, so do resources. The commitment required of voluntary and community sector representatives, often working with disparate constituencies and on a steep learning curve, is immense. But the staff and information back-up that statutory partners take for granted is rarely available for community and voluntary sector participants. In research we were told:

> There is no-one to take up the slack if you stop work for your community to talk to a statutory body or work with them on an issue. You need to feel that something of real benefit to your community is going to happen in the foreseeable future to compensate your community for the loss of your skills.

The growing demand for partnership intensifies the problem. There is a danger that partnership will be the victim of its own success – one current study reports 42 different forums in one locality (Deakin and Gaster, 1998). The time considerations involved in this overloading certainly coopt people's energies, leaving little time to consider issues in depth, much less to be briefed by, or accountable back to, local constituencies.

The overloading of agendas and pressures on time often means that voluntary and community sector representatives find themselves party to decisions that they do not feel they have had sufficient time to consider, or may not even have been present to consider. They are rushed through crowded agendas under severe pressure. It means that the all-important detail of plans and programmes is left to the paid professionals – usually from the statutory side – to flesh out, with little time for voluntary and community partners to consider its implications. And it leaves little time for accountability back to the communities they are there to represent.

Who plays?

Under these circumstances voluntary and community sector participants in partnership tend to be the 'usual suspects'. The commitment of time required means that representatives need to be people who can 'hit the ground running' and that the 'real communities' (often reflected in the informal end of the voluntary and community sectors) that government is anxious to reach remain on the outside.

Representation is always a thorny issue for partnerships and there are often issues about the accountability of representatives to their constituencies. But respondents in our studies argued that statutory partners prefer to consult with people who speak their language and play by their rules. They argued that representativeness only becomes an issue for statutory partners when voluntary and community sector partners disagree with their agenda. The point has also been made that the legitimacy of 'representatives' from other sectors is rarely questioned.

The cards are stacked

Voluntary and community organisations often feel that they are not in the right game and that the real decisions are taken elsewhere. Within any partnership, there may be tensions when community organisations are funded by the authority with which they are seeking to develop a partnership. Voluntary and community organisations report an element of 'he who pays the piper' calling the tune and explicit or implicit censorship (Craig *et al.*, 1999). Many feel that they will not have real power until they have independent assets of their own to bring to the partnership.

Few respondents in the studies reported here believe there is a conspiracy to exclude voluntary and community organisations – although black voluntary organisations did argue that there was systematic discrimination. There was, however, a more general concern with stereotypes of the voluntary sector as amateurish and as 'moaners', and of excluded communities as 'problems', especially amongst politicians. A respondent in one study spoke of the 'contempt' which local statutory bodies had for the voluntary sector (Craig *et al.*, 1999). Technical complexity is often used as a reason to exclude communities (Atkinson and Cope, 1997) and yet there are many examples of community and voluntary organisations developing sophisticated alternative plans and measures of policy impact.

Central government policy can also create problems for partnership. Pressure on mainstream budgets can outweigh the financial gains brought in by special initiatives while the sheer pace of change can destabilise the networks and relationships that partnership requires. Respondents in a number of our studies referred to the impact of local government reorganisation which had often brought with it insecurity on both sides, changes in personnel and changes in funding arrangements. Whilst it is only in laboratory conditions that all extraneous factors can be controlled, the implications of such parallel initiatives do have to be considered. Current changes in regional government and the health service are likely to create further waves for organisations in the regeneration and community care fields.

Alternative futures

Are the prospects for the future, then, as negative as they appear? In finding partnership wanting in so many respects, are the voluntary and community sectors and, indeed, researchers, crying 'wolf'? Are their expectations realistic and are they being fair to statutory partners who are themselves engaged in a considerable process of change?

Marsh and Rhodes (1992) suggest that policy networks can serve to ride out change: to constrain, contain and redirect it. 'Similarly, Atkinson (1999) argues that the current language and discourse of partnership are framed in ways which reinforce existing power relations and that this determines 'the terms in which individuals and groups "think" about what is possible' (see also Stewart and Taylor, 1995). Pluralist models of decision-making, along with proposals for associational democracy (Hirst, 1994), have been heavily criticised for their failure to acknowledge power differences between groups and their assumption that voluntary organisations are themselves democratic.

Pessimists might argue, then, that cooption is inevitable, drawing on the work, for example, of the social movement theorists who report a tendency for such movements to go through a cycle from protest to incorporation (Tarrow, 1994; Fainstein and Hirst, 1995). They might also argue, echoing the Community Development Projects in the 1970s, that the structural forces of globalisation far outweigh the tinkering at the margins that partnerships might achieve.

But there are many who would argue against this pessimistic point of view. At a theoretical level, power does not have to be conceptualised as a zero-sum commodity. It can be a productive and regenerative force (Clegg, 1989). At a more practical level, participants in partnership are gaining in skills and influence, although the experience has been painful. Partners from all sides have been on very steep learning curves and some participants in the research covered here feel that difficulties are being ironed out. There is evidence that the New Deal for Communities[2] has learnt at least some of the lessons from the past and there is a strong drive from central government for community-led partnerships in this and other policy areas.

As sectors interact more, crossovers in personnel are increasing understanding between partners. Informal links are being built. And the opportunities that partnership has provided for people in the voluntary and community sectors to become involved in implementation should not be underestimated. In MacFarlane's view (1993), this is as important in empowering people as being involved in meetings and strategic decision-making.

There is also considerable variation between policy areas and between local authority areas. Where there has been a history of public investment in the development of voluntary and community organisations and a history of engagement across the sectors, the evidence suggests that progress is being made. It may be that as examples of effective practice spread, the problems identified here will be seen as no more than teething troubles.

Beyond the purely pessimistic and optimistic approaches to the problems of partnership is the pragmatic one. If the pessimists are over-deterministic, it can equally be argued that the optimists are over-romantic. Even if the teething troubles of partnership can be overcome, the evidence provided here suggests that there are very real tensions to be resolved. These include:

- the tension between the need to account for public money and the flexibility that is required if voluntary and community organisations are to have a real input into partnership;
- tensions between leadership, representation and the wider participation that is needed to put issues on the agenda, to legitimate them, to generate ideas for change and to engage

communities and organisations in the implementation of programmes;
- the tension between integration and diversity – the need, as Claus Offe describes it (1987, p. 65): 'to maintain the diversity within civil society while creating some measure of unity, of bindingness, of political authority'.

A pragmatic response would acknowledge that policy-making is not so clear-cut as the pessimists argue, but is a process of paradoxes, contradictions and balancing acts. This is critical to theoretical approaches to policy-making and implementation such as chaos theory, complexity theory and 'garbage can' theory. Social movement theorists highlight the importance of political opportunity structures (Tarrow, 1994) – the windows and cracks that appear when political systems change. They also emphasise the importance of alliances, formal and informal, as do complexity theorists. Current interest in capacity-building and 'social capital' (Putnam, 1993) is encouraging investment in community development and related activities. The New Deal for Communities is said by policy-makers to come with permission to do things differently.

Exploiting the opportunities

How then can voluntary and community organisations exploit these opportunities? The first condition is that they need to develop the skills to spot opportunities, widen cracks in the system, build alliances and generate different ways of engaging – building genuine new forms of governance with allies across the sectors. Often partnership becomes too dependent on a particular committee or board, which limits opportunities for engagement and thus limits sustainability. Effective partnership will require a variety of routes to engagement and a rich pattern of connections within and across organisations at different levels, through working groups, workshops, task forces and joint projects (Haynes, 1999).

A second condition is that voluntary organisations need to be strategic in their choice of partnerships. This means being clear about their 'bottom line', what their rules of engagement are and what the price is for their involvement. It also involves a recognition that policy influence is most likely to be achieved where there are insiders *and* outsiders. It is likely that many organisations over time will play both roles, but if those which become more established (and potentially coopted) are to be kept on their toes, they require a 'Greek chorus' (Milofsky and Hunter, 1994) of the less institutionalised and the angry. In the environmental field, Murphy (1997) argues that insiders, who have often entered negotiations in the teeth of opposition from other campaigners, have been successful because of the threat that outsiders have posed to business interests in terms of unwelcome global publicity and the disruption of trading.

A third condition is an effective and adequately resourced voluntary sector infrastructure (see also Chapter 6 in this book). Balancing participation with effective representation and entrepreneurial leadership will require an imaginative approach to ways of engaging people as participants. It will require dynamic, responsive and accountable community structures, which have the confidence of all parts of the community and can also deliver. It will also require skills in conflict mediation and working with diversity, including a recognition *within* the sector that different interests may need different channels for engagement. There is still a lot to learn about how such structures can be built.

A final condition is to press – as the price of participation in partnership – for the continued and long-term investment in social capital that will spread involvement and bring in new voices and new groups, even if they do not sing from the same hymn sheet as those who are already established. This will require investment from government as well as from the sector itself.

Notes

1. The findings of two of these studies have been published as Taylor *et al.*, 1998, and Craig *et al.*, 1999. I would like to acknowledge the contribution of other members of the various research teams to these studies. However, the conclusions drawn here are solely mine.

2. The New Deal for Communities is a £800 million central government programme to tackle multiple deprivation in the most disadvantaged areas of the UK. The aims of the programme are to bring together spending on housing and regeneration into a

single strategy, to extend economic opportunities for local people and to improve the delivery of local services.

References

Atkinson, R. (1999) 'Discourses of partnership and empowerment in contemporary British urban regeneration', *Urban Studies*, 36(1): 59–72.

Atkinson, R. and S. Cope (1997) 'Community participation and urban regeneration in Britain', in P. Hoggett (ed.) *Contested Communities: Experiences, Struggles, Policies*, Policy Press, Bristol.

Clegg, S. (1989) *Frameworks of Power*, Sage, London.

Commission on the Future of the Voluntary Sector (1996) *Meeting the Challenge of Change: Voluntary Action into the 21st Century*, NCVO Publications, London.

Craig, G., M. Taylor, C. Szanto and Wilkinson, M. (1999) *Developing Local Compacts: Relationships Between Local Public Sector Bodies and the Voluntary and Community Sectors*, York Publishing Services, York.

Crook, J. (1995) *Invisible Partners*, Black Training and Enterprise Group, London.

Deakin, N. and L. Gaster (1998) 'Local government and the voluntary sector: who needs whom, why and what for?', paper presented at the Third International Conference of the International Society for Third Sector Research, Geneva, 8–11 July.

Fainstein, S. and C. Hirst (1995) 'Urban social movements', in D. Judge, G. Stoker and H. Wolman (eds) *Theories of Urban Politics*, Sage, London.

Hastings, A., A. McArthur and A. McGregor (1996) *Less Than Equal: Community Organisations and Estate Regeneration Partnerships*, Policy Press, Bristol.

Haynes, P. (1999) *Complex Policy Planning: The Government Strategic Management of the Social Care Market*, Arena, Aldershot.

Hirst, P. (1994) *Associative Democracy: New Forms of Economic and Social Governance*, Polity Press, Cambridge.

Home Office (1998) *Getting It Right Together: Compact on Relations Between Government and the Voluntary and Community Sector in England*, Cm 4100, Stationery Office, London.

Hulme, D. and M. Edwards (1997) *NGOs, States and Donors: Too Close for Comfort*, Macmillan in association with Save the Children, Basingstoke.

Jeffrey, B. (1997) 'Creating participatory structures in local government', *Local Government Policy Making*, 23(4): 25–31.

Knight, B. (1993) *Voluntary Action*, Home Office, London.

Labour Party (1997) *Building the Future Together: Labour's Policies for Partnership between Government and the Voluntary Sector*, Labour Party, London.

MacFarlane, R. (1993) *Community Involvement in City Challenge: A Good Practice Report*, NCVO Publications, London.

Maloney, W., G. Jordan and A. McLaughlin (1994) 'Interest groups and public policy: the insider/outsider model revisited', *Journal of Public Policy*, 14(1): 17–38.

Marsh, D. and R. Rhodes (1992) *Policy Networks in British Government*, Oxford University Press, Oxford.

Milofsky, C. and A. Hunter (1994) 'Where non-profits come from: a theory of organizational emergence', paper presented to the Association for Research on Nonprofit Organizations and Voluntary Action (ARNOVA), San Francisco, October.

Murphy, D. (1997) 'The partnership paradox: business–NGO relations in sustainable development in the international policy arena', PhD thesis, University of Bristol.

Offe, C. (1987) 'Challenging the boundaries of institutional politics: social movements since the 1960s', in C. Maier (ed.) *Changing Boundaries of the Political*, Cambridge University Press, Cambridge.

Putnam, R. (1993) *Making Democracy Work: Civic Traditions in Modern Italy*, Princeton University Press, Princeton, NJ.

Stewart, M. and M. Taylor (1995) *Empowerment and Estate Regeneration: A Critical Review*, Policy Press, Bristol.

Tarrow, S. (1994) *Power in Movement: Social Movements, Collective Action and Politics*, Cambridge University Press, Cambridge.

Taylor, M. (1998) 'Influencing policy: a UK voluntary sector perspective', in D. Lewis (ed.) *International Perspectives on Voluntary Action*, Earthscan, London.

Taylor, M., A. Mills and L. Seymour (1998) *The Voluntary and Community Sectors in Brighton and Hove: Support and Representation*, Health and Social Policy Research Centre, University of Brighton, Brighton.

Wistow, G., M. Knapp, B. Hardy and C. Allen (1992) 'From providing to enabling: local authorities and the mixed economy of social care', *Public Administration*, 70: 24–45.

8

Providers of Care for Older People: The Experience of Community Care

Jeremy Kendall and Martin Knapp

Introduction

Many changes in community care in the UK are currently under way, prompted by the 1990 National Health Service and Community Care Act. Final implementation was in 1993, but the full impacts are still working their way through. The 1990 Act aimed to alter four balances:

- between institutional and community-based care;
- between supply-led, provider-dominated services and needs-led, purchaser-dominated services;
- between NHS and local government responsibilities for decision-making and funding; and
- between public and independent (voluntary and private) sector provision.

To encourage the shift from public to private and voluntary provision, the legislation contained concrete incentives and legally backed regulations. Local authorities were required to spend 85 per cent of the Special Transitional Grant (STG) of transferred social security funds on private and voluntary services. A Direction on Choice required authorities to offer users a range of residential care or nursing home placements and, under reasonable circumstances, meet their choices. Private sector involvement in the annual round of community care planning was also required, building on voluntary sector involvement established in the 1980s.

Local authorities *initially* gave greater emphasis to community development or governance, and central government to market creation (Wistow *et al.*, 1994). Subsequent responses represented a sea change. Most authorities now (across the political spectrum) want to encourage market-like forces capable of raising service volume from available budgets. Whilst there has been growth in 'market pragmatism' (Wistow *et al.*, 1996), these same authorities recognise the need to promote quality of care and quality of life. Consequently, most have held back from encouraging highly competitive 'free' markets, and favoured active market management and more 'relational' styles of working.

These changes to local authority roles had considerable potential implications for voluntary organisations, a quarter of whose revenue in 1990 came from public sector sources, more than half of it from local government (Kendall and Knapp, 1996). By 1995, the voluntary social services sector was significantly larger, with employment and real operating expenditure growing annually at around 5 per cent (Kendall and Almond, 1998). Recent growth has been largely public sector-led, with income from the public sector accounting for 39 per cent of all income in 1995.

The broad effects of these funding changes are often discussed under the (misleading) heading of 'the contract culture' (Kendall and Knapp, 1996; 6 and Kendall, 1997; Walsh *et al.*, 1997). Our intention is not to revisit these issues (they are addressed by Scott and Russell in Chapter 4), but to offer a more specific account by focusing on providers of care for older people, a user group that accounts for the vast bulk of social services public expenditure (Evandrou and Falkingham, 1997). We review *comparative* evidence on the impacts on the voluntary and private sectors, in the context of local authority attitudes and actions regarding their roles. Local authorities have always been important as agenda-setting regulators and funders, and in shaping the environment in which providers operate. The new stream of reforms makes them yet more powerful. After considering the *actual* policy environment and (where possible) the impacts of the legislation, we turn to *potential* future consequences.

Changing local authority perspectives

Views of social services chairs and directors

Our own Personal Social Services Research Unit work at the London School of Economics, in collaboration with the Nuffield Institute for Health, Leeds University, gives us a decade-long perspective on a representative sample of local authorities (Wistow *et al.*, 1994, 1996). As well as collecting statistical data, we have conducted in-depth interviews with Social Services Committee chairs (elected members), social services directors and/or other senior managers.

In 1991, voluntary organisations were often already working closely with local authorities, in contrast with the private sector. But this was not a 'golden age' for the voluntary sector. As late as the mid-1980s there was still local authority hostility to 'organisations that they associated with middle-class charity' (Wistow *et al.*, 1996, p. 91; also see Challis *et al.*, 1988). Nevertheless, there was mutual learning (often facilitated by overlapping membership of governing bodies), participation in joint planning, and a relatively relaxed grant-based funding environment. Local authority doubts focused mainly on the sector's capacity to respond to new supply opportunities. In 1991, many chairs and directors of social services departments thought that voluntary organisations lacked experience and expertise in managing contracts, as well as a supporting 'infrastructure'. They saw unevenness in the balance of available services and shortages of volunteers. But they were also aware of, and respected, the decisions of some voluntary bodies not to become heavily committed through contracting, sketchily referring to the dangers of threats to autonomy and independence.

At the same time, there was much misunderstanding and mistrust of the private sector, perhaps fuelled more by anecdote and ideology than experience or evidence. A common view, less often voiced today, was that it was inappropriate to gain financially from the suffering of others. In contrast, there was widespread 'goodwill trust' for voluntary organisations but not always 'competence trust' (Sako, 1992). The distinction continues to have relevance, as noted below.

By 1993, most authorities still tended to cultivate links with voluntary rather than private sector providers. The former were more likely to be involved in community care planning, received significant amounts of grant funding, and were sometimes given special status when authorities were establishing new services or floating off in-house provision. But over the next three years there were major shifts in positions and perspectives followed by less dramatic changes to late 1998. By 1996, some degree of purchaser/provider separation was common and – throughout the UK – purchasers were now much more likely to agree contracts with both voluntary and private providers (Walsh *et al.*, 1997). The imperative of involving the private sector which followed from the legal requirements noted earlier often revealed to authorities that previous anxieties about 'care for profit' and opportunism were groundless. Instead, they found widespread adherence to appropriate caring and professional values, particularly in the 'small businesses' that dominated (and still dominate) the private sector. Although some authorities remarked that 'ideally' they would prefer to work more closely with the voluntary sector, they simply could not find the appropriate services.

Field-level staff views

No longitudinal research evidence exists on the views and actions of social services staff below senior management level. However, 1988/9 data from operational-level staff about the roles and contributions of the voluntary and private sectors in care for older people is instructive (Allen *et al.*, 1992). The main advantage of voluntary residential care services was seen to be 'providing an environment which either met an elderly person's particular needs as a member of a fraternal or religious group, or enabled them to engage in a more independent lifestyle' (p. 272). Perceived disadvantages were that homes tended to be selective in admissions (not taking people who were 'too physically or mentally frail'), supply was heavily constrained (waiting lists too long) and 'an aura of charity might remain in some [homes]' (p. 273). When asked about private residential care, field-level professionals pointed to advantages that small facilities could bring through their 'domestic character', but expressed anxieties about user vulnerability if financial support was not forthcoming, lack of access to other services, and concerns about quantity and quality of care staff (p. 272).

As regards non-residential services, most professionals recommended voluntary services to their clients because they encouraged local networking, brought together people in similar circumstances, and offered access to volunteers for specific tasks. In contrast, private non-residential care generated a 'less favourable response' (p. 223). The assumption seems to have been that the cost would be borne by the user (with resources presumably not made available from the Social Services Department budget), a situation that has now changed.

Local authority budgets are increasingly being devolved from the centre to areas, teams or care managers. Consequently field-level staff perspectives of this kind are of growing importance. For example, Mannion and Smith (1998) report how the relevant decision-makers – increasingly care managers – take prices set higher up in an authority as given 'constraints', and concentrate on maximising 'quality' (p. 128). Yet because quality defies 'definition, measurement and monitoring', these decision-makers 'have to rely on informal information, status, trust and reputation as a basis of assessing' it (p. 125).

Lapsley and Llewellyn (1998) found considerable variety in how residential care 'quality' was interpreted by field staff, although local decision-makers invariably claimed to be concerned with maximising user choice and dignity, and meeting needs and preferences (the values promoted so strongly by their professional training). The cost information in which purchasers were interested (other than the overall price level – which was generally fixed at Department of Social Security levels) was that relating to paid labour. They concluded that

> the beginnings of a new way of thinking [were emerging], characterised by a commitment to the idea of a balanced provision of care across all sectors (local authority, private, voluntary), a willingness to consider the costing dimension, and a sensitivity to the concept of the budget constraint. However, these changes should not be overstated. (p. 150)

Voluntary sector responses in comparative perspective

Partly as a result of the changes outlined above, local authority social services expenditure on the voluntary sector grew significantly during the 1990s. How was this experienced on the provider side? Aside from the rapid fall in the proportion of services provided directly by local authorities, examination of national data on market shares reveals interesting changes.

Residential care

After providing an almost unchanging absolute number of places in a rapidly expanding market prior to the 1990 Act, the voluntary sector's market share has shown signs of recovery, although this may primarily reflect the creation of hybrid 'not-for-profit' trusts whose place in 'the voluntary sector' is contested (Kendall and Knapp, 1994). It is still dwarfed by the private sector, which is primarily composed of providers which were already operating before 1990. In all areas of residential care, both sectors have become increasingly reliant on local authority funding. In the voluntary sector, the proportion of older residents supported by local authorities grew from 20 per cent in 1994 to 29 per cent in 1996, and in the private sector from 18 per cent to 37 per cent.

Home (domiciliary) care

Many voluntary sector services for older people at home are low-intensity, low-visibility, volunteer-led activities. They are often beyond the purview of local authorities, and not thought of as 'care' by participants. It is not clear how these services have been affected by the 1990 Act, although annual Department of Health data show that the scale of purposively contracted voluntary home care services has grown since 1992. However, the considerable increases in local authority funding have been absorbed almost entirely by the private sector. Existing providers have expanded, and a very large number of new private providers have joined this market since 1993.

Day care

Voluntary sector day services are well established and well regarded. Department of Health statistics show that the sector has consolidated its position. The private sector has begun to grow at the margins and is apparently keen to gain a more secure foothold in this market (Laing and Saper, 1998); but its contribution remains relatively small compared to that from the voluntary sector and local authorities.

A view *across* social services for older people indicates that the voluntary sector is operating distinctively from the private sector in a number of ways. We describe these briefly under twelve heads, where possible making contrasts over time.

1. Diversified portfolios of care

The voluntary sector has more multi-field organisations than the private sector, including long-established generalist organisations and those which have recently diversified (for example 'social entrepreneur-led' housing associations developing home-care or residential services). In contrast, the private sector has to date mainly comprised (somewhat isolated) small businesses. However, there has recently been noticeable growth, from a low base, in corporate ownership – particularly of residential and nursing care facilities.

2. Longevity and linkages

The voluntary sector's long tradition of care provision gives it a fuller track record upon which to draw, as well as, in some cases, greater intimacy and experience of joint working and overlapping governance with the public sector. However, most users of voluntary sector residential care have *not* been (and still are not) sponsored by local authorities.

3. Quality of care

The private and voluntary sectors typically deliver different combinations of activities and these could generate quality-of-care differences. In residential care, for example, evidence from the

1980s shows that there were greater opportunities for recreation, leisure and visiting in voluntary sector homes compared to private, after controlling for resident dependency (Kavanagh and Knapp, 1997). Conversely, voluntary home care services in 1995 offered a more restricted range of services, being less likely to provide day-sitting, night-sitting or live-in services.

4. Staffing

Residential care staffing patterns differed a little between the private and voluntary sectors in terms of retention and qualifications. Staff turnover was lower in the voluntary sector in 1996 (15 per cent of current staff started or left in the previous year, compared to 22 per cent of private sector staff). Private sector staff are slightly more likely to have a professional qualification, most commonly RGN or NVQ (30 per cent compared to 27 per cent). Across social care as a whole, 6 per cent of private sector employees and 5 per cent of voluntary had full NVQs. The proportions of residential care staff with, or currently studying for, social work qualifications were also similar (13 per cent private sector, 15 per cent voluntary) (LGMB, 1997).

5. Rates of pay

Care staff salaries are significantly higher in the voluntary than in the private sector. Analyses of pooled data for 1995–97 from the *Labour Force Survey* found a mean wage rate of £5.61 in the voluntary sector compared to £3.98 in the private sector for employees in the 'social work with accommodation' category (roughly equivalent to residential care); and in 'social work without accommodation' (non-residential social care), a voluntary sector mean wage of £6.02, compared with £4.32 in the private sector (Almond and Kendall, 1999).

6. Volunteers

Volunteers supporting older people are formally organised by voluntary organisations, by the public sector (particularly through social services departments), and through private organisations. It is not known exactly how these are distributed by sector within this field but we do know in general (across all fields) that volunteering takes place primarily through the voluntary sector (Davis Smith, 1998). Cutting across the sectors, volunteer inputs are heavily concentrated in day care and social activities, with more limited contributions to home care (Ware, 1997; Curtice *et al.*, 1997) and very little to residential care (LGMB, 1997).

7. Prices

Other things being equal, including user dependency, residential care prices tend to be lower in the voluntary than the private sector, and home-care prices higher (Forder *et al.*, 1999; Forder and Netten, 1999). In the mid- to late 1980s, private sector residential and nursing home fees were tightly bunched around Income Support (social security) rates, whereas voluntary sector fees varied rather more (Kavanagh and Knapp, 1999).

8. Costs and mark-ups

These fee differences are interesting given the voluntary sector's lesser propensity to pay low wages. Staff wages account for a high proportion of the total cost of care services, so that wage differences directly influence overall costs and (potentially) also fees. In the residential sector, voluntary homes may have a lower rate of price–cost mark-up ('profit' or 'surplus') than their private sector counterparts (see 'top-ups' below). There can also be motivational differences between the sectors: on average, voluntary sector managers place slightly less emphasis on financial reward for themselves than their private sector owner–manager counterparts (even if field-level staff, including care assistants, are paid more, as noted above). However, the relationship between sector and manager motivation is complex and far from deterministic: there is certainly no 'clean' self-selection of empathic entrepreneurs into the voluntary sector and opportunistic, profit-obsessed entrepreneurs into the private sector.

9. Top-ups

The voluntary sector is more likely than the private to 'top up' local authority residential care fees – that is, cross-subsidise from other sources – and increased its apparent willingness to do so between 1994 and 1997. In the latter year, three-quarters of all homes claimed to do this (Kendall, 1999). The difference is made up from revenue from other services, net revenue from other publicly funded residents (health authorities are often prepared to pay higher fees than local authorities) and 'external sources'.

10. Dependency

There have been significantly lower levels of resident dependency in voluntary than private residential homes for some time (Townsend, 1962). Since the early 1990s, however, there have been 'pronounced increases' in dependency across all sectors but particularly in the voluntary sector (Darton, 1998). At the end of the decade, average dependency levels have more or less converged. Our research suggests that average dependency levels in home care are lower in the voluntary that the private sector.

11. Admissions policy

The voluntary residential care sector more often than the private sector operates an admissions policy on the basis of the religious, ethnic or professional backgrounds of users. This result applied in both 1994 and 1997 (Kendall, 1999).

12. Perceived competition

Voluntary sector residential care providers report being subjected to competitive forces to a lesser degree than their private sector counterparts, even when located in the same geographical (local) markets. However, the absolute amount of reported competition experienced by the voluntary sector has grown. In 1994, while private sector providers almost all described themselves as operating in an environment characterised by some competition, a third of voluntary homes indicated that they experienced no competition. By 1997, only one in ten voluntary sector homes were claiming to be free of competitive pressures (Kendall, 1999).

Discussion

The voluntary social services sector in general has grown over the 1990s, encouraged particularly by the 1990 NHS and Community Care Act. Support for older people has been part of this development. Much of this growth has been stimulated by local authorities spending more on external services and the preference of some for links with voluntary rather then private providers. Changes in funding availability have been accompanied by changes in funding *route*. Formal service-level agreements or contracts are now more common, with their accompanying monitoring requirements, and spot contracting is increasingly prevalent in some service areas, with implications for administrative load and (potentially) for demand fluctuations.

What do the recent experiences described in this chapter suggest for the future? When it comes to be viewed historically, the late 1990s and early 2000s will probably be characterised by two major features, one relating to the public sector and one to the private.

Over the next few years, local authorities will probably divest themselves of even more of their provider responsibilities, and there may soon remain only 'niche' or symbolic public sector provision for older people. At the same time, corporate (private) providers are likely to gain significant shares of the residential care and nursing home business for older people. In the process, many small family-business (private) homes could be squeezed out, unable to compete on price or to convince potential residents that they offer superior quality. Many purchasers hold these smaller homes up as models of quality provision, but they find it increasingly difficult to justify paying the higher fees that some homes need in order to remain solvent. Nevertheless, new residents (or maybe it is their relatives) often seem to favour the new facilities now opening across the country: purpose-built, chain hotel-like in design and décor, functional and large enough to reap economies of scale.

Where will this leave the voluntary sector? Much activity may continue to take place at some remove from local authorities, with many organisations continuing to provide, in their own way, valued services and support to private users. Others are choosing, and will continue to choose, to deliver services regulated and/or funded by local authorities. Voluntary social services organisations certainly have more public sector business to bid for than ever before, but often face tough competition as they do so, particularly from corporate private providers. The possible consequences should not be exaggerated, as many voluntary sector providers are strong in particularistic and specialist markets in which, to date, the private sector has shown little interest. The most obvious example is publicly funded (but not otherwise regulated) day care (but see Laing and Saper, 1998). In fields insulated from direct competition, the challenge will be to negotiate robustly and fairly with purchasers, rather than to respond competitively to other suppliers' strategies.

Voluntary providers that do have to compete with others will have to continue to persuade purchasers of their trustworthiness. Field-level professionals couch their 'quality' judgements in these terms, but this may be less of a *fait accompli* than in the past. While some voluntary providers have rightfully attracted greater 'competence trust' from purchasers, their *comparative* advantage over the private sector in terms of 'goodwill trust' may be eroding as the latter build better relations with authorities. Furthermore, formal contractual funding undertaken in the context of extensive regulation arguably offers less scope for the cultivation of 'goodwill trust' than traditional styles of grant funding. This is an area where one of the 1998 White Paper proposals may have sectoral implications: the intention systematically to regulate domiciliary care on a national scale may increase purchasers' overall confidence in working with private providers. Conversely, by the same logic, the decision to leave day care unregulated leaves voluntary organisations at an advantage.

The picture is more complex yet. The 1990 legislation encouraged local authority devolution of decision-making *and purchasing*. The extent of budgetary devolution varies, but across all localities potential providers must now demonstrate their care-quality abilities to a larger set of decision-makers or stakeholders. Field-level decision-makers are becoming increasingly cost-conscious. They are also placing emphasis on traditional, professionally driven, and therefore user-focused, concepts of quality in which relations with care staff occupy centre stage. The evidence on relative cost and quality and the sector's apparently relatively strong position on both staff turnover and pay augur well, helping to compensate for the withering of an assumed 'goodwill trust' cushion. A contrary view of the future would be that financial pressures on authorities might encourage recentralisation of budgets, or use of near-monopsonistic purchasing powers to negotiate favourable terms for block contracts. Either would limit the influence of 'street-level bureaucrats' (Lipsky, 1979).

Service users and their families also have a growing voice in social care (and growing powers of exit, in fact, although the personal risks of moving between services can be high). The specialist and new social entrepreneur elements of the voluntary sector in particular have enjoyed good user relations. But some of the older and more conservative elements in the sector, including some which still have rather traditional attitudes to users, will need to demonstrate greater willingness to respond to users' and carers' preferences.

The present variation in provider types *within* the sector (Kendall, 1999) will presumably continue because of organisational sunk costs, legal status, and differentiated ('niche') demands. But there will undoubtedly be pressures for organisational change. Will single-home organisations survive in the increasingly tough competitive environment? Are mergers like those that have become so prevalent in the social housing field desirable (see Chapter 11)? What will happen if local authority externalisation takes the form of large-scale transfers or sales of services?

The 1998 White Paper's emphasis on prevention, with ring-fenced funds, may be greeted by critics as 'too little, too late'. Yet this could disproportionately benefit the voluntary sector since it is much more active than the private sector in day care and (on average) supporting less dependent users.

Finally, both so-called 'independent' sectors have become more dependent financially on local government over the 1990s and this trend looks set to continue. In fact, the private sector is (for now) more vulnerable: it is less well positioned to cross-subsidise, a higher proportion of its users are sponsored by local authorities, and it is more dependent on spot contracts. The voluntary sector has more users not sponsored by local authorities at all; avoids the problem of 'all eggs in one basket' by (often) securing an array of funding arrangements, contract types and grants; and more commonly works with more than one authority, reflecting in part its greater volume of activity outside residential and home care and its specialist and niche market roles. If we compare the voluntary sector over time rather than with other sectors today, it is clear that it is increasingly likely to be buffeted by the fiscal winds of change blowing through the public sector. Whereas in the past a bad central government grant settlement for a local authority would lead to the slashing of voluntary sector grants, today's contractual environment may give voluntary bodies slightly more security. However, it is a form of security that, through the commitment it implies and demands, could prove damaging. Local authorities need to keep their independent providers happy, but more importantly, they need to provide their populations with services which meet assessed needs. The results could be the uncomfortable squeezing of existing relations.

References

Allen, I., D. Hogg and S. Peace (1992) *Elderly People: Choice, Participation and Satisfaction*, Policy Studies Institute, London.

Almond, S. and J. Kendall (1999) 'Low pay in the UK: the case for a three sector comparative approach', PSSRU Discussion Paper 1529, London School of Economics and Political Science, London.

Challis, L., S. Fuller, M. Henwood, R. Klein, W. Plowden, A. Webb, P. Whittingham and G. Wistow (1988) *Joint Approaches to Social Policy*, Cambridge University Press, Cambridge.

Curtice, L., F. Fraser and T. Leca (1997) *The Range and Availability of Domiciliary Care Services in Scotland*, Scottish Office Home Department Central Research Unit, Edinburgh.

Darton, R. (1998) 'PSSRU survey of residential and nursing home care', *Mental Health Research Review*, 5: 26–30.

Davis Smith, J. (1998) *The 1997 National Survey of Volunteering*, Institute for Volunteering Research, London.

Evandrou, M. and J. Falkingham (1997) 'The personal social services', in H. Glennerster and J. Hills (eds) *The State of Welfare*, 2nd edition, Oxford University Press, Oxford.

Forder, J. and A. Netten (1999) 'The price of placement in residential and nursing home care: the effects of contracts and competition', PSSRU Discussion Paper 1263, London School of Economics and Political Science, London.

Forder, J., B. Hardy, J. Kendall, M. Knapp and G. Wistow (1999) *Residential Care Providers in the Independent Sector: Motivations, Pricing and Links with Purchasers*, Report to the Department of Health.

Kavanagh, S. and M. Knapp (1997) 'The costs of external services for elderly people living in institutions', in A. Netten and J. Dennett (eds), *Unit Costs of Health and Social Care*, PSSRU, University of Kent at Canterbury.

Kavanagh, S. and M. Knapp (1999) 'Cognitive disability and direct care costs for elderly people', *British Journal of Psychiatry*, 174: 539–46.

Kendall, J. (1999) 'The contribution of the voluntary sector to social care for older people: from origins to the mid 1990s', in B. Hudson (ed.) *The Changing Role of Social Care: Research Highlights in Social Work*, Jessica Kingsley, London.

Kendall, J. and S. Almond (1998) *The UK Voluntary (Third) Sector in Comparative Perspective: Exceptional Growth and Transformation*, PSSRU, University of Kent at Canterbury.

Kendall, J. and M. Knapp (1994) 'A loose and baggy monster: boundaries, definitions and typologies', in J. Davis Smith, C. Rochester and R. Hedley (eds) *An Introduction to the Voluntary Sector*, Routledge, London.

Kendall, J. and M. Knapp (1996) *The Voluntary Sector in the UK*, Manchester University Press, Manchester.

Laing, I. and P. Saper (1998) 'Promoting the development of a flourishing independent sector alongside good quality public services', in M. Henwood and G. Wistow (eds) *With Respect to Old Age: Long Term Care – Rights and Responsibilities*, Community Care and Informal Care Research, Volume 3, A Report by the Royal Commission on Long Term Care, CM 4192 – 11/3, The Stationery Office, London.

Lapsley, I. and S. Llewellyn (1998) 'Markets, hierarchies and choices in social care', in W. Bartlett, J. Roberts and J. Le Grand (eds) *A Revolution in Social Policy: Quasi-Market Reforms in the 1990s*, Policy Press, Bristol.

LGMB (1997) *Independent Sector Workforce Survey 1996: Residential and Nursing Homes in Great Britain*, Local Government Management Board, London.

Lipsky, M. (1979) *Street Level Bureaucracy*, Russell Sage Foundation, New York.

Mannion, R. and P. Smith (1998) 'How providers are chosen in the mixed economy of community care', in W. Bartlett, J. Roberts and J. Le Grand (eds) *A Revolution in Social Policy: Quasi-Market Reforms in the 1990s*, Policy Press, Bristol.

Sako, M. (1992) *Prices, Quality and Trust*, Cambridge University Press, Cambridge.

6, Perri and J. Kendall (eds) (1997) *The Contract Culture in Public Services*, Arena, Aldershot.

Townsend, P. (1962) *The Last Refuge*, Routledge & Kegan Paul, London.

Walsh, K., N. Deakin, P. Smith, P. Spurgeon and N. Thomas (1997) *Contracting for Change: Contracts in Health, Social Care and Other Local Government Services*, Oxford University Press, Oxford.

Ware, P. (1997) 'Independent domiciliary services and the reform of community care', PhD thesis, Department of Law, University of Sheffield.

Wistow, G., M. Knapp, B. Hardy and C. Allen (1994) *Social Care in a Mixed Economy*, Open University Press, Buckingham.

Wistow, G., M. Knapp, B. Hardy, J. Forder, J. Kendall and R. Manning (1996) *Social Care Markets: Progress and Prospects*, Open University Press, Buckingham.

9

Grant-Making Foundations: Policy Shapers or Policy Takers?

Diana Leat

Introduction

This chapter moves the spotlight away from organisations which provide services or undertake other activities for the benefit of groups of users to those whose function is to provide funds to operating organisations of that kind. Like operating charities grant-making foundations work in the 'space' between market and state (Deakin, 1996; Kendall and Knapp, 1996; Knight, 1993). The size, shape and nature of that 'space' in large part determines what foundations do and the demands made upon them. In that respect, foundations are policy *takers*. But many foundations have pioneered the funding of new approaches and services which have subsequently been incorporated into statutory provision. In that respect, foundations have been policy *shapers*. At the same time, however, grant-making foundations have traditionally claimed that they have nothing to do with the state.

While the claims of foundations to have influenced social policy echo those of other voluntary organisations (Bruce, 1994), there is a significant difference in their circumstances. Foundations are not dependent on the state for funding. Given that much of the debate concerning the influence of the state on voluntary organisations revolves around the latter's resource dependence, this is a crucial difference and might be taken to suggest both that foundations have greater power for independent influence on social policy and that foundations are less likely to be affected by changes in social policy.

Forming a judgement on the role of foundations in influencing social policy is difficult because charitable grant-making foundations in the UK have received remarkably little attention both within public policy debate and within voluntary sector research. In part this may be because foundations have shunned publicity, including the attentions of researchers, and most have kept themselves formally aloof from public policy debate. In part, lack of attention to UK charitable grant-making foundations may stem from their small numbers and modest resources compared with their counterparts in the United States.

The resources and power of foundations

According to information provided by the Association of Charitable Foundations an estimated 8,800 charitable grant-making foundations currently distribute around £1.25 billion per annum in grants to other bodies. Although this sum is small relative to total voluntary sector income it is of increasing importance to large parts of the voluntary sector. In addition, the National Lottery Charities Board (NLCB) alone gave £680 million to nearly 12,000 projects between 1995 and 1997 and the total figure given is further swelled by the contribution (around £280 million in total) of a dozen large operating charities which give grants in addition to providing services (Pharoah and Siederer, 1997; Fitzherbert *et al.*, 1996).

The size of foundations' wealth is perhaps less important in policy terms than their power. The perceived power of foundations does not rest primarily on the size of their funding capacity which, in the UK, is relatively small – the Lottery Boards aside (Leat and CAF, 1996). Foundations are uniquely powerful because they are seen to possess 'constantly replenishable pools of organised but uncommitted money that can be freely and, if need be, quickly deployed to meet existing or new social needs' (Pifer, 1984, p. 7). Foundation money may be spent irrespective of legislative mandate and the constraints of political legitimacy. It is this which gives them their largely unrecognised and unaccountable power to influence social development. 'Not bound by voters, shareholders, or customers – and with only feather-light oversight by government – they couldn't possibly be allowed to exist with such potential power and such utter freedom of action in a democracy. But they do' (Nielsen, 1996, p. 6).

Unlike their counterparts in the United States British charitable foundations have never been the subject of a major policy debate. In the USA the freedom of charitable foundations – created by resource independence – has been the subject of heated public policy controversy. Throughout the 1960s attacks on the power of foundations came from both the right and left of the political spectrum. The right criticised foundations as seedbeds of subversion and 'social-science-ism'; the left accused them of elitist grant-making and of forming a cartel grabbing for power over the American economy (Simon, 1965). In the light of anxieties concerning the power of foundations, the American Tax Reform Act 1969 introduced a new regulatory system with sanctions, a new tax on investment income and new restrictions on the deductibility of property gifts (Simon, 1996).

Social policy change and foundations

Despite their resource independence and their policy-shaping role, foundations have increasingly found themselves in recent years in the role of policy-takers rather than policy-makers. UK foundations have been affected by the broad and specific policy changes described elsewhere in this volume (see, for example, Chapters 2 and 5).

The 1980s was a decade in which the state, in effect, expanded the 'space' and role of foundations as it attempted to shrink its own 'space' and responsibilities (Commission on the Future of the Voluntary Sector in England, 1996). Central and local government funding were restricted, with knock-on effects on operating voluntary organisations and on many statutory organisations. The old consensus on 'statutory responsibilities' and 'what the state normally funds' began to crumble. Operating voluntary organisations not only found that there was no new money but some also had their existing grants cut. And when they tried to raise money from other sources there was increasing competition from new fund-raising players in the shape of hospitals and schools (Wilson, 1992). One effect on foundations was an 'often dramatic increase in the volume of applications and ... a change in the purposes for which funds are sought' (ACF, 1991).

Although increased demand on foundations was perceived largely as the result of cuts in government funding, the reality was almost certainly more complex. The role of the state appeared to be diminishing in some spheres but many voluntary organisations were in fact receiving larger quantities of statutory funding (Mocroft, 1997; Russell *et al.*, 1996; also Chapter 4 in this volume). Foundations were experiencing the impact not merely of government policies concerning the scale of funding but also of changes in the terms and culture of government spending.

Much of the increase in central and local government funding of voluntary organisations was related to special programmes for carefully designated areas of work (see also Chapters 4 and 7). Most of these special programmes were designed to achieve aims narrower or wider than, or different from, the particular purposes of the recipient organisations. The culture of government spending on the voluntary sector had changed from one in which voluntary organisations were supported as broadly 'good organisations doing good works' to one in which voluntary organisations were supported as vehicles for the delivery of specific statutory objectives (Commission on the Future of the Voluntary Sector in England, 1996).

This fundamental change in government policy was most clearly demonstrated in the efficiency scrutiny of government funding for the voluntary sector (Home Office, 1990). Ten or twenty years earlier the words 'efficiency' and 'voluntary sector' would not have been linked in the same sentence. In addition to the new emphasis on 'efficiency' in funding voluntary organisations, much central government spending on voluntary organisations in this period was experimental, short-term funding designed to 'demonstrate' and 'innovate'. It was almost as if government had decided to adopt the role of foundations, leaving foundations, in effect, in the former role of government as continuing funder of someone else's bright ideas.

In the 1990s a range of policy changes, unrelated to foundations, had further effects on demand, grant-making and effectiveness. For example, periodic crises in local authority spending, with some authorities completely running out of money and making huge cuts in their funding of voluntary organisations and other expenditures, not only increased demand on foundations but also undermined the assumptions and effectiveness of some of their existing grants. For example, changes in housing benefit rules in the mid-1990s had obvious effects on homelessness in general and refugees and asylum-seekers in particular – groups in which some foundations had a particular interest. Changes in university funding meant that foundations funding research were under pressure to provide what had previously been seen as overhead costs. In medical research the effect was such that the Association of Medical Research Charities issued a statement reaffirming its policy that

> charities should not pay the indirect costs of research they support in universities, even though changes in statutory funding are creating severe difficulties in maintaining the research infrastructure to support external funding. The difficulties appear to be most acute in providing major equipment and maintaining buildings, but it is also apparent that some essential laboratory facilities and staff are often not in place. (AMRC, 1996, p. 2)

The implementation of the NHS and Community Care Act in 1993 and the arrival of the contracting out of statutory services has created further new dilemmas for foundations. They are increasingly being asked for funds to pay for activities which cannot be costed into contracts, but which are nevertheless essential to the contracted organisation's capacity and competence. Aside from making such specific decisions concerning what is, or should be, paid for by the contractor, foundations are now beginning to ask themselves whether it is appropriate for them to give grants to organisations working under contract to the state. Are such grants, in effect, disguised subsidies of statutory services and responsibilities? And how should foundations respond to requests both from 'independent trusts' floated off from statutory bodies and from thinly disguised charitable arms of, for example, hospitals and schools?

These changes in social policy have had effects not merely on what foundations do but on how they do it. In recent years many foundations have been reexamining their grant-making processes and practices. One set of factors encouraging reassessment relate to changes in funding of what were previously seen as statutory responsibilities. As noted above, these changes create new demands for trust funding: more applications; applications for items and activities previously funded by the state; applications for larger sums; applications for longer-term revenue funding; and applications for core rather than project funding (Leat, 1992).

Larger and longer-term grants, as well as greater demand relative to available resources, raise new considerations. Such grants are thought to require more careful assessment and greater emphasis on reducing, if not avoiding, risk. As a result, many of the larger foundations now require more information, and different types of information, from applicants. They are increasingly using formal application forms. Some are also using core and freelance staff to telephone or visit applicants in order to verify and amplify written information provided by the applicant (Leat, 1998). Grant-making in some foundations is no longer seen as simply a matter of spending money on good works undertaken by well-intentioned and worthy organisations. Increasingly, foundation grant-making is seen as a risky business requiring detailed knowledge and professional judgement (Leat, 1998).

Knowledge for grant-making is not only a matter of obtaining more information about applicants and their proposed projects but also about keeping up with the sheer quantity of regulation and legislation in specific areas. For example, apart from the implications of the NHS and Community Care Act, foundations giving grants to organisations working with children have had to be familiar with the Children Act 1989, and those giving grants to a wide range of organisations have had be aware of the Food Safety Act (see also Chapters 5 and 12). Foundations need knowledge of such regulations not only to assess the increasing number of grant requests to facilitate compliance with these regulations but also in order to assess the viability of projects proposed by applicants who may be unaware of such regulations.

Other pressures on foundations

In addition to responding to the changing social policy environment of recent years, foundations have had to deal concurrently with other major changes in their environment, including the National Lottery, the Charities Act 1992 and tax changes.

1. The National Lottery

Under the National Lottery etc. Act 1993 five distributing boards were created to facilitate giving to the Arts, Sport, Heritage, Charities and the Millennium – collectively generally referred to as 'the good causes'. Whereas operating charities have complained most vociferously about the Lottery's income-generating activities and their effects on fund-raising, foundations have been much more concerned with the Lottery's spending practices.

The effects of the creation of these distributing boards on foundations vary depending in large part on the particular grant-making policies and practices of the individual boards. One general effect of the creation of the five boards, however, is to dwarf the contribution of foundations and thereby radically alter the ecology and the balance of power in charitable grant-making. Foundations, once accused of being able to upset the priorities of government by creating, but not following through, new responsibilities, suddenly find themselves being given a taste of their own medicine. There's a new and very rich gang on the block changing the rules of the game without consulting the old players.

One area in which existing foundations have felt the wind of change blown in by the National Lottery especially fiercely is the arts. The number of foundations giving to the arts is fairly limited, probably including no more than about fifty foundations with incomes in excess of £100,000 per annum and perhaps a further thirty or so much smaller trusts with some record of giving to the arts. When it became clear that the arts would be one of the five 'good causes' to benefit from a portion of the proceeds of the National Lottery, many foundations giving to the arts welcomed the proposals, expecting that this would relieve them of some of the demand for funding and solve the longer-term problems of keeping arts companies going.

The effect of the National Lottery on foundations funding the arts has, however, been rather less straightforward than anticipated. The National Lottery distributing board for the arts requires matching funding before Lottery funding is released. This means that the effect of the very large sums available for distribution to the arts has not been to decrease the demand on foundations but rather to increase it. This impact is exacerbated by the huge disparity between available Lottery funding and available funding for the arts from traditional foundations. Furthermore, Lottery funding for the arts has significantly raised the stakes in the game and has encouraged arts organisations to employ high-powered (and often well-paid) fund-raisers, a large part of whose job is to approach the same small number of foundations.

National Lottery giving to the arts, and in particular the matching funding requirement, has not only increased rather than decreased, as expected, the pressure on foundations giving to the arts, it has also fundamentally disturbed their old roles. As one foundation member writes:

> One of the great merits, in my view, of the trust world is its independence and extraordinary diversity ... There is a further enormous advantage in not having to conform to agendas or policies, politically correct or otherwise, of Government funded bodies such as the Arts Council or Regional Arts Boards. Trusts are understandably wary of supplementing Lottery grants as this allows the Lottery distributors to become dominant in terms of policy as well as cash. (Haldane, 1997, p. 17)

Unlike the distributing board for the arts, the National Lottery Charities Board does not require its grant recipients to raise matched funding, and it can make funds available for revenue costs, and not simply for capital. But its effect on foundations working in the broad field of social welfare has nevertheless been immense. In 1996/7 the NLCB made grants exceeding £300 million to charities and other good causes (Unwin and Westland, 1997). The very size of the NLCB's grant-making capacity is sufficient for its weight to be felt, dwarfing the contribution of other foundations. Its more tangible effects on other foundations are that it has led to an increasing number of applications to other foundations for grants to assist in applying for NLCB funds. Its large grants have also raised expectations and aspirations among voluntary organisations which have then been reflected in applications to other foundations. Some foundations argue that the NLCB has effectively encouraged small organisations to grow too far too fast, and that foundations are then asked to fund the associated support and infrastructure costs.

But the greatest concern for foundations in all fields covered by the Lottery distributing boards has been how the initiatives spawned by the Lottery will be sustained and on whom that ongoing demand will fall (Unwin and Westland, 1997; Haldane, 1997; ACF, 1997a). The fear is that the Lottery boards have created large and small organisations, buildings, programmes, staff numbers, and so on, which will require ongoing revenue funding from other foundations. There are two issues here. One is a matter of principle. Many foundations are unwilling to pick up the Lottery's priorities and have made it a positive principle to stick to their own priorities, refusing, for example, to provide matched funding. The other issue is one of arithmetic. Even if foundations were willing, in effect, to trail along in the wake of the Lottery, they simply do not have the resources to do so.

2. The Charities Act 1992

Legislation directly and specifically related to charities obviously has a major impact on grant-making foundations as charities. Recent charities legislation is another example of the 'risk reduction' culture described by Rochester in Chapter 5 in that it aimed to regulate charities more closely in order to reduce the risk involved in charitable giving. Clearly, charity legislation is designed to regulate all charities. However its impact on foundations is not necessarily in the same areas or at the same level as on operating charities. The Charities Act 1992 illustrates the way in which different aspects of charities legislation may have very different levels of significance for different types of charity. It also illustrates the ways in which foundations are not only influenced by new legislation but may also actively influence the form and content of legislation.

Different parts of the Act had different degrees of relevance for foundations as compared with operating charities. For example, the clauses of the Act dealing with control of fund-raising were highly relevant to most operating charities but of little relevance to the majority of endowed foundations. Conversely, those parts of the Act which dealt with investments were central to the operation of endowed foundations but of much more limited relevance to many operating charities. The Charities Act 1992 was in part the result of growing disquiet concerning the regulation and supervision of charities in general. In 1987 the government conducted an Efficiency Scrutiny of the Supervision of Charities

(HMSO, 1987) and, in the following year, a Public Accounts Committee report (Committee of Public Accounts, 1988) expressed views little short of horror concerning the level of accountability required of charities by the Charity Commission. In 1989 a White Paper, *Charities: A Framework for the Future*, was published. The recommendation in the White Paper of most relevance to foundations was that: 'regulations should require all statements of account to give details of grants made by charities out of their income and property. In particular, they should disclose the names of their institutional beneficiaries, together with the amount of grant paid' (Home Office, 1989).

Although this proposal was publicly welcomed by the Association of Charitable Foundations (ACF, 1991), many foundations viewed it as an unwarranted interference with their privacy. Traditionally, foundations have been seen as highly secretive organisations. Some have positively rejected the notion that they should be publicly accountable on the grounds that the money they spend is private money and what they do with that money is their own private business. Others have argued for 'secrecy' on moral or semi-religious grounds. They have avoided publication of their good works on the grounds that advertising one's altruism undermines the moral worth of the gift. Some have gone to considerable lengths to preserve their anonymity. Other foundations have argued against public disclosure on more practical grounds. One argument is that publication of the foundation's existence and its specific activities would lead to a flood of applications with which the foundation could not deal (Fitzherbert and Forrester, 1991). Another argument, from a minority of large foundations, is that full disclosure of grants given is simply impractical. BBC Children in Need, for example, gives in excess of 13,000 grants per annum and would thus require a document the size of a telephone directory to present the full list.

Despite these objections ACF broadly supported the White Paper proposals on disclosure and concentrated its efforts on their implementation, focusing in particular on the income level at which the requirements on accounts became operational. ACF worked hard briefing members and lobbying the House of Lords Committee on the Bill, as well as working with a joint working group convened by the National Council for Voluntary Organisations, to secure various amendments which were of particular interest to foundations. When the Act was finally passed it was clear that foundations were not only subject to significant legislative change but that they (via ACF) had played an important part in influencing the nature of that change. Foundations were both change-takers and change-shapers.

In the event, the main requirements of the Charities Act 1992 of particular relevance to foundations included the duty to publish an annual report (something relatively few foundations had previously done and to which, as noted above, some foundations objected for different reasons) and a statutory duty to keep accounts in the form specified in regulations to be based on the Statement of Recommended Practice (SORP) 2. The accounting rules required grant-making foundations to list the grants given to organisations but not to individuals, thus meeting one objection from foundations. Even more radically, perhaps, foundations were required to make their accounts available to any member of the public who asked for them and paid a reasonable fee. And both annual reports and accounts were to be available for inspection at the Charity Commission. The Act also required an annual return to the Charity Commission from all foundations. Those which broke the new and more stringent accounting rules were likely to be specially marked. In addition the 1992 Act gave the Charity Commission statutory powers to demand information from charities and to hold formal enquiries, as well as legal authority to exchange information with other government bodies, including the Inland Revenue. Where a charity had been mismanaged or where the interests of the charity required it the Charity Commission could appoint, suspend or remove trustees or appoint a receiver or manager. The Act also excluded certain people as trustees. Although some of these provisions had always been regarded as 'good practice' by the Charity Commission, the 1992 Act made it a criminal offence to fail to fulfil the requirements of the Act.

These provisions of the Act concerning accountability and openness marked a radical change in the requirements on foundations, bringing them very clearly into public light. They marked the end of an era of privacy for foundations. The arguments outlined above against disclosure might still be viewed as having some moral force but the 1992 Act removed any legal credibility they might have had.

In addition to requiring greater openness and accountability, the 1992 Act had effects on the way in which foundations handled their investments and income. Under the Act charities were given the freedom to lease or sell land or real property without special permission from the Charity Commission, provided that the proper professional advice was obtained and that the terms were the best that could be procured. The investment-holding functions of the Official Custodian for Charities ceased except in special circumstances. Once investments were transferred from the Official Custodian, each foundation itself had to reclaim tax from the Inland Revenue. The Act also made it easier to incorporate a charity under the Charitable Trusts Incorporation Act 1872 and allowed an incorporated charity to execute legal documents and institute legal proceedings in its own name rather than the joint names of trustees. Although this did not limit the liability of trustees it was seen as particularly useful to foundations holding stocks and shares.

If the accountability requirements of the 1992 Act took a degree of freedom away from foundations these financial investment provisions increased their freedom. But the most eagerly awaited freedom – reform of the Trustee Investments Act 1961 – turned out to be a longer story.

3. The other financial and tax changes

The Charities Act 1992 and an attempted subsequent reform of the Trustee Investments Act 1961 were examples of policy and legal changes which were specifically related to charities, and as such to foundations. By contrast, but also relating to foundations' investments, various tax changes introduced by the new Labour government provide interesting examples of legal and policy changes which are not intentionally directed at foundations but which nevertheless have indirect and unintended effects on foundations.

In July 1997 in its first budget the new government abolished Advance Corporation Tax credit. This was a measure designed to encourage reinvestment by businesses which was not intended to have any effect on charitable giving. But abolishing the credit had an effect on tax-exempt investors and some foundations forecast that their investment income would drop by 10 per cent or more (ACF, 1997b). Anticipating this change the Association of Charitable Foundations made representations in advance to the Chancellor of the Exchequer, pointing out that charities would be caught in a net not primarily designed to affect them and that charities would be adversely affected by the rumoured change. This secured a transitional arrangement for charities which meant that the abolition of the tax credit was delayed for two years and then phased in over a further five years giving time for charities to re-order their investments.

By the autumn of 1997, however, there was a further twist in the tale, illustrating the complex routes by which apparently unrelated legal and policy changes may have effects on foundations. It became apparent that a growing number of UK multinationals were starting to pay foreign income dividends (FIDs) which, unlike traditional dividends, do not allow tax-exempt investors to reclaim tax. Companies paying FIDs included many of the 'blue-chip' investments favoured by foundations. The practice of paying FIDs had come about as an indirect result of the abolition of Advance Corporation Tax credit. Companies had previously been reluctant to pay FIDs because their biggest shareholders, the pension funds, could reclaim tax on traditional dividends. When this ability to reclaim tax on traditional dividends was abolished in the July budget there was nothing to stop companies switching to FIDs.

The effect on foundations (and charities in general) was to undermine the transitional arrangement negotiated by ACF and to significantly reduce many foundations' investment income. For example, the Wellcome Trust estimated that Glaxo Wellcome's decision to pay an FID instead of a traditional dividend would reduce the Trust's income by £5 million.

The 1997 July budget also contained a promise of a review of charities taxation arrangements which was widely believed to herald the possibility of some change in the amounts of irrecoverable VAT paid by charities. Although this review has at the time of writing been further delayed the issue of VAT provides a nice illustration of the ways in which legal and policy changes affecting the bulk of charities may have little relevance to foundations. Few foundations pay very much VAT and therefore had little direct interest in such a change. ACF nevertheless welcomed the review as an opportunity to open up discussion of the effects of taxation on gifts to charity and, more specifically, on the formation of foundations.

Conclusion

UK foundations' traditional position on relationships with government is nicely summed up in ACF's first annual report: 'Foundations are independent grant-givers, who determine their own agenda. Although such an agenda may take account of Government thinking and practice, foundations' relationship with Government is not necessarily a close one' (ACF, 1992, p. 8). Although this may still be the 'official' position, foundations have become increasingly aware of the ways in which government policies have direct and indirect effects on the demands made upon them and on the effectiveness of their grant-making. Foundations are realising that, however much they might wish it were otherwise, they do not work in isolation. Government policies impact on them directly and deliberately via charity law, as well as directly but less deliberately through changes in legislation and policies relating to tax and investment issues. In addition, the areas, levels, terms and general culture of government funding of both statutory and voluntary services and individuals (via the benefit system) impact on operating voluntary organisations which in turn bring those impacts to the desks of foundations.

One interesting development in the 1990s was the creation of the Association of Charitable Foundations. Why was ACF finally formed at the beginning of the 1990s? One answer might be that foundations realised that the world had changed. While foundations had been sitting on the sidelines maintaining their independent aloofness from government, government had stolen the foundations' clothes, casting itself in the role of definer of the necessary, short-term funder and innovator, leaving foundations with the more onerous and less attractive task of picking up the longer-term bill. Arguably, the creation of ACF was, in part, a means of regaining lost ground, providing a vehicle through which foundations could collectively make their voices heard in influencing policy.

The erosion of clear boundaries between the state, market and voluntary sectors and their respective roles and responsibilities, as well as increased emphasis by the Labour government on partnerships and alliances, is likely to mean that foundations will need further to rethink their roles and relationships with government in the coming years. The old 'them and us' position may come to be seen not merely as unrealistic but also as outdated and precious.

Furthermore, the creation and activities of the National Lottery distributing boards, especially perhaps those of the NLCB, and the creation of the Diana, Princess of Wales Memorial Fund have brought grant-making to charities into the media and political limelight. As yet, the stories about both grant-making and the way in which foundations operate are crude and heavily personalised. But local authorities are beginning to express their concerns about the effects of grants made by the Lottery on democratically determined plans and priorities (Unwin and Westland, 1997). If the Diana, Princess of Wales Memorial Fund fails to satisfy the expectations of those sections of the public who believe that they, in some way, 'own' the Fund, questions regarding the public accountability of foundations may gain a higher profile. Charitable foundations in the UK may yet find themselves in the position, familiar to their US counterparts, of having to explain their 'power without responsibility' in a modern democracy.

References

Association of Charitable Foundations (ACF) (1991) *Annual Report 1991*, ACF, London.
Association of Charitable Foundations (ACF) (1992) *The First Three Years 1989–1992*, ACF, London.
Association of Charitable Foundations (ACF) (1997a) *Promoting the Effectiveness of UK Grant-Making Trusts, Annual Review 1996–97* ACF, London.
Association of Charitable Foundations (ACF) (1997b) *Trust and Foundation News*, June/July.
Association of Medical Research Charities (AMRC) (1996) *Policy Statement*, AMRC, London.
Bruce, I. (1994) *Meeting Need: Successful Charity Marketing*, ICSA, London.

Commission on the Future of the Voluntary Sector in England (1996) *Meeting the Challenge of Change: Voluntary Action into the 21ˢᵗ Century*, NCVO Publications, London.

Committee of Public Accounts (1988) *Monitoring and Control of Charities in England and Wales*, HMSO, London.

Deakin, N. (1996) 'The devil's in the detail: contracting for social care by voluntary organisations', *Social Policy and Administration*, 30(1): 20–38.

Fitzherbert, L., C. Giussani and H. Hunt (eds) (1996) *The National Lottery Yearbook*, 1996 edition, Directory of Social Change, London.

Fitzherbert, L. and S. Forrester (1991) *A Guide to the Major Trusts*, Directory of Social Change, London.

Haldane, D. (1997) 'The Lottery and the arts', *Trust and Foundation News*, June/July, p. 17.

HMSO (1987) *Efficiency Scrutiny of the Supervision of Charities*, HMSO, London.

Home Office (1989) *Charities: A Framework for the Future*, HMSO, London.

Home Office (1990) *Profiting from Partnership: Efficiency Scrutiny of Government Funding of the Voluntary Sector*, HMSO, London.

Kendall, J. and M. Knapp (1996) *The Voluntary Sector in the UK*, Manchester University Press, Manchester.

Knight, B. (1993) *Voluntary Action*, Home Office, London.

Leat, D. (1992) *Trusts in Transition: The Policy and Practice of Grantmaking Trusts*, Joseph Rowntree Foundation, York.

Leat, D. (1998) *Faith, Hope and Information: Assessing a Grant Application*, Joseph Rowntree Foundation, York.

Leat, D. and CAF Information Unit (1996) 'CAF's top 500 grantmaking trusts', in *Dimensions of the Voluntary Sector 1996*, Charities Aid Foundation, Tonbridge.

Mocroft, I. (1997) 'The survey of local authority payments to voluntary and charitable organisations for 1995–96', in C. Pharoah and M. Smerdon (eds) *Dimensions of the Voluntary Sector*, 1997 edition, Charities Aid Foundation, Kent, pp. 41–51.

Nielsen, W.A. (1996) *Inside American Philanthropy*, University of Oklahoma Press, Norman and London.

Pharoah, C. and N. Siederer (1997) 'Number, income and assets – new estimates', in C. Pharoah and M. Smerdon (eds) *Dimensions of the Voluntary Sector*, 1997 edition, Charities Aid Foundation, West Malling.

Pifer, A. (1984) *Speaking Out: Reflections on Thirty Years of Foundation Work*, Council on Foundations, Washington, DC.

Russell, L., D. Scott and P. Wilding (1996) *Funding the Voluntary Sector*, University of Manchester, Manchester.

Simon, J.G. (1965) 'The Patman report and the Treasury proposals', *Proceedings of the Seventh Biennial Conference on Charitable foundations*, New York University, Matthew Bender, Albany, NY.

Simon, J. (1996) 'The regulation of American foundations: looking backward at the Tax Reform Act of 1969', *Voluntas*, 6(3): 243–54.

Unwin, J. and P. Westland (1997) *Local Funding: The Impact of the National Lottery Charities Board*, Association of Charitable Foundations, London.
Wilson, D. (1992) 'The strategic challenges of co-operation and competition in British voluntary organisations: towards the next century', *Nonprofit Management and Leadership*, 3(2): 239–54.

10

International Development NGOs: Policy Conflict and Convergence

David Lewis

Introduction

This chapter is concerned with UK-based voluntary organisations involved with the provision of international development assistance to poor countries – sometimes called non-governmental international aid agencies – and explores the ways in which they both shape and are shaped by development policy. It will use the term 'development NGOs' to refer to organisations which are neither governmental nor commercial businesses and which are linked with the international development community of organisations and institutions – the 'aid industry'. Non-governmental organisations (NGOs) are viewed as part of a 'third sector' which, despite its blurred boundaries, can be seen to have local, national and international dimensions. The chapter also makes a distinction between 'Northern NGOs' (NNGOs) which have their roots in the industrialised countries but which undertake development or emergency relief work in aid-recipient countries, and 'Southern NGOs' (SNGOs) which are non-governmental organisations which have emerged locally in the countries where NNGOs are active.

The chapter argues that while the growth of these international development NGOs has been in large part due to increases in government funding (which has brought not only opportunities but also pressures and constraints), NGOs have nevertheless contributed to changing wider development policy agendas. It examines the ways in which the changing funding policies are impacting upon NNGOs by looking at the growth of direct funding of SNGOs and the post-Cold War prioritisation by governments of NGO humanitarian emergency relief. The chapter then reflects on ways in which NGO approaches to development have influenced official donors through a 'reverse agenda' and suggests that this is partly evident in the 1997 British government White Paper (DFID, 1997). Finally, the chapter moves from a discussion of the implications of the issues raised for international development NGOs to a consideration of their importance for the wider study of social policy.

Background

The 1990s have seen a rapid growth of interest among policy-makers and researchers in what have been variously termed 'NGOs', and 'non-profit' and 'voluntary' organisations in both the industrialised 'North' and the aid-recipient countries of 'the South' (Smillie, 1995; Lewis, 1999). This has been reflected in a growth of interest in these types of organisations amongst activists in both domestic and international contexts. Within the academic field of social policy, the growth of interest in the 'third sector' has mainly been associated with a restructuring of welfare policies in industrialised countries (Smith and Lipsky, 1993; Kramer *et al.*, 1993). More recently, emerging ideas about the need to build a global social policy perspective have led to a new interest in development policy processes including the roles of NGOs, development institutions such as the World Bank and the United Nations (Deacon *et al.*, 1997). Across a number of other disciplines, the renewed interest in the concept of 'civil society' has also focused considerable research attention on the third sector (for example, Brown and Tandon, 1994; Chambre, 1997; Burbidge, 1997).

The new interest in NGOs in international development circles has arisen in response to a set of related trends, such as the perceived failure of state-led development approaches which were common during the 1970s and 1980s. The so-called 'new policy agenda' for development for the 1990s combined neo-liberal economic policy prescriptions with a stated commitment to 'good governance'. It projected development NGOs as efficient and responsive alternatives to the state in the delivery of services and as organisational actors with the potential to strengthen democratic processes (Robinson, 1993). In addition to increased roles in longer-term development work, international NGOs have also been highly visible in the response by Western citizens and governments to crises in the developing world and the former communist countries, such as the famine in Ethiopia or ethnic violence in the former Yugoslavia (Fowler, 1995).

Although figures on global NGO numbers and resources are notoriously difficult to gauge with any accuracy, the numbers of development NGOs registered in Organisation for Economic Co-operation and Development (OECD) countries is believed to have increased from 1,600 in 1980 to nearly 3,000 by 1993 and the expenditure of these organisations has grown in the same period from US$2.8 billion to US$5.7 billion (Hulme and Edwards, 1997). It is estimated that in the early 1970s about 1.5 per cent of total NGO income was drawn from official bilateral and mul-tilateral donor sources, and that this figure had risen to about 30 per cent by the mid-1990s (ODI, 1996).

Development NGOs are an extremely diverse group of organi-sations which range from large formal, professional, bureaucratic agencies such as the British NGO Oxfam (UK/Ireland) to small, informal, voluntaristic groups composed of a handful of people with little in the way of organisational structure or funds such as Vetwork UK, a largely 'structureless' organisation in which members and users support each other with ideas and informa-tion using new electronic communication technologies (Blakeway, 1998). The activities undertaken by NGOs include self-help, as-sistance to members, the provision of services to particular sections of the wider community and campaigning work at the local, na-tional or international level. NGOs may be active in the health, education, agriculture or industrial sectors, or they may be con-cerned with wider human rights, gender or environmental issues. They may work locally, nationally or, as is increasingly the case, on a global level.

By the late 1990s, NNGOs found that, despite new opportuni-ties for funding and influence, they were operating within an increasingly complex and difficult policy environment. There are at least three main dimensions to this changing environment. First, while the 'new policy agenda' has brought NGOs more resources and a higher profile, there is now a trend towards direct funding of SNGOs by official donors, rather than routing aid through NNGO intermediaries. Second, the increase in funds has brought organisational pressures in the form of organisational change and formalisation (Billis and MacKeith, 1992). For example, NGOs are required to manage a larger and more complex scale of operations and to develop more sophisticated systems of accountability. Third, problems of NGO goal displacement as a result of changing patterns of funding availability have become more acute. For example, while official resources available for emergency relief work (as opposed to longer-term development work) by NNGOs increased dramatically in the post-Cold War period, there are now signs that this is again being reduced (ODI, 1998).

In addition to these quite formidable difficulties, the picture is further complicated by the fact that the identities of NNGOs appear increasingly fragmented and unclear (Smillie, 1994; Lewis, 1998). For example, NNGOs may profess long-term development principles but may at times be given funding incentives by official donors to undertake short-term humanitarian relief work. During the 1990s, there was a growth in the profile of intrastate conflicts, often referred to as 'complex political emergencies' (Duffield, 1993), usually in marginal areas of the global economy and frequently fuelled by predatory state structures. NGOs have been considered by policy-makers to have a special contribution to make in meeting the humanitarian needs created by these wars and in 'containing' the resultant disorder (Fowler, 1995). In addition, NNGOs' identity crisis is heightened by the fact that while they are organisations of the North, they work mainly in the South. Some NNGOs do not always have clear roots either in the 'domestic' voluntary or non-governmental sector or recognisable roles in the countries in which they work.[1]

From indirect to direct funding

Many NNGOs have now made the transition from implementing their own projects to working with and funding Southern 'partner' NGOs, often with government development funds. However, official funding policy towards NNGOs is changing. The role of NNGOs as channels for funds for SNGOs is being displaced. Instead of working through NNGOs as intermediaries or 'brokers' (Smillie, 1994) some Northern governments are choosing instead to go directly to the SNGOs to develop funding relationships (Bebbington and Riddell, 1995; Edwards, 1996). These changes, while proceeding at a very different pace in different parts of the world, have profound implications for the relationships between NNGOs, SNGOs and donors.

There has been a growth in direct funding of Southern NGOs by the DFID (Department for International Development) in recent years although precise figures are very difficult to come by due to the variety of different routes through which international development funds are channelled to NGOs (ODI, 1996). Approximately 9.3 per cent of British aid to developing countries (amounting to £180 million) was spent through British NGOs in 1995–6, one-third of which was emergency assistance. Since 1994 there have been several new ways in which SNGOs began to receive funds directly. The Direct Funding Initiative was established by the DFID in East Africa in 1994 and by 1997 £6 million was being committed through this route. The British Partnership Scheme which is administered through British embassies disbursed £9 million to local NGOs in the same year (German and Randel, 1999). There is a plan, currently pending approval, to commit £5 million per year to support for local NGOs and civil society organisations in India.

A similar pattern of changing funding relationships has occurred in Sweden, where the process of change and its effects have been better documented than in the UK. Thus, while approximately half of the Swedish government's assistance to the Bangladesh NGO sector is transferred through Swedish NGOs, the other half is now provided directly to Bangladeshi NGOs by the Sida (Swedish International Development Agency) office in Dhaka (Lewis and Sobhan, 1999).

The rush by donors to fund NGOs directly raises a number of questions. Bebbington and Riddell (1995) conclude their discussion of the changing relationships between NNGOs, SNGOs and donors with three main issues for further consideration: (i) that donor support to NNGOs has tended to rest on a view of NNGOs as effective aid delivery mechanisms rather than as organisations capable of assisting SNGOs in the wider strengthening of 'civil society'; (ii) that there may be a danger in direct funding that SNGO agendas will be distorted to fit offfficial donor objectives; and (iii) that while trends towards increased direct funding are sometimes perceived as a 'threat' to NNGOs they may also be viewed as an opportunity for creative thinking about enhancing the effectiveness of donor, NNGO and SNGO roles and relationships. Edwards (1996) has drawn attention to a potential crisis of identity and legitimacy among NNGOs as increasingly effective SNGOs take over most of the activities previously carried out by organisations from the North. In some developing countries (such as India or Bangladesh) there may be very little an NNGO can bring to a third sector which is increasingly dominated by a range of highly professional local organisations and a set of innovative development and policy ideas.

From development to emergency work?

A second area of policy change affecting NNGOs is the changing global context of relief and development. In the post-Cold War political and economic order, the growth of the concept of 'complex political emergencies' led Western governments to fund NNGOs to undertake humanitarian emergency work which serves the purposes of both meeting immediate humanitarian needs and 'containing' the spread of instability and disorder. During the early 1990s the volume and the proportion of such overseas development assistance devoted to emergency work increased significantly in line with the numbers of humanitarian emergencies in the Horn of Africa, Central Africa and the Balkans (Randel and German, 1997). According to Burnell (1997, p. 238) the quantity of aid intended for disaster relief and emergency assistance 'more than trebled' between 1988 and 1993 to reach approximately one-tenth of total flows of overseas development assistance. Hoffman (1997) calculates that US$5 billion worth of emergency assistance is now channelled through NGOs each year.

This policy trend led NNGOs into a period of soul-searching about the relationship between long-term development work and short-term emergency humanitarian assistance. With increased government funding available for relief, some NNGOs have been tempted to expand their emergency work – even while carrying misgivings about the implications. Burnell (1997, p. 182), for example, quotes the head of one British NGO lamenting the increasing diversion of NNGOs' work towards 'emergency relief with a strong political flavour' and the associated threat to NGO independence. Other organisations such as Children's Aid Direct have evolved as specialist organisations and grown substantially to move into the emergency 'market' generated by these wider policy changes. In the words of one NGO observer there is a very real danger that NNGOs may lose their relative independence as development organisations and become merely 'ladles for the global soup kitchen' (Fowler, 1995). In this view more funding for NNGOs will become available as levels of global stability decline: ... 'in a quest to guide stability in favour of those vying for power, finance will become increasingly available to agencies who can deliver "stabilising" social services' (Fowler, 1997, p. 229).

For NNGOs which have taken up the challenge of relief and emergency work there have been difficult lessons to be learned, particularly in the period since the Rwandan genocide in 1994. They have had to face the fact that NNGOs can become substitutes for political solutions, that they can contribute to a worsening of ongoing conflict by providing resources, and that they can be manipulated by governments (Cushing, 1995; Hoffman, 1997). Since the mixed experiences of NNGO operations in Somalia and Rwanda there are signs that the international humanitarian system is being reassessed and restructured and that overall funding levels have begun to decline since 1995 (ODI, 1998).

The 'reverse agenda' and the UK White Paper

According to some observers of the changing relationship between NGOs and official donors there has been a phenomenon in recent years which has been termed the 'reverse agenda' (ODI, 1996). While official donors and NGOs have traditionally espoused different approaches to development, it has been observed that the very policy priorities emphasised by NGOs have now begun to influence aid policy. For example, official aid programmes are now far more concerned with the concept of participatory planning, the gender dimensions of development and environmental concerns than they were during the 1980s and part of the explanation for this lies in the efforts of NGOs to influence and transform official policy. For example, Norway consulted many NGOs when drawing up its bilateral programmes in Nicaragua and Ethiopia in 1993. The World Bank now includes NGOs in the implementation of many of its projects. Donors' concerns with human rights and 'strengthening civil society' is another reflection of this reverse agenda.

Objectives now overlap to a significant extent and some donors take over and expand projects started by NGOs under an official umbrella. However, significant numbers of NGOs in both the North and the South (particularly those which are long established) remain wary of these developments. Some see it more as a convergence of 'language about development' rather than overall approaches to development. For example, NGOs such as Oxfam remain highly critical of World Bank structural adjustment policies.

In Britain, the White Paper on International Development – published in 1997 and the first since 1975 – reflects a major change in emphasis in development policy (DFID, 1997). The White Paper consists of four sections. The first of these speaks of a refocusing of development efforts on the 'elimination of poverty and the encouragement of economic growth which benefits the poor' (p. 3). The second section talks of building 'partnerships' with other donors and development organisations. New ways of working with both the private and the voluntary sectors in the UK, and with researchers, are to be put in place, along with reform of the Commonwealth Development Corporation into a public/private partnership. The third section focuses on creating a new consistency of government policies to favour 'sustainable development', pointing specifically to human rights, labour standards and accountability and transparency in government. It is here that gender issues are most clearly articulated. Violence against women, for example, is seen as a human rights issue. The White Paper also commits the government to promoting political stability, to responding 'effectively' to conflict and to the reduction of developing country external debt to 'sustainable levels'. Finally, the fourth section speaks of the need for increasing public understanding of international development and ensuring the accountability of resources intended for development. The paper ends with a promise to reverse the decline in British aid levels and reaffirms commitment to the UN target of 0.7 per cent of GDP.

The reverse agenda is evident in many issues raised in the White Paper (such as debt relief, gender issues and human rights) and formal consultation processes have now been set in motion with development NGOs and other community-based organisations. For example, the Aid and Trade Provision (ATP) was formally ended by the White Paper which states (p. 45) that 'no more applications will be accepted for ATP assistance, and the scheme will be closed'. This has long been a central criticism of the NGO community. For years this policy tied British aid to the provision and subsidy of British products and services and provided what amounted to an export subsidy, despite the rhetoric of market competition embodied in the UK Conservative government's domestic policy and the requirement to remove subsidies in developing countries undergoing structural adjustment plans. The percentage of bilateral aid which was tied to the purchase of goods and services from the UK was 73 per cent in 1991 and 54 per cent in 1994 (Curtis, 1997). The change now removes the link between aid and the funding of British exports and in theory at least frees governmental funds to be applied to less self-interested purposes.

Not that NGOs take the White paper at face value. Some see the challenge of the next few years as one of maintaining pressure on the government to ensure that the White Paper's concerns become a reality and are not simply forgotten. Thus Whaites (1998, pp. 203–4) argues from an NGO perspective:

> The mere completion of the first international development White Paper in 20 years has therefore rightly been seen by most NGOs as a sign of progress ... [it] has the potential to leave a real mark ... we must seek to provide real scrutiny and constructive input on how government can translate good intentions into real actions for the poor.

Equally important is the fact that the White Paper also acknowledges that there is a need to build a stronger public understanding of, and constituency for, British aid so as to overcome the relative marginality of development issues in public life.

Conclusion

This chapter has argued that UK development NGOs, like other NNGOs, are currently caught in a turbulent development policy environment in which their roles are increasingly being redefined at national and global levels. At the same time, NGOs are themselves helping to shape the changing development policy agenda. The issues discussed here have important implications for the future of international development NGOs; they also raise issues central to the study of social policy. For example, the relationship between organisations such as NGOs and the wider framework of institutions through which policy is produced might be conceptualised within a model that is analogous to Giddens's (1979) theory of structuration. NGOs are constrained in important ways by the institutional policy environment in which they operate, yet at the same time they help create that framework through the actions they undertake, such as contracting, lobbying and negotiation. Far from being stable or static, there is a dynamic and changing relationship between organisations and policy.

In many ways NGOs themselves are in a precarious position, as Edwards (1996) has argued. NNGOs – and for that matter many SNGOs – may have to choose between selling their development services (such as training, information, expertise) in the market-place and becoming contractors for government – increasingly to 'mop up' during or after conflicts and emergencies. If they move towards the former they may reach a position where they can reduce their dependence on foreign aid or public giving and improve their organisational sustainability, but in doing so they will move much closer to the private sector and may lose some of their distinctiveness as value-driven organisations. They are likely to achieve only a low level of development impact in terms of poverty reduction because only better-off sections of the community will be able to pay for such services. If they opt for the latter route, they may move closer to government and lose their ability to act as independent pressure groups, to generate alternative development ideas and to pursue longer-term poverty reduction agendas. While it has probably never been appropriate to see any NGOs as truly 'autonomous' organisations, the future may hold a significant reduction in 'room for manoeuvre'. The possibility of a 'third way' as NGOs move closer to, and perhaps become part of, wider 'social movements' (Korten, 1990; Sennilosa, 1998) remains a possibility for some organisations in the future, although evidence for such a transition remains rather limited.

There are also implications for wider social policy research in the North. A recent overview of global social policy issues undertaken by Deacon *et al.* (1997) points to the need for the study of social policy in the North to take a more international perspective. As national governments have undergone relative decline in relation to private capital flows, the traditional frameworks for social policy analysis in the North are in need of rethinking. In particular they point to the need to acknowledge and examine the growing role of global policy actors – such as intergovernmental organisations, NGOs, transnational companies – beyond rich country welfare states, in attempts to understand changing social policy at a global level. It is sobering to note that this has long been acknowledged as a central social policy concern among many Southern social policy researchers (Onimode, 1989; Kanji *et al.*, 1991).

Supranational 'public' institutions such as the International Monetary Fund (IMF), the World Bank and NNGOs all have key roles in policy formation and implementation particularly in areas of the world with high concentrations of poverty and conflict. The concept of a 'globalising civil society' outlined by Macdonald (1994) may become more relevant as new types of NGOs from both North and South work locally and internationally to safeguard human rights and democratic processes. Deacon *et al.* (1997) suggest that social policy as a discipline needs to draw far more upon work in development studies than it has done to date in order to make sense of these global issues. This chapter has argued that the analysis of the changing roles of NNGOs in international development could provide a useful starting point.

Note

1. In order to adjust to the new challenge of globalisation, there are some NNGOs such as Oxfam which have begun to work with excluded or marginalised communities 'at home' rather than working to an agenda which implies that poverty is only found in the 'third world' (Lewis, 1999).

References

Bebbington, A. and R. Riddell (1995) 'The direct funding of Southern NGOs by donors: new agendas and old problems', *Journal of International Development*, 7(6): 879–94.

Billis, D. and J. Mackeith (1992) 'Growth and change in NGOs: concepts and comparative experience', in M. Edwards and D. Hulme (eds) *Making A Difference: NGOs in a Changing World*, Earthscan, London.

Blakeway, S. (1998) 'A brand new resource for community animal health'. *Appropriate Technology*, 25(1): 6–8.

Brown, L. and R. Tandon (1994) 'Institutional development for strengthening civil society', *Institutional Development*, 1(1): 3–17.

Burbidge, J. (1997) *Beyond Prince and Merchant: Citizen Participation and the Rise of Civil Society*, Institute of Cultural Affairs International, Brussels.

Burnell, P. (1997) *Foreign Aid in a Changing World*, Open University Press, Buckingham.

Chambre, S. (1997) 'Civil society, differential resources, and organizational development: HIV/AIDS organizations in New York City', *Nonprofit and Voluntary Sector Quarterly*, 26(4): 466–88.

Cushing, C. (1995) 'Humanitarian assistance and the role of NGOs', *Institutional Development*, 2(2): 3–18.

Curtis, M. (1997) 'OECD country profile: the United Kingdom', in *The Reality of Aid: An Independent Review of Development Cooperation*, Earthscan, London.

Deacon, B. with M. Hulse and P. Stubbs (1997) *Global Social Policy: International Organizations and the Future of Welfare*, Sage, London.

DFID (1997) *Eliminating World Poverty: A Challenge for the 21st Century*, CM 3789, The Stationery Office, London.

Duffield, M. (1993) 'NGOs, disaster relief and asset transfer in the Horn: political survival in a permanent emergency', *Development and Change*, 24(1): 31–57.

Edwards, M. (1996) 'International development NGOs: legitimacy, accountability, regulation and roles', discussion paper for the Commission on the Future of the Voluntary Sector and the British Overseas Aid Group (BOAG), London.

Fowler, A. (1995) 'Capacity building and NGOs: a case of strengthening ladles for the global soup kitchen?', *Institutional Development*, 1(1): 18–24.

Fowler, A. (1997) *Striking A Balance: A Guide to Enhancing the Effectiveness of Non-Governmental Organizations in International Development*, Earthscan, London.

German, T. and J. Randel (1999) 'Country Study 23: United Kingdom', in I. Smillie and H. Helmich (eds) *Stakeholders: Government–NGO Partnership for International Development*, Earthscan, London.

Giddens, A. (1979) *Central Problems in Social Theory: Action, Structure and Contradiction in Social Analysis*, Macmillan, London.

Hoffman, M. (1997) 'Doing no harm? Rethinking the role of aid agencies', *LSE Magazine*, 9(1): 4–7.

Hulme, D. and M. Edwards (eds) (1997) *Too Close for Comfort: NGOs, States and Donors*, Macmillan, London.

Kanji, N., N. Kanji and F. Manji (1991) 'From development to sustained crisis: structural adjustment, equity and health', *Social Science and Medicine*, 33(9): 985–93.

Korten, D. (1990) *Getting to the 21st Century: Voluntary Action and the Global Agenda*, Kumarian, Hartford.

Kramer, R., H. Lorentzen, W. Melief and S. Pasquinelli (1993) *Privatisation in Four European Countries: Comparative Studies in Government–Third Sector Relationships*, M.E.Sharpe, New York.

Lewis, D. (1998) 'Development NGOs and the challenge of partnership: changing relations between North and South', *Social Policy and Administration*, 32(5): 501–12.

Lewis, D. (ed.) (1999) 'Introduction' to *International Perspectives on Voluntary Action: Reshaping the Third Sector*, Earthscan, London.

Lewis, D. and B. Sobhan (1999) 'Routes of funding, roots of trust? NNGOs, SNGOs, donors and the rise of direct funding', *Development In Practice*, 9(1–2): 117–29.

Macdonald, L. (1994) 'Globalising civil society: interpreting international NGOs in Central America', *Millennium*, 23(2): 267–85.

ODI (1996) 'NGOs and official donors',Briefing Paper No. 4, August, Overseas Development Institute, London.

ODI (1998) 'The state of the international humanitarian system', Briefing Paper No. 1, March, Overseas Development Institute, London.

Onimode, B. (ed.) (1989) *The IMF, the World Bank and the African Debt: The Social and Political Impact*, Zed Books, London.

Randel, J. and T. German (1997) *The Reality of Aid: An Independent Review of Development Cooperation*, Earthscan, London.

Robinson, M. (1993) 'Governance, democracy and conditionality: NGOs and the new policy agenda', in A. Clayton (ed.) *Governance, Democracy and Conditionality: What Role for NGOs?*, INTRAC, Oxford.

Senillosa, I. (1998) 'A new age of social movements: a fifth generation of non-governmental organisation in the making?', *Development in Practice*, 8(1) (February): 40–53.

Smith, S. and M. Lipsky (1993) *Non-Profits for Hire: The Welfare State in the Age of Contracting*, Harvard University Press, Cambridge, Mass.

Smillie, I. (1994a) 'Changing partners: Northern NGOs, Northern governments', *Voluntas*, 5(2): 155–92.

Smillie, I. (1994b) *The Alms Bazaar: Altruism under Fire–Nonprofit Organisations and International Development*, Intermediate Technology Publications, London.

Whaites, A. (1998) 'The new UK White Paper on International Development: an NGO erspective', *Journal of International Development*, 10(2): 203–13.

11

Non-profit Housing Agencies: 'Reading' and Shaping the Policy Agenda

David Mullins and Moyra Riseborough

Introduction

This chapter reviews the way in which changing social policies in the UK, particularly those developed by a 'modernising' Labour government elected in 1997, have impacted on the role of non-profit housing organisations. It challenges the view that housing associations are merely the agents of government and discusses the ways in which they have also helped to shape the policy agenda for social housing.

The chapter begins with an account of the changing role played by non-profit housing organisations since 1978. It then introduces the more recent social policy agenda through an analysis of the 'policy signals' read by key actors involved in research undertaken at the University of Birmingham between 1997 and 1999.[1] Finally it uses this research to indicate the ways in which non-profit housing organisations are shaping policy today.

The changing role of non-profit housing organisations

We use the term 'non-profit housing organisations' to describe a group of about 2,000 organisations registered with the Housing Corporation, the government agency responsible for funding and regulating social housing outside of the local government sector. These organisations are non-profit in that 'surpluses' cannot be distributed to shareholders. They are also voluntary bodies, in the sense that they are governed by boards of volunteers although, as we discuss, the term 'voluntary housing movement' is now rarely used. Finally, we adopt the more widely used collective term of 'housing associations' throughout, preferring this to their 1996 Housing Act designation – 'registered social landlords'.

The English non-profit housing sector today is almost unrecognisable from that of 1978. Then there were fewer than 400,000 homes in the sector which accounted for just 7 per cent of all social rented homes. Today, there are well over a million homes, which account for nearly one in four social rented homes in England. The largest organisation now has over 40,000 homes, more than most local authorities, and there are 15 associations with more than 10,000 homes, together accounting for a quarter of the sector. Increasingly, non-profit housing is dominated by a small number of national or regionally based associations and by a growing number of new non-profit landlords set up to receive housing stock from local authorities. Indeed in the 1990s the sector grew more through stock transfers from local authorities than from new development by existing associations (Spencer *et al.*, 1995; Mullins, 1998).

There are also some important continuities, particularly the large number of small local organisations (the majority own fewer than 250 homes). Also constitutional forms remain the same: associations are either industrial and provident societies, registered charities or companies limited by guarantee. They continue to be regulated by a single industry-based body, the Housing Corporation, and represented by a trade body, the National Housing Federation (NHF). Despite the role of the NHF in forging a common identity as a 'movement', the diversity of these organisations remains a distinguishing feature.

The history of housing associations helps to explain this diversity. Malpass (1997) refers to their 'discontinuous history', with new organisations established to meet the new policy objectives of each epoch. Social origins of associations may be linked to changing 'welfare regimes' (Esping-Anderson, 1990; Salamon and Anheier, 1998). Thus we may associate medieval almshouses and nineteenth-century philanthropic trusts with distinct social and political circumstances of 'liberal' pre-industrial and urbanisation periods. Similarly, the majority of recent stock transfers by local authorities to newly established organisations may be linked to a move away from the 'social democracy' of the post-war period in which state investment had 'crowded out' the voluntary sector. Nevertheless, it is interesting to observe the ability of some organisations to adapt and transform to meet requirements of new epochs (Mullins, 1998).

Incorporation by the state

The process of 'incorporation' of associations by the state through public subsidy of new development has been occurring since 1974. The 1970s saw considerable expansion in the work of housing associations supported by funding from the Housing Corporation and local authorities. During this period public funding was generous, covering virtually 100 per cent of costs and cushioning associations from risk. It was available only to organisations regulated by the Housing Corporation.

It can be argued that in this period of incorporation, resource dependency (Aldrich, 1976) on public funding had the effect of increasing the isomorphism (DiMaggio and Powell, 1983) of non-profit housing organisations through regulatory mechanisms and through the strengthening of sectoral identity and networks. Regulation played an important part in promoting 'coercive iso-morphism' since in order to secure public subsidy, housing associations were required to conform with what some saw as a prescriptive regulatory regime operated by the Housing Corporation. However, this view may underplay the extent to which housing associations themselves influenced and benefited from this regime, for example, through the reenforcement of sectoral norms relating to meeting housing needs and equal opportunities, and by involving users and excluding potential profit-distributing competitors. The term 'regulatory capture' provides a good description of the ways in which housing associations actively used policy networks such as trade associations to shape this regulatory regime (Mullins, 1997).

Re-privatisation and displacement of state housing provision

The sector's continued expansion in the 1980s was increasingly at the expense of, rather than complementary to, the state housing sector. However, it was not until 1988 that a mainstream role for housing associations was embraced by the radical right through the introduction of private finance to complement public subsidy in what has been described as the 're-privatisation' of housing associations (Randolph, 1993). In this period the boundaries between the public and other sectors were redrawn as housing associations became the chosen vehicle for decentralisation of state housing through transfer of development activity and assets from local government.

Growth in the late 1980s and early 1990s was again very rapid. However, the terms on which housing associations expanded were very different. Private finance introduced powerful new stake-holders (banks and building societies), increased risk, and involved the adoption of business techniques. Those involved got used to growth, and growth itself became a major rationale for some organisations. This attitude was captured by the early 1990s industry expression 'develop or die' when associations competed on price to attract public subsidy, even if this meant charging higher rents or dipping into reserves.

Walker (1998) has described this period of transformation of non-profit housing as a move from 'comfort to competition', detecting conflicting objectives for voluntary organisations arising from this increased emphasis on competitiveness. One indicator of change was the decreasing importance placed on the 'voluntary' label, with many associations preferring to be seen as social entrepreneurial bodies, approaching social purposes in a business-like way.

Ten years after their move to the mainstream of new social housing provision heralded by the 1988 Housing Act, housing associations faced a much reduced supply of public funding (between 1993 and 1998 subsidy available from the Housing Corporation fell by 60 per cent (Wilcox, 1997)). They also faced challenges to their legitimacy as 'local public spending bodies' (Committee on Standards in Public Life, 1996) and an uncertain political agenda. Most were busily repositioning themselves in relation to central government and local authorities, many were involved in possible mergers (Mullins 1999a) and some were diversifying into other activities – particularly regeneration and care (Riseborough, 1998). Market segmentation was the order of the day and a few were planning to drop the housing association

label altogether in search of new roles and resources. Figure
11.1 synthesises the literature to highlight the main changes in
the role and purpose of housing associations in the 1990s and
their possible future directions (Cope, 1990; Housing Corporation, 1990; National Federation of Housing Associations, 1990;
Langstaff, 1992; Spencer *et al.*, 1995; Davis and Bacon, 1996;
Best, 1997).

Since 1978 the housing sector has exemplified the ability of
non-profit organisations to respond flexibly to a rapidly changing
policy context. Best (1997, p. 119) highlights the chameleon nature
of the sector:

> without housing associations politicians of the right would be
> dependent on an owner occupied sector which may have passed
> the limits of its sustainability, and a private rented sector re-
> luctant or unsuited to take responsibility ... without housing
> associations politicians of the left would be stuck with the model
> of council housing.

Such flexibility can also be a liability, particularly when there
is a lack of trust in non-profit organisations (National Council
for Voluntary Organisations, 1998) and when questions of
underlying values are raised (Spencer and Davis, 1995). It also
carries a political risk, as the next section indicates.

The policy context for nonprofit housing in the 1990s

In this section of the chapter we are particularly concerned with
the emergent policy agenda of the New Labour government. This
may be summarised by the well-used straplines 'the Third Way'
and 'modernisation'.

The 'Third Way' concept has been fleshed out by Giddens
(1998) as characterising the space occupied by New Labour thinking at the 'radical centre', as distinct from either old left social
democracy or new right neo-liberalism. The 'Third Way' appears
to stand for a new version of the mixed economy, an increased
role for social enterprises, better regulation, new forms of democracy with a greater role for localities and for the 'cosmopolitan
nation', and a new ethic of 'no rights without responsibilities'.

Figure 11.1 *Changing directions for housing associations in the 1990s*

- Competition increasing, public funding declining
- Increasing divide between large developers and the rest
- Medium and small associations seeking new roles through diversification and consolidating community bases
- Diversification occurring into regeneration, care and special needs activities, and management of housing for other landlords
- Partnerships with new stock transfer landlords expected to be important
- Mergers and group structures of increasing importance
- Increasing emphasis on strategic planning and long-term business planning
- Increasing concerns about accountability
- Possibility that larger associations will become more like private companies (full re-privatisation a possible political agenda in early 1990s)
- Stock reinvestment increasing in priority
- Emphasis on independence and autonomy of sector by both NHF and Housing Corporation
- Move from voluntary sector to non-profit sector; some associations expected to give up charitable status to become more commercially orientated
- Relationship with local authorities changing
- Involvement in market renting a possibility

Sources: Housing Corporation, 1990; NFHA, 1990; Spencer *et al.*, 1995; Davis and Bacon, 1996.

In social policy terms this may represent a move from the welfare state to the 'social investment state' with the emphasis on risk management.

The concept of 'modernisation' presents structural adaptation to global economic change as an imperative for both the private and the public spheres, including local government and the voluntary sector (Mullins, Reid and Walker, 1998). 'Modernisation' of local government is presented as involving new forms of democracy (such as elected mayors and citizens' juries), and the introduction of a 'Best Value' regime for service provision. This seems likely to reinforce the regulatory and enabling role of the local state and create new opportunities for social entrepreneurship.

Another feature of the emerging policy context for non-profit housing has been the blurring of the concept of housing policy. Aside from the largely symbolic policy of releasing capital receipts from council housing sales (while reducing overall housing expenditure), there has been very little attention to address housing *per se*. Instead, housing organisations have been looking to wider emerging agendas around regeneration, social exclusion and social care. While housing has always been 'the wobbly pillar under the welfare state', to quote Torgerson's (1987) evocation of Beveridge's pillars of welfare, it has never been more so in Britain than in the late 1990s (Mullins and Niner, 1998).

So which are the main policy agendas of relevance to non-profit housing providers? The most obvious is the New Deal for Communities which promotes action on the 'worst estates' through continuation of stock transfers, which had been encouraged by the previous Conservative government. Others include community regeneration, social investment, tackling social exclusion, health action zones and 'welfare to work'. Moreover, since housing associations had already diversified into activities such as the provision of residential and day care, employment and training initiatives, a wide range of policy streams affect their non-housing activities. The ways in which non-profit housing organisations have sought to engage with this new policy context are discussed next.

How non-profit housing organisations are reading policy signals

Our recent research sought to identify how decision-makers in non-profit housing organisations were interpreting this emerging policy agenda. The studies spanned the change of government, but focused particularly on the period between July 1997 and January 1999 during which the incoming government reviewed almost every aspect of public policy and spending. We use the notion of 'policy signals' to indicate the ways in which decision-makers scanned the policy environment to detect changes in emphasis rather than waiting for policies to be dried and dusted before responding to them. Figure 11.2 summarises the main

Figure 11.2 *Policy signals and housing association responses*

Period 1 **1995–1996**	• Uncertain pre-election period – some HAs are busy producing adaptable 'election-proof' corporate plans • Critical discussion on quangos including housing associations is influenced by the Labour Opposition • HAs respond by defending their accountability and governance arrangements, by making improvements and by beginning to embrace 'stakeholding' • Some HAs attempt to distance themselves from the previous government's anti-local government agendas
Period 2 **January–May 1997**	• Pollsters predict Labour landslide – HAs become more committed to responding to themes which will appear in Labour manifesto • HAs 'broadcast the good news' about their works • HAs emphasise partnership with local government, and the need to build sustainable communities and to combat social exclusion. • More overt messages about need for investment in social housing, retention of housing benefit, and measures to address 'affordability problem'
Period 3 **May 1997–May 1998**	• Labour government returned – a window for potential influence opens – HA Chief Exec's join the queue to meet the minister • Slogan 'what matters is what works' seen to provide opportunities for HAs to present the minister with 'solutions' and thereby shape the agenda • Government announces Comprehensive Spending Review • Message-making and networking activity intensifies – 'the window doesn't close'
Period 4 **Summer 1998–** **spring 1999**	• Comprehensive spending Review results are partial • Correctness of HA strategy of courting local authorities is confirmed, but welfare reform, social care and housing benefit issues are still unclear • The 'Third Way' begins to be interpreted. Particular policy themes confirmed as important: community and accountability (localism); opportunity and citizenship (tackling social exclusion); renewing social responsibility and democracy and welfare reform (no rights without responsibilities), and efficiency and user involvement (Best Value) • Best Value illustrates the continued 'open window' – broad principles are established by government and Housing Corporation, associations are encouraged to make policy through pilots

policy signals that our 'Delphi panel'[2] attached greatest importance to and how they were planning to respond to these signals.
This summary indicates the relatively high levels of uncertainty
and instability which characterised the period of study. Decision-
makers were initially wary of being seen as 'contaminated' by a
close association with the outgoing Conservative government. This
was perceived as the main danger arising from the historical
flexibility noted in the first part of this chapter. Later, instability
was associated with an unexpectedly long period in which they
perceived an opportunity to shape policy rather than simply
respond to new government directives. The ways in which new
policy agendas such as 'Best Value' have rolled out exemplify
an approach in which the 'policy signals' metaphor appears particularly apposite.

Decontamination – presenting a more accountable image

At the start of our research the image of housing associations
was tarnished because they had been favoured by the former
government and criticised by the Nolan Committee for their lack
of transparency and oligarchic tendencies (Committee on Standards
in Public Life, 1996). Therefore in the period before the election
some housing associations began to reposition themselves as
organisations prepared to change and become more accountable.

As clearer policy signals began to appear (for example, in the
Labour Party's manifesto), key phrases were replicated in the
messages that housing associations broadcast about themselves.
Small and medium-sized associations repositioned themselves as
local or regional agencies where this was possible. Meanwhile
some national associations re-presented themselves as organisations with local links and local responsibilities, for example, by
adopting regional structures or cultivating relationships with
specific local authorities.

One example of this type of activity was a study undertaken
in a black and minority ethnic (BME) housing association in
London to identify strengths and weaknesses in its relationships
with local authorities. The survey was used by the association to
improve its image and to consolidate its relationships with certain authorities. The association had successfully interpreted the
importance of local authority relationships ahead of the new

government being returned to office. It has subsequently built on this to ensure that its position as a leading BME organisation is recognised, and it has thereby shaped partnerships between local authorities and BME associations in London more generally. The second example concerns an association established in the early 1990s in a predominantly rural area, which later had transferred to it all of the District Council's housing. This association sought to respond to criticisms of stock transfers as exemplifying an 'accountability deficit'. In this case repositioning involved emphasising the association's strengths in terms of local community ties and an understanding of the needs of rural areas (for example, by publicising new activities on tenant participation and meeting housing and training needs of young people tailored to a rural context).

One may question the extent to which these responses to policy signals constitute 'window dressing' or more profound changes in values and practices. We would argue that such a distinction is difficult to maintain, since non-profit organisations like housing associations are constantly engaged in strategic positioning activities such as those described above.

The open window – a new policy environment?

The second feature of uncertainty was observed in the last two phases shown in Figure 11.2. Delphi panel members had initially assumed that the election of the new government presented a 'window of opportunity' to convince ministers and senior civil servants that they had a useful role to play in the new policy agenda. In this period they not only counteracted negative images associated with the 'quango' debate, but also successfully resurrected policy themes out of favour in the later days of the outgoing government such as the BME housing policy (Housing Corporation, 1998a). They also began to demonstrate their role by engagement in the pilot stages of emerging programmes such as Welfare to Work – demonstrating that 'what mattered was what worked'.

By the summer of 1998 it was becoming apparent that this window was going to remain open longer than had been anticipated. While some broad themes such as continued government support for stock transfers and increased support for resident involvement had been clarified, there were still many issues on which the new government appeared to have an open mind. Moreover, the style of policy-making seemed to some panel members to have changed subtly to involve a greater element of networking. Some concluded that they could play a part in shaping policy options through their own networks. This can be illustrated by the example of Best Value.

While the Best Value regime was initially developed as a replacement for compulsory competitive tendering in local government, its principles of challenging services, consulting users, comparing performance and considering the use of competition were regarded as having a wider applicability across public services (Blair, 1997). In the housing sector, the Housing Corporation announced that it did not intend to regulate to require housing associations to deliver Best Value. Instead it sought to encourage them to identify effective practices by piloting and by exchange of good practice through survey and review (Housing Corporation, 1998b). Some associations saw this as a real opportunity to make policy, and there was no shortage of applications for the pilot programme, which consisted of 46 housing associations working either individually or in partnership on 23 pilots. However, there were lingering suspicions that sooner or later the window would close and thus it would be unwise to go too far out on a limb before the government clarified 'the new rules' – perhaps through regulation. Thus one respondent to a survey on associations' Best Value plans commented that: 'we don't want to fall into the trap of rushing documents out which will need to be dumped when the next stage arrives' (Mullins, 1999b).

Shaping policy themes

So far we have explored the ways in which housing associations sought to reposition themselves after the 1997 election as a response to their reading of the policy signals. However, the Best Value example indicates the possibility that non-profit organisations have a more active role to play than this. Rather than being passive agents as theorised in principal/agent economics (Hughes, 1994), we saw many of these organisations as active agencies in their own right, selecting themes from their scanning of the policy environment but also seeking to influence and shape that environment through individual and collective action (Clegg, 1990).

The most striking example of policy-shaping involved a large generalist association in the Midlands. It took a decision to predict the evolution of policy on housing and regeneration and transformed its structure to become a 'social investment agency' with housing as only one of its 'social businesses'. This was a high-risk strategy, launched a few weeks after the General Election when it was still unclear what response housing associations would receive from the new government. However, the notion of 'social investment' has since been elaborated as a key policy theme in the 'Third Way' agenda (Giddens, 1998). There is little doubt that this organisation has influenced the way that 'social investment' is being interpreted.

Another example concerns a national housing association that provides housing and care services for older people. The association, like many others with sheltered housing stock, was finding that this form of provision was becoming less popular with older people. Standards and facilities were falling below people's expectations (Riseborough and Murphy, 1998). In 1996 the association decided to review the purpose of sheltered housing and the role of scheme managers and to adopt a high profile on this. It also embarked on an expensive programme to demolish or remodel housing stock to modern standards. This was a bold step, since future revenue and capital arrangements for housing and care were by no means certain and were the subject of a number of policy reviews, including a Royal Commission. This association was seeking to shape future policy through publicising its own activity. The chief executive took the view that 'It's no use waiting – you have to force the pace'.

Another association involved in the same subsector, housing and care for older people, took a slightly different tack to the first by correctly predicting that Health Authority and Trust funding would be devolved in such a way that housing associations could access it. The association positioned itself in think-tanks and advisory bodies at the highest levels and set up secondment exchanges of senior personnel between the association and the Department of Health. It thereby learned about an unfamiliar institution and its operations and gained access to insider information. In contrast to others, this association is not publicising this strategy despite its significance to the association and its potential impact on the wider policy context.

A final example of policy-shaping activity involves a long-established philanthropic trust which had decided it was 'making the move towards being even less reactive to what the Housing Corporation or Government says – we are determined to develop as a charitable body' (first interview before 1997 election). However, this association is a large landlord and is involved in local authority regeneration partnerships. It took a strategic decision to engage with government agendas to deal with run-down housing estates. As noted earlier, this is probably the only new government policy theme that has a clear housing focus: attending to 'worst estates' was one of the first three areas identified by the newly established Social Exclusion Unit. During 1996 the association successfully obtained European and Lottery funds to provide community development services and training opportunities for its residents as part of its intention to create sustainable communities. During 1997 the association indicated that it was willing to respond to some elements of the New Deal but also set out its stall on how it thought that community development and training schemes should be done. This association, therefore, sought to influence and shape policy being developed by the new government, while retaining its cherished independence.

Conclusion

This chapter has outlined the development of the non-profit housing sector and some of the ways in which it has interacted with social policy. Historically, the sector has displayed many of the flexible characteristics which, advocates argue, make the voluntary sector an attractive vehicle for governments of whatever persuasion to deliver social policy objectives. It has grown through significant engagement with the state in a number of policy eras. In particular it prospered in a period of full public sector subsidy between 1974 and 1988 and then again in the early 1990s as a prime example of the mixed economy of welfare approach favoured by the then Conservative government. However, critics argue that this engagement and growth have caused it to lose other special characteristics, particularly those associated with its links with voluntarism and civil society.

By considering in some detail the terms of engagement between the sector and the incoming Labour government during a relatively short and unstable period of policy we have gained a more complete understanding of the role of non-profit agencies in social policy. This has led us to reformulate our ideas in relation to policy, to the role of agency and to social theory.

In relation to policy processes, the research supports post-structuralist critiques which contest the notion of the state as a unified, albeit contradictory and complex entity. Instead we interpret the state as disconnected and erratic and politics as a set of contests over meaning (Hillyard and Watson, 1996). In this context, positioning and broadcasting activity by housing associations, which might easily be written off as rhetoric and window dressing, are interpreted as strategic contests over meaning.

Hierarchical modes of regulation assumed in principal/agent models of policy implementation (Hughes, 1994) have been increasingly displaced by markets and networks, often coexisting in complex delivery systems in the new fragmented state (Levacic, 1993). Policy can no longer be seen as a top-down process, and analysis of decision-making must encompass a series of levels or sites of influence, including organisations themselves. This is particularly apparent in some of the new elements of the policy agenda such as 'Best Value' and tackling social exclusion.

Our research also identified the role of agency, by exploring the ways in which key actors in housing associations have been 'reading' the policy environment and by observing the strategies they are adopting to shape it. These organisational agents can be seen as 'practical experimentalists 'confronted by uncertainty, ambivalence, contradiction and ambiguity, seeking to impose their own 'circuits of power' on a chaotic canvas (Clegg, 1990).

We conclude that policy is being made in the social housing sector by a complex interplay between organisations and actors at many different levels. We have been able to observe quite closely the mode of operation of one group of actors: decision-makers in housing associations. It is clear from this study that while these decision-makers take a very close interest in government policy formation this is not simply so that they can better implement policies handed down to them. Instead, by reading policy signals from the earliest stage these actors feel able to shape the policy process using both the resources of their organisations to demonstrate capacity to deliver and their external network resources to lobby and influence. Moreover, there are signs that the policy processes which they seek to influence have been open to such piloting and influencing activities.

Some would argue that this is a temporary phase associated with the first change in political control at national government level for eighteen years. However, a similarly close study of interaction between the non-profit housing sector and the state in the glory days before the 1988 Housing Act might have led to a similar conclusion about a regime which brought housing associations maximum subsidy and minimal risk.

Notes

1. This research project 'Changing with the Times' has benefited from grant funding from the Housing Corporation. It has involved the use of innovative research methods, particularly a longitudinal 'Delphi panel' of decision-makers from 15 housing associations. We are grateful for this funding and for the active participation of senior actors in the non-profit housing sector which this facilitated. However, we accept full responsibility for errors, omissions and differences of interpretation.

2. A Delphi panel is a research method used in futures research to refine concepts, make realistic predictions about future change and to test the impact of external change on participants' views. Panels are usually recruited from experts or leading actors whose confidentiality is preserved, while allowing close interaction and dialogue through playing back and refining ideas on an anonymous basis.

References

Aldrich, H. (1976) 'Resource dependence and interorganizational relations', *Administration and Society*, 7(4): 419–54.

Best, R. (1997) 'Housing associations: the sustainable solution?', in P. Williams (ed.) *Directions in Housing Policy. Towards Sustainable Housing Policies for the UK*, Paul Chapman, London.

Blair, T. (1997) *'Leading the Way. A New Vision for Local Government*, Institute for Public Policy Research, London.

Clegg, S. (1990) *Modern Organizations. Organization Studies in a Post-Modern World*, Sage Publications, London.

Committee on Standards in Public Life (1996) *Second Report. Local Public Spending Bodies*, HMSO, London.

Cope, H. (1990) *Housing Associations: Policy and Practice*, Macmillan, Basingstoke.

Davis, R. and A. Bacon (1996) *Future Directions for Housing Associations*, Housing Corporation, London.

DiMaggio, P. and W. Powell (1983) 'The iron cage revisited: institutional isomorphism and collective rationality in organizational fields', *American Sociological Review*, 48: 147–60.

Esping-Andersen, G. (1990) *The Three Worlds of Welfare Capitalism*, Princeton University Press, Princeton, NJ.

Giddens, A. (1998) *The Third Way. The Renewal of Social Democracy*, Polity Press, Cambridge.

Hillyard, P. and S. Watson (1996) 'Postmodern social policy: a contradiction in terms', *Journal of Social Policy*, 25(3) (July): 321–44.

Housing Corporation (1990) *Into the Nineties. Opportunities and Challenges for the Housing Association Movement*, Housing Corporation, London.

Housing Corporation (1998a) *Black and Minority Ethnic Housing Policy*, Housing Corporation, London.

Housing Corporation (1998b) *Draft Guidance on Best Value*, Housing Corporation, London.

Hughes, O. (1994) *Public Management and Administration*, Macmillan, Basingstoke.

Langstaff, M. (1992) 'Housing associations: a move to centre stage', in J. Birchall (ed.) *Housing Policy in the 1990s*, Routledge, London.

Levacic, R. (1993) 'Markets as coordinative devices', in R. Maidment and G. Thompson (eds), *Managing the United Kingdom*, Sage, London, pp. 30–50.

Malpass, P. (1997) 'The discontinuous history of housing associations in England', Housing Studies Association Conference, Cardiff, September 1997.

Mullins, D. (1997) 'From regulatory capture to regulated competition', *Housing Studies*, 12: 301–19.

Mullins, D. (1998) 'Interpreting the changing role of English housing associations social origins and transformations', Third International Conference of the International Society for Third Sector Research, Geneva, July 1998.

Mullins, D. (1999a) 'Managing ambiguity: merger activity in the nonprofit housing sector', *Journal of Nonprofit and Voluntary Sector Marketing*, 4(4): 349–64.

Mullins, D. (1999b) *Survey of Best Value Activity*, National Housing Federation, London.

Mullins, D. and P. Niner (1998) 'A prize of citizenship? Changing access to social housing', in A. Marsh and D. Mullins (eds) *Housing and Public Policy. Citizenship, Choice and Control*, Open University Press, Buckingham.

Mullins, D., B. Reid and R. Walker (1998). 'Modernising housing. Organisational change in social housing in England and Wales. Towards an agency/structure approach', European Network for Housing Research Conference, Cardiff, September 1998.

National Council for Voluntary Organisations (1998) 'Theorising trust and confidence in the voluntary sector', Plenary Session, NCVO Research Conference, London.

National Federation of Housing Associations (1990) *Towards 2000. The Housing Association Agenda*, NHFA, London.

Randolph, B. (1993) 'The re-privatisation of housing associations', in P. Malpass and R. Means (eds) *Implementing Housing Policy*, OUP, Buckingham.

Riseborough, M. (1998) 'Social housing landlords and housing plus', discussion paper for Joseph Rowntree Housing Trust, School of Public Policy, University of Birmingham, Birmingham.

Riseborough, M. and F. Murphy (1998) *Integrating Care Housing and Community. A Fresh Approach for Older People*, Abbeyfield Society, St Albans.

Salamon, L. and H. Anheier (1998) 'Social origins of civil society: explaining the nonprofit sector cross-nationally', *Voluntas*, 9(3): 213–48.

Spencer, K. and R. Davis (1995) *Housing Associations and the Governance Debate*, School of Public Policy, University of Birmingham, Birmingham.

Spencer, K., D. Mullins and B. Walker (1995) *Voluntary Housing Today and Tomorrow*, Occasional Paper 1, School of Public Policy, University of Birmingham, Birmingham.

Torgerson, U. (1987) 'Housing: the wobbly pillar under the welfare state', in B. Turner, J. Kemeny and L. Lundquist (eds) *Between State and Market. Housing in the Post-Industrial Era*, Almquist & Wiksell, Stockholm.

Walker, R. (1998) 'New public management and housing associations: from comfort to competition', *Policy and Politics*, 26(1): 71–87.

Wilcox, S. (1997) *Housing Review 1996/97*, Joseph Rowntree Foundation, York.

12

Boards: Just Subsidiaries of the State?

Margaret Harris

This chapter focuses on the governing bodies of voluntary organisations – their 'boards', 'councils', 'trustees' and 'management
committees'. These bodies are a key organisational and legal component of voluntary agencies (Harris, 1996) and experience in
the USA suggests that successful implementation of social policy
is often dependent on their capacity and cooperation (Saidel and
Harlan, 1998). How, then, have UK voluntary boards experienced
recent changes in social policy? This chapter seeks to answer
this question.

Voluntary governing bodies

A 'voluntary governing body' or 'board' is the group within a
voluntary agency which carries 'ultimate responsibility for what
the organization does' (Dartington, 1995, p. 208). In addition to
being a point of legal accountability, a board is charged with
establishing and maintaining a voluntary agency's mission and
with achieving legitimacy amongst its internal and external 'constituencies' or 'stakeholders' (Stone and Wood, 1997).

In fact, from an organisational point of view, boards constitute the very heart of voluntary agencies.[1] Voluntary agencies
may, or may not, involve volunteers in their operational work;
they may, or may not, have voluntary members; and they may,
or may not, benefit from voluntary donations of money. But if
they do not have a (largely) volunteer governing body they are

missing a key qualification for being included in the voluntary sector. Similarly, if an agency has a board whose independence is in doubt – say because members can be appointed or removed at the will of a powerful governmental or commercial stakeholder – then its claim to be part of the voluntary sector must also be in doubt (Billis, 1993; Salamon and Anheier, 1992).

The functions performed by the boards of charities and other voluntary agencies can be broadly classified under five headings: being the employer; formulating and monitoring adherence to agency goals; securing and safeguarding resources; being the point of final accountability; and providing a link or buffer between the agency on the one hand and its external stakeholders and environment on the other hand (Harris, 1996). Changing social policies have affected the performance of all these, but the extent of impact has varied between functions and the experiences of national and local boards have generally been rather different.

Social policy and voluntary boards

Unlike volunteers and users (the subjects of Chapters 13 and 14), voluntary boards have not received much direct attention from politicians and policy-makers. Recent changes in social policy *have* impacted on them in numerous ways but the impacts have reached them indirectly rather than directly through initiatives, projects, legislation or regulations specifically addressed to them.

Social policy trends such as welfare pluralism, care in the community and 'marketisation' have led to an expansion of the welfare service-providing role of the voluntary sector, an expansion which began in the mid-1980s and accelerated during the 1990s. A corollary of this expanding role of the voluntary sector in welfare provision has been new challenges for voluntary agencies themselves; coping with organisational growth and change has become a major preoccupation (Billis and Harris, 1992; Lewis, 1993). The consequences of growth have had to be faced by paid staff and service volunteers as well as board members but, as this chapter will show, there are indications that it is boards who have struggled most with the challenge of change, especially in smaller, local voluntary agencies. Often adaptation to the new era of welfare pluralism has been led by paid staff keen to respond to the wishes of powerful governmental funders and to put their agencies in the forefront of social policy implementation. Board members, on the other hand, have often 'found themselves' managing large-scale service provision for vulnerable people and carrying accountability for complex budgets and major fund-raising. As signatories to contracts and 'service-level agreements' they may be subject to tight, even intrusive, monitoring and regulation. They may also experience the knock-on effects of performance evaluation schemes imposed on the governmental sector – from CCT (compulsory competitive tendering) to 'Best Value'.

Thus social policies which have precipitated voluntary sector growth have impacted on voluntary boards substantially but indirectly. In addition, board members have been affected by the changing needs and demands of other key groupings within their voluntary agencies. As paid staff and service volunteers have adapted to the changed social policy environment, board members have had to take on new supporting and leadership roles. Old understandings about the sharing of responsibilities between boards and staff have had to be renegotiated (Harris, 1993) and informal relationships have had to be formalised or made more 'business-like'. New understandings about the management of service volunteers have had to be reached.

Similarly, the new social policy emphasis on consumerism and responsiveness to 'customers' has pushed boards into rethinking the way in which they are linked to their agencies' service users. As in the governmental sector, the professional model of service provision to 'clients' has given way to more participative approaches to service users. For voluntary boards this has posed new organisational challenges: ensuring that their own composition is representative, involving users in the work of the board itself and developing additional means of uncovering user needs.

Voluntary boards have also been affected by new legislative and regulatory frameworks. With the exception of the Charities Acts of 1992 and 1993 and SORP[2], the new frameworks have not been directed specifically at voluntary boards and their work. Yet in recent years the boards of voluntary agencies in the welfare field have had to get to grips with a plethora of new regulations and laws, all of which have reflected changing trends in social policy (see Chapter 5). For example, the implementation of the NHS and Community Care Act 1990, the Carers (Recognition and Services) Act 1995, the Children Act 1989, the Education Acts of 1993 and 1996, and the Disability Discrimination Act 1995 have been important milestones in the work of many voluntary agencies. In governmental welfare agencies and in the largest of the national voluntary agencies, organisational resources (including training officers and training budgets) are generally available to assist in the process of adapting to new legislation and new policy trends. But in smaller voluntary agencies, and especially in those which are not affiliated to strong national headquarters organisations, boards as well as staff and volunteers have to make necessary adaptations with little or no resources except their own pooled expertise.

In concluding this résumé of the many ways in which voluntary sector boards may feel the impact of social policy implementation and social policy change, it should be noted that boards, like paid staff and service volunteers in welfare voluntary agencies, have been affected by numerous social policy currents *in addition* to those such as welfare pluralism, marketisation and community care which have been key drivers of expansion in the voluntary sector. Especially at the local level, voluntary agencies in the 1990s have had to grapple with the implications of such diverse policies as the ending of DSS long-term care funding; the pressure for people to be discharged early from NHS hospitals to release beds; government emphasis on encouraging volunteering; the implementation of 'New Public Management;[3] and fund-raising via the National Lottery.

Voluntary board members, then, are a key element in the policy implementation process in the era of welfare pluralism and they have been exposed to numerous social policy changes and demands. How have they experienced this turbulent social policy environment? In addressing this question, this chapter draws primarily on data from a recent study of local and national voluntary boards (the Voluntary Governing Bodies or VGB study) but those data are supplemented by findings from earlier work by the author and colleagues.[4] Throughout the chapter quotations from the VGB study interviews are inserted to illustrate key points and convey the flavour of board members' experiences.[5]

Maintaining organisational integrity

In an uncertain and rapidly changing social policy environment voluntary boards have faced a number of issues surrounding the survival of their agencies and the maintenance of their organisational integrity.

One constant preoccupation of boards in recent years has been securing resources in the face of uncertain funding streams from governmental agencies. This has been especially the case for *local* voluntary agencies in which organisational survival itself can be threatened by sudden cuts in funding from public sector agencies (themselves suffering serious resource constraints) or by major changes in funding conditions such as a switch from grants to contracts. Boards have become increasingly concerned about maintaining good relationships with public bodies and the need to compete and 'jostle' for funding. Some voluntary agencies have tried to diversify their funding sources in order to shield themselves in the future but, as Gronbjerg (1993) found in her US studies, this can cause further problems for boards who have then to conform with multiple monitoring requirements.

Although national boards have generally not felt quite so concerned about the very survival of their agencies, they too have experienced pressures to compete for governmental funding and a subsequent quest within their own agencies for internal economies and new funding sources. Increasingly resources have been channelled into marketing and public relations activities in order to raise the profile of national agencies. In tandem with a growing concern about securing resources, voluntary agencies have faced increasing demands from public sector funders to demonstrate 'public accountability'. Thus boards have had to be aware of, and monitor adherence to, laws and public regulations relevant to their agency's work and status. In addition to the broad body of employment law, anti-discrimination legislation and health, safety and food regulations, boards of welfare agencies may need, for example, to be aware of charity law; company law; community care, child care and housing legislation; and EU regulations on the handling of people with disabilities.

As well as meeting these regulatory requirements, voluntary agencies have also had to meet the monitoring requirements of their funders. In general, senior members of local boards cooperate with paid staff in ensuring that funders' monitoring requirements are met. But in smaller local voluntary agencies with few paid staff it may fall to board members themselves to provide the often detailed information required:

> At the last monitoring visit, the Grants Officer [from a local government department] wanted to know how many games of dominoes members had played in the inter-borough competition, how many outings and holidays were organized, numbers of telephone calls made, numbers of callers to the office, numbers of people receiving the newsletter and number of publicity leaflets distributed.

In the larger voluntary agencies, board members may need to keep in close touch with the day-to-day work of paid staff in order to ensure that funders' accountability requirements are met. Where they are signatories of contracts, boards have become more aware of their role as monitors of their agencies' work and as the point of final accountability for both the quality of services and the proper use of resources. And they are increasingly aware of the heavy sanctions available for those boards which do not live up to expected standards of accountability (Sargant and Kirkland, 1995).

At the local level, the role of funders' representatives on boards can be problematic. Now that governmental agencies have often become 'purchasers' of services from voluntary agencies, the role of their representatives on boards can be ambiguous. Are they there to support the voluntary agency? Or are they there to monitor how 'their' money is being spent and report back if they are not satisfied about the agency's efficiency and effectiveness?

> [When the local authority representatives on the board] became Monitoring Officers it was made very clear that this was now a contractual relationship. They no longer had the time to be an adviser, a friend ... We feel much more inspected, regulated, mistrusted. We just want to be left to get on with it.

Another organisational preoccupation of boards in the new policy era has been maintaining services. Many voluntary agencies which were formerly providing services that complemented or supplemented governmental provision have moved into the mainstream of service provision for their client group. Often such services are funded by short-term contracts with no guarantee of renewal. While they were pleased to have secured contracts, many local board chairpersons interviewed for the VGB study reported that their boards were increasingly concerned about ensuring the continuity of services for vulnerable users. In line with their role as guardians of their agencies' mission and representatives of their stakeholders (Ben Ner and Van Hoomissen, 1994; Harris, 1994), board members feel an ongoing concern about the welfare of those to whom they provide services. But this can be at odds with market principles now underlying social policy which assume that services will be provided by whichever agencies (in any sector) are most 'competitive' or 'best value' at any one time.

In the face of these multiple and growing demands, especially from governmental funders, boards can find themselves struggling to maintain their freedom to identify and meet needs in their own way.

For us it's about autonomy and us laying our own priorities. It's them setting the agenda, which has brought out issues like are we an independent organization.

The composition and work of boards

In addition to threatening the organisational integrity of voluntary agencies and thereby raising major issues for boards, the changing social policy climate has had important implications for the functioning of boards as collectivities and for the work and role of individual members of boards.

The VGB study confirmed earlier suggestions (Marsden, 1996; Tumim, 1992) that potential board members can be frightened off by a social policy environment which emphasises voluntary sector accountability and legal responsibilities. However, it seems people are now disinclined to be a board member not so much because of accountability requirements and legal responsibilities, but because of the growing need for specialist expertise and skills. As was found by Russell and Scott (1997) in their study of the impacts of contracts on volunteers, VGB study findings suggested that an increasingly common source of problems over recruit-ment and retention of board members is the growing *complexity* of board responsibilities (see also Chapter 4). As voluntary agencies move into larger-scale and mainstream welfare provision so does the need increase for specialist understanding of financial sys-tems, legislation, social policy and strategic planning. At the local level particularly, board members may also need to understand the financial, accounting and monitoring implications of contracts and 'community care' policies.

Again like Russell and Scott, the VGB study found that this complexity has led some voluntary agencies to narrow the range of people they consider suitable for board membership; increas-ingly they look for people with specialist skills – especially 'business' skills – for whom there is much competition. Ironically, this response to the complex social policy environment may in fact militate against the achievement of another social policy goal – involving users in service planning and provision (see Chapter 14). As professionalisation increases within voluntary agencies, it may become harder to also increase user involvement. Special efforts have to be made to recruit user members and non-pro-fessionals on to boards and then help them to get to grips with the intricacies of the work and responsibilities. And despite these efforts, boards which comprise both user representatives and people who are welfare professionals may become polarised between those whose prime concern is meeting specialist needs and those who are knowledgeable about the 'contract culture' and who want to push their voluntary agency towards embracing it.

Increasing complexity of work and responsibilities and rising demands from governmental funders can have the effect of in-tensifying calls on the volunteer time of individual board members, particularly the more senior ones. Although paid staff may take over some of the more onerous accountability-related tasks as voluntary agencies grow, this can be counterbalanced by the increasing amounts of time needed for board members to develop strategies; to negotiate contracts; to comprehend complex funding arrangements; to liaise with other agencies; to manage staff; to prepare funding applications; and to lobby funders. The need for board members to give more of their voluntary time can be a special problem because of the personal circumstances of many of those who volunteer for board service:

> The squeeze on resources has directly affected me as a parent of a child with special needs, and has meant that I feel less able to give the time and energy needed [as chairperson of a national board] because I am always battling for my own child.

In addition to the increasing demands on personal time, members of boards often experience high levels of anxiety because of the rapid growth of their agencies, insecure funding and onerous accountability demands. Some board members may try not to think about their responsibilities: 'we would be scared out of our lives if we really thought about it'. Others may feel over-whelmed. Chairpersons in the VGB study talked about being 'increasingly nervous' about the many responsibilities they faced. Several mentioned the less trusting and more punitive climate that had developed as social policy had changed and which could impact on them as board members ultimately accountable for their agencies' work.

In these circumstances, some board members are asking themselves why, as volunteers, they should be subject to so many expectations and regulations – many of which are both time-consuming and anxiety-provoking. In many cases, they feel that their own efforts are not matched by the governmental agencies which are funding and regulating them:

> People are asking why we have to do this when we are an independent organization... Why are we giving our time for nothing if we're not being allowed to make decisions?

Irrespective of how much satisfaction they got from performing their role, most of the chairpersons interviewed for the VGB study were very concerned about the broader implications of changing social policies, not just for themselves, their boards and their agencies, but for the voluntary sector generally and for the specialist need groups it has traditionally served. Of par-ticular concern was the way in which voluntary sector agencies were being pushed into becoming mainstream service-providers, raising major issues about the role of government in welfare and its relationship with the voluntary sector.

[We have to] come to a decision about the role of the organization; is it to be a statutory body, a voluntary body, to do preventative work or only work in acute cases?

Charities like ourselves have long ceased to be charities in the true sense of the word; just subsidiaries of the state, that's what we are.

Discussion and conclusions

In addressing the question 'how have UK voluntary boards experienced recent changes in social policy?', this chapter raises a number of implications for those who make and implement social policy.

First, it seems that social policies can impact differently on the national and local levels of the voluntary sector. It is largely the national voluntary agencies and the national levels of multi-layered agencies which have a high media profile and whose officers regularly interact with government ministers and senior civil servants. Thus it might be tempting for social policy-makers to assume that the views and experiences of national agencies reflect those of the voluntary sector as a whole. However, the VGB study suggested that their perspectives may not reflect experience at the 'cutting edge' of welfare policy implementation. For in the UK it is largely at the *local* level that welfare policies are implemented. Thus policy-makers need to pay more attention to how their policies impact on *local* voluntary agencies and how they are perceived by the board members and staff whose commitment is ultimately a crucial factor in successful policy implementation in the welfare field.

Second, the findings reported in this chapter suggest that it is not so much policy change in itself which is problematic for voluntary boards. Rather, changing social policy is experienced as problematic to the extent that it is seen as threatening the essentially voluntary and independent nature of the role of the board and the role of the third sector in welfare provision. Board members accept that they have a part to play in the implementation of social policy but they do not expect this to be at the expense of the traditional role of the voluntary sector in identifying social need and deciding how best to meet that need (Commission on the Future of the Voluntary Sector, 1996).

Social policy-makers need to appreciate the exchange which is implicit in the willingness of people to serve on voluntary boards. They are prepared to give their time and expertise to, in effect, smooth the process of policy implementation; they do this by 'interpreting' new policies to staff, working out the organisational implications for their voluntary agencies and generally sharing with staff the job of responding to a turbulent environment. However, they do expect to enjoy some power and/or prestige in exchange.

The implementation of new social policies may be threatening this delicate balance, especially at the local level. Competition for resources, monitoring and accountability demands, complying with legislation and regulations – all of these place heavy burdens on local voluntary boards. Increasingly boards feel that they need people with specialist skills in areas such as financial management, advocacy and fund-raising. For some members of local boards, the pressures have become so heavy and the counterbalancing rewards so few that they are demoralised. Boards are having problems in recruiting new members as the burdens associated with board membership at the local level become more widely known. Whereas board members at the national level may feel that there are compensations in the form of honour and excitement, local board members generally appear resentful and anxious, hanging on only because of a lingering commitment to the client group served by their agencies.

Those charged with implementing social policy need to take note of the fact that overzealous direction, control or monitoring of voluntary boards may have the perverse effect of *discouraging* the impulse to active citizenship – on which the very survival of the voluntary sector depends. Successful implementation of social policy in the age of welfare pluralism is unlikely to be associated with 'top-down' approaches (Sabatier, 1993). It is more likely to be associated with an approach which accepts the essentially 'political' and contingent nature of the policy implementation process (Ham and Hill, 1984) and the need to negotiate and compromise with, rather than to instruct and control, key actors in the non-governmental sectors.

There are indications that the New Labour government is

moving closer towards an understanding of voluntary agencies as equal partners in the drive to tackle social exclusion and other social problems (Filkin *et al.*, 1999; Home Office, 1998). This vision of partnership needs now to move beyond a generalised respect for the third sector and towards a deeper understanding of the key organisational elements which make up voluntary agencies, including not only service volunteers, paid staff and users, but also volunteer boards.

The boards of voluntary agencies have mostly escaped the spotlight of social policy-makers up to now. Yet they are a crucial link in the chain of welfare policy implementation and a vital element in newly emerging forms of governance and partnership. The many ways in which social policies impact on voluntary boards – as individuals and collectivities – need to be taken into account by those who make social policy and those who ensure it is implemented.

Notes

1. This chapter uses the terms 'voluntary agencies' and 'voluntary sector' to refer broadly to non-governmental, not-for-profit organisations which provide services in the welfare field at the national and local levels.

2. The Charities Acts of 1992 and 1993 emphasised and reinforced the accountability functions of board members who are charity trustees. SORP is the Statement of Recommended Practice for Accounting by Charities which became applicable from 1996.

3. 'New Public Management' is a contentious term but is used here broadly to refer to a move away from traditional principles of 'public administration' and towards running public sector organisations using business sector principles (Ferlie *et al.*, 1996). For a fuller discussion see Chapter 2 of this book.

4. Other sources in addition to work specifically cited in the text include work by the author and colleagues on the links between public policy and the performance of local voluntary agencies in the UK (Billis and Harris, 1992) and an exploratory study of the way in which local voluntary boards were affected by the introduction of the 'contract culture' (Harris, 1997).

5. The VGB study was conducted in two phases during 1996 and 1997. Phase One examined the boards of eleven local voluntary agencies in the South-East of England. All agencies had at least one paid member of staff, they were all operating broadly in the

'welfare' field and they were all receiving substantial local governmental funding – although many also had income from other sources. Agencies were selected such that they varied with respect to size, sources of income and other key organisational variables. Phase Two of the study examined twelve national agencies; again all were in the welfare field and were varied organisationally. In both phases of the study, board chairpersons were questioned about the impact of public policies and about the changes their boards had experienced in the previous few years. This was roughly from 1992 onwards, a period which saw the implementation of many facets of welfare pluralism including an increasing number of voluntary agencies taking on provision of mainstream welfare services; changes from grants to contracts as a mechanism of government funding; rising demands for non-governmental agencies to demonstrate public accountability; the imposition of tight monitoring and regulatory procedures; and increased competition between non-governmental agencies. The interviews were semi-structured.

References

Ben Ner, A. and T. Van Hoomissen (1994) 'The governance of nonprofit organizations: law and public policy', *Nonprofit Management and Leadership*', 4(4): 393–414.

Billis, D. (1993) 'Sector blurring and nonprofit centres', *Nonprofit and Voluntary Sector Quarterly*, 22(3): 241–58.

Billis, D. and M. Harris (1992) 'Taking the strain of change: UK local voluntary agencies enter the post-Thatcher period', *Nonprofit and Voluntary Sector Quarterly*, 21(3): 211–26.

Commission on the Future of the Voluntary Sector (1996) *Meeting the Challenge of Change: Voluntary Action into the 21st Century*, ('The Deakin Commission'), NCVO Publications, London.

Dartington, T. (1995) 'Trustees, committees and boards', in J. Davis Smith, C. Rochester and R. Hedley (eds) *An Introduction to the Voluntary Sector*, Routledge, London.

Ferlie, E., L. Asburner, L. Fitzgerald and A. Pettigrew (1996) *The New Public Management in Action*, Oxford University Press, Oxford.

Filkin, G., L. Bassam, P. Corrigan, G. Stoker and J. Tizard (1999) *Starting to Modernise*, Joseph Rowntree Foundation/New Local Government Network, London.

Gronbjerg, K. (1993) *Understanding Nonprofit Funding*, Jossey Bass, San Francisco.

Ham, C. and M. Hill (1984) *The Policy Process in the Modern Capitalist State*, Wheatsheaf, Brighton.

Harris, M. (1993) 'Exploring the role of boards using total activities analysis', *Nonprofit Management and Leadership*, 3(3): 269–82.

Harris, M. (1994) 'The power of boards in service providing agencies: three models', *Administration in Social Work*, 18(2): 1–15.

Harris, M. (1996) 'Do we need governing bodies?', in D. Billis and M. Harris (eds) *Voluntary Agencies: Challenges of Organisation and Management*, Macmillan, London.

Harris, M. (1997) 'Voluntary management committees: the impact of contracting in the UK', in Perri 6 and J. Kendall (eds) *The Contract Culture in Public Services*, Arena, Aldershot.

Home Office (1998) *Compact on Relations between Government and the Voluntary and Community Sector in England*, Cm 4100, The Stationery Office, London.

Lewis, J. (1993) 'Developing the mixed economy of care: emerging issues for voluntary organisations', *Journal of Social Policy*, 22(2): 173–92.

Marsden, Z. (1996) *A Beneficial Experience: A Study of Business People on Voluntary Management Committees*, Working Paper 17, Centre for Voluntary Organisation, London School of Economics, London.

Russell, L. and D. Scott (1997) *Very Active Citizens? The Impact of Contracts on Volunteers*, Department of Social Policy and Social Work, University of Manchester, Manchester.

Sabatier, P. (1993) 'Top-down and bottom-up approaches to implementation research', in M. Hill (ed.) *The Policy Process: A Reader*, Harvester Wheatsheaf, London.

Saidel, J. and S. Harlan (1998) 'Contracting and patterns of nonprofit governance', *Nonprofit Management and Leadership*, 8(3): 243–60.

Salamon, L. and H. Anheier (1992) *In Search of the Nonprofit Sector 1: The Question of Definitions*, Working Paper 2, The Johns Hopkins Comparative Nonprofit Sector Project, Baltimore, Md.

Sargant, N. and K. Kirkland (1995) *Building on Trust: Results of a Survey of Charity Trustees*, Trustee Services Unit, National Council for Voluntary Organisations, London.

Stone, M. and M. Wood (1997) 'Governance and the small, religiously affiliated social service provider', *Nonprofit and Voluntary Sector Quarterly*, 26, S44–S61.

Tumim, W. (1992) *On Trust: Increasing the Effectiveness of Charity Trustees and Management Committees*, National Council for Voluntary Organisations/Charity Commission, London.

13

Volunteers: Making a Difference?

Justin Davis Smith

Introduction

Governments have long been interested in volunteering. From the Good Neighbour Campaign in the late 1970s through the Active Citizen and Make a Difference initiatives in the 1980s and 1990s to New Labour's 'Giving Age', successive administrations of both left and right have sent out a clarion call for people to play a more active role in their communities (Sheard, 1986, 1992; Deakin, 1995). Alongside these high-profile generic campaigns governments have also adopted more targeted approaches, seeking to involve volunteers from particular groups in society in pursuit of specific policy objectives. The precise focus of these initiatives has been determined by the specific policy concerns of the day. Sheard (1995) has argued that governments have viewed volunteering as 'a panacea for whatever society's current ills happen to be' (p. 116). Thus in the 1960s the focus of attention was on youth disaffection; in the 1980s it shifted to mass unemployment; while in the late 1990s volunteering is seen as having a key role to play in combating social exclusion.

Sheard has summarised some of the issues arising from increased government attention: first, the danger that government might seek to coopt, or take over, volunteering for its own purposes; second, the gap between rhetoric and reality, with funding consistently falling short of requirements; and third, a failure by government to recognise the links between broader social (and economic) policy and people's ability and willingness to volunteer.

This failure of governments to think through the implications of wider policy for specific initiatives has been marked in relation to volunteering. For example, throughout the 1980s and 1990s the tightening up of welfare benefit eligibility made it increasingly difficult for unemployed people to volunteer – at a time when government was specifically targeting this group for volunteering (Davis Smith, 1997). Similarly New Labour's proposals to charge volunteers for having their criminal records checked would seem to cut across the professed desire to widen the socio-economic base of volunteering (Howlett and Locke, 1999).

A further inconsistency can be seen in relation to contracting. By expanding the role of voluntary agencies, contracting could have been expected to increase the contribution made by volunteers. In practice, however, volunteers have remained marginal to many voluntary agencies and have in some instances been squeezed out by paid staff (CSV, 1993; Russell and Scott, 1997). Moreover, the contracting out of local government services has meant that support for public sector volunteering has been greatly reduced (Presland, 1993). A similar displacement phenomenon has been noted as a consequence of the New Deal, where voluntary agencies have taken on people on work placements under the voluntary sector option – sometimes at the expense of traditional volunteers (Sibley, 1999).

Despite these examples there is some evidence that New Labour has begun to address the need to 'join up' policies. The Social Exclusion Unit was set up with a specific brief to coordinate government action to combat social exclusion, and the new Active Community Unit at the Home Office has been given a similar remit to work across government to promote volunteering and community activity (Webber, 1999).

Sheard also argues that government policy has had an impact on the values of volunteering. The linking of volunteering and unemployment in the 1980s and 1990s, through such programmes as Opportunities for Volunteering and Voluntary Projects Programmes, led to a confusion between paid work and volunteering and an attempt by some 'to seek to redefine volunteering so as to accommodate the blurring of boundaries which was taking place' (Sheard, 1995, p. 22).

This chapter looks at government policy on volunteering through the lens of one initiative, the Make a Difference programme, which was established under the last Conservative administration. Of all recent initiatives on volunteering Make a Difference was the highest-profile (it had the personal backing of the Prime Minister, John Major) and, at least in principle, the most strategic, as it moved beyond the simple exhortation to volunteer to focus on the infrastructure required to underpin any such development (Russell and Scott, 1997). It thus provides an ideal example through which to examine the strengths and limitations of government ability to influence individual action and organisational policy. It also offers lessons to New Labour about how best to take forward its own volunteering initiatives. The review here of Make a Difference draws on a variety of sources: unpublished reports and working papers; press coverage and official government releases; official and independent evaluation reports; as well as a new survey of volunteer-involving organisations carried out by the author at the Institute for Volunteering Research.

The Make a Difference initiative

The Make a Difference initiative was announced by the Home Secretary, Michael Howard, during his St Stephen's Club Disraeli Lecture on the 'Conservatives and Community' on 28 February 1994, and formally launched the following day. It was heralded by the government in its publicity leaflet as 'an integrated approach to increasing individual involvement in the community', its main aims being to 'promote the value of community involvement'; to 'make it easier for people to volunteer'; and to 'involve volunteers in a wider variety of activities which benefit both themselves and their communities' (Home Office, 1994).

Amongst a plethora of plans, 'the government announced the setting up of a new telephone helpline to publicise volunteering opportunities and a new independent working group, the Make a Difference Team, to develop a volunteering strategy for the UK. Further initiatives were announced in 1995. These included plans to provide a volunteering opportunity for all young people aged 15–25; the funding of 70 new local volunteer development agencies (LVDAs); a media campaign to promote volunteering; and the setting up of a new England-wide body, the Volunteering Partnership, to advise government on volunteering issues.

Although the initiative was on the whole warmly welcomed, some reservations were expressed. The Director of Volunteer Development Scotland, herself a member of the Make a Difference Team, argued for a note of realism to be injected into the debate. 'Volunteering', she said, 'is not a quick fix for social and organizational ills, nor should it be seen mainly as a tool, either in the management of the unemployed, or in the delivery of public services' (Burns, 1995, p. 2). There was a suggestion that some volunteer coordinators had been angered 'by the negative image of non-supportive and ineffective organizers ascribed to them in the Report' (Wardell *et al.*, 1997, p. 31).

The most trenchant opposition was expressed in *The Voice*, Britain's leading black newspaper, where it was claimed that it is 'those people with the lowest stake in society that are being asked to give up even more'. 'The government', the author continued, 'has the gall to pontificate about creating a neighbourly society by suggesting that we who have so little to give in the first place should now do more.' It was concluded that 'to suggest that voluntary activity is the answer is ludicrous – a case of fiddling while Rome burns . . . and the government abdicating all responsibility' (Azeez, 1995, p. 14).

Evaluating make a difference

What impact did the Make a Difference programme have? Did it encourage more people to volunteer? Did it strengthen the volunteering infrastructure? Did it indeed *make a difference*? On the surface the results are disappointing. When the 1997 National Survey of Volunteering was published at the beginning of 1998 it showed that overall levels of volunteering had actually gone down over the period covered by Make a Difference, with a particularly steep fall in participation by young people, one of the programme's key target groups (Davis Smith, 1998). But these statistics, while disappointing, do not in themselves prove that the programme was a failure. It is possible that without Make a Difference the decline might have been even greater. Moreover, it could be reasonably argued that much of Make a Difference was geared to the long-term improvement of the infrastructure of volunteering and that results therefore would take some time to show through. Amongst the range of initiatives and projects launched under the programme three stand out as worthy of closer scrutiny: the national volunteer helpline; the media campaign and the programme of support for LVDAs (local volunteer development agencies – discussed further below).

Volunteering helpline

In February 1996 Roger Tarling, Chief Research Officer within the Research and Statistics Directorate at the Home Office, reported on a review of the operation of the national volunteering helpline, some 11 months after its establishment (Tarling, 1996). The original estimate had been for 12,000 calls per year. The annual running costs were approximately £150,000 per year. Tarling concluded that after some initial 'teething problems' the service was now 'operating successfully' (p. 6). The aim of the service was to put people in touch not with actual volunteering opportunities but with local intermediary agencies such as volunteer bureaux who could direct them to appropriate opportunities in their area. An initial problem was insufficient and inaccurate data. Tarling reported that to begin with 'callers were sometimes given the wrong information or no relevant information' (p. 6). But by the time of the review it was Tarling's belief that these problems had been largely overcome. A database with some 1,500 entries had been developed 'and appeared to be working satisfactorily' (p. 7).

In terms of overall numbers the helpline had met and indeed exceeded targets, with over 15,000 calls recorded in the first ten months of operation, although 4,500 of these were reported to be calls left on the answerphone or 'lost calls', and a further 3,000 'non-interactive' calls where the caller was 'silent and rang off', got the wrong number or 'had misunderstood the kind of information available'. Actual 'interactive calls' during this period numbered less than 7,000, somewhat down on initial estimates of 12,000 a year.

Information from the helpline operator Network Scotland's own routine analysis suggested that the overwhelming majority of callers were satisfied with the service they received, with two-thirds saying they had contacted the referral agency and, of these, 40 per cent saying they had started volunteering. The feedback from the referral agencies was less encouraging, with one in six saying that the callers to the helpline had been given the wrong information about the organisation.

Tarling's conclusion was that the helpline, at £13 per call, was probably not the most cost-effective way of helping people find out about volunteering. Most people in fact got involved locally through word of mouth or in response to a perceived local need and a better option was felt to be 'developing and supporting the local infrastructure to promote volunteering' (p. 17). The helpline reduced its hours to cut costs and closed in September 1997.

Media campaign

In March 1996 a pilot campaign to promote volunteering was launched in the Central television area to run for six weeks. The market research company BMRB International was con-tracted to evaluate its effectiveness. Two waves of research were carried out: the first in advance of the campaign and the second immediately following it. The results were not encouraging. The evaluation (BMRB, 1996) found 'no change in overall awareness of advertising for voluntary work between the pre and post waves' (p. 3), and only 3 per cent spontaneous recall of the Make a Difference advertising, although this rose to 14 per cent after prompting by the researchers. There was no suggestion from the research that the advertising had led people to think more about volunteering. Indeed the report concluded that the 'propensity to volunteer in the future was lower at the second wave' (p. 3), although this was explained not as a negative reaction to the advertisements (indeed those that had remembered seeing them actually quite liked them) but as a result of seasonal variations.

The conclusion drawn was that given 'the diverse nature of volunteering and the heterogeneity of the population' a 'national advertising campaign with a broad focus might not be the most appropriate means of encouraging voluntary activity, either via a direct response or by influencing attitudes'. 'At the very least', the report suggested, 'a national campaign is likely to need a strong co-ordination with local activity' (p. 7).

Local volunteer development agencies

The evaluations of both the helpline and the media campaign had pointed to the weakness of the volunteering infrastructure at local level. The programme of funding for the development of new LVDAs was a deliberate attempt to put this right.

In 1997 the Community Development Foundation produced a review for the National Association of Volunteer Bureaux of the LVDAs set up under Make a Difference, based on telephone interviews with 12 of them (CDF, 1997). An initial cohort of 17 LVDAs had been established in 1995, followed by two further cohorts of 21 and 22 in the following two years. The first round had focused mainly on rural areas; the second round mainly on metropolitan areas; and round three on mixed areas. Funding varied between £85,000 and £120,000 per agency over two years.

The evaluation reported that 'LVDA staff generally felt that the agencies had had a considerable beneficial impact on volunteering in their area, and this was borne out by the figures collected' (p. 3). Some agencies had started from scratch and built up to a large throughput. Islington Volunteer Centre, for example, interviewed 970 potential volunteers in the first year. Some agencies exceeded targets but most did not and felt they were unrealistic:

> Agencies made clear that many enquiries failed to lead to a placement, and that follow-up of contacts was not always successful but there was usually a gradually rising rate of success. In addition to specific placements, an increasing number of people were made aware of the benefits of volunteering. (p. 4)

The report found that projects successfully targeted unemployed people, although 'the rate of participation from [other] disadvantaged populations and minority ethnic groups was low' (p. 4). The LVDAs felt they had played an important role in improving networks. 'We have drawn local organisations together, which was not happening before', commented one (p. 5). Another said:

> Networking is a vital feature which has been lacking here. People have often not known what else is available in their area and

who is doing what. Now they are beginning to contact each other more and to see opportunities for collaboration. (p. 5)

Despite the overall favourable review, difficulties were noted. For some new projects the start-up time could be up to six months, a quarter of the overall project period. And tensions could arise between the new project and the host organisation. There was also some criticism of the application process as 'having encouraged bidding organizations to make unrealistic promises' (p. 6). Funding was seen as the key issue for the future. 'Agencies felt that a period of three to five years' tapered funding would have been fair in order to give the projects more credibility and more chance to attract other funders' (p. 8). Many options for funding had been explored, including local authorities and the National Lottery. But the report found that 'whilst most agencies were willing to try all avenues to supplement a core grant, there was a feeling that survival was only possible through a measure of central government support' (p. 9).

LVDAs had done some good work, but the future was uncertain. The report concluded that there 'needs to be a long-term government commitment to funding local volunteering infrastructure' (p. 13). There was a very real danger of short-termism 'which raises and then confounds expectations and reduces agency credibility' (p. 13).

The view from the field

How did volunteer-involving organisations themselves rate the programme? In 1998 the Institute for Volunteering Research undertook a postal questionnaire survey of some 1,200 volunteer-involving organisations to look at a range of volunteering-related issues, such as methods of recruitment, training and support, and also perceptions of the value of Make a Difference. The survey provides a useful source of information on the organisational impact of the programme.

The sample for the survey was drawn primarily from the customer database of the National Centre for Volunteering, topped up by the leading 200 charities (in terms of income) taken from the Charities Aid Foundation *1997 Dimensions* publication. The following analysis is based on 400 returns of which 85 per cent were from voluntary organisations, 14 per cent from statutory bodies and 1 per cent from private companies. In terms of organisational structure, 17 per cent were national organisations, 13 per cent local branches of national or regional groups, 57 per cent local independent organisations, and 13 per cent 'other'. As for area of interest, 15 per cent were volunteer placement agencies such as volunteer bureaux, 13 per cent were involved primarily in giving advice and information, 10 per cent in community development activities, and between 6 per cent and 8 per cent in the fields of health, befriending, people with disabilities, young people and older people.

Knowledge of and involvement in Make a Difference

Asked whether they had ever heard of the Make a Difference programme, 78 per cent said yes, 21 per cent no. Not surprisingly, perhaps, voluntary organisations were the most likely to have heard of the programme (79 per cent), with slightly lower figures recorded for statutory bodies (75 per cent) and private companies (60 per cent). However, such figures are misleading and do not reflect the true *recognition* levels within the statutory and private sectors (nor indeed within the voluntary sector) as a whole. The sample was drawn largely from the National Centre for Volunteering's database and was therefore biased towards those who could be expected to have an interest in volunteering matters. Local independent organisations (81 per cent) were slightly more likely than national organisations (76 per cent) to have heard of the programme, with local branches of national or regional groups the least well informed (62 per cent). Not surprisingly volunteer placement agencies (87 per cent) were the most likely group to have heard of Make a Difference.

Of those that had heard of the programme 41 per cent said they had made use of it. Many had received funding through the various Challenge or LVDA schemes. Others pointed to less specific usage, particularly the use of the programme in helping to raise awareness of volunteering and in using 'the guidelines to formulate our own policy'. Again, voluntary organisations were more likely than statutory or private agencies to have made use of the programme, and local independent voluntary agencies were more likely to have done so than branches or national head-quarters. The major difference was in fields of interest, with over 71 per cent of volunteer placement agencies saying they had used the programme, compared with 43 per cent of those involved in advice and information, 34 per cent in befriending, and 28 per cent in work with young or older people.

The value of the programme?

Those organisations which had heard of the programme were asked what they felt about it 'as a whole'. For those who had used it, there was much favourable comment, ranging from 'brilliant' to 'a positive move forward'. There was also recognition that it was 'good to have top down endorsement of volunteering'. But there was also much disquiet, which tended to focus on two issues: lack of funding and poor organisation. Organisations bemoaned the lack of money overall for the project and also the lack of thought given to continuation funding, with common complaints along the lines of 'inadequate in establishing long term initiatives' and 'level and length of funding makes sustained change difficult'. One organisation felt that 'One year projects probably cause more problems than they alleviate'. There was also a feeling that things could have been better organised, with some criticism levelled at 'Home Office administration'.

Opinion was equally divided among those that had heard of the programme but not taken part in it. For some it was 'a good idea', 'encouraging and thought provoking', and 'good to see government appearing to take an interest in volunteering'. While for others it was 'confusing', 'difficult to make use of', 'low profile', 'remote', and 'too short-sighted'. One organisation pointed to the reluctance 'by some to be involved in a government scheme', and another dismissed it as 'political posturing'.

Organisational impact

Organisations which made use of the programme were asked to give details of the impact on their organisation. 'For some the impact was 'little', 'minimal', 'not much', or 'hard to assess'. For others it was 'very significantly positive', 'vital', and 'massive'.

Some organisations owed their very existence to Make a Difference, or had expanded their operations considerably with programme funds. One organisation said it had been 'able to take on new workers and offer more support to volunteers', while another said that it had provided 'a real boost to growth and development'. Others said that Make a Difference had 'allowed us to update and professionalise', to 'cooperate with other organizations', 'to expand procedures and raise volunteers' profile', and 'to tighten up policies'. For one the 'impact was likely to be long-term – a steady trickle', and another commented that there had been 'none so far', but expressed hopes 'it will make a difference soon'.

Lessons for government and policy

In the light of their experience of Make a Difference, organisations were asked what they felt the New Labour government could do to 'promote volunteering most effectively'. The responses provide an indication of what governments can and cannot do in this area.

A number of organisations suggested that government should do nothing. Their comments included 'Leave it alone', 'Support others to do it', and 'Do not politicize'. Of those who saw a more positive role for government several strands can be identified, including: support for the local infrastructure; general financial support; removing obstacles (such as those built into the social security benefits system); enhancing national awareness (through advertising campaigns); linking volunteering to the school syllabus; and, generally, promoting a more positive image of volunteering. There was some scepticism about creating 'another development programme', and a plea to use 'established links' and to 'support existing organisations in a sustained and committed fashion'.

A number of organisations felt more attention should be paid to making volunteering attractive to young people – 'Make it more fun, trendy, show gains', was the view of one respondent – while another felt that 'more work in schools' might help to redress the 'skewed perception of voluntary work and young people'. There was some support for a renaming or 're-branding' of volunteering. 'Improve its street cred', was the advice of one, with another advocating 'something more attractive', and 'asking young people what they'd like'.

A key element of any government strategy, it was felt, should be to place more emphasis on the benefits to the volunteer. 'Show what people gain, dispel cheap labour myth', suggested one respondent, with another saying it was vital to 'attach value to it; through awards; qualifications and counting in the labour market'. There was a call for greater clarity from government, which needed to 'understand the concept of volunteering' and 'not to confuse the issue with New Deal'. But, perhaps not surprisingly, the greatest demand was 'to put more money into it' and 'provide more financial input'.

Conclusion

What then was the value of Make a Difference? Did it result in a significant boost for volunteering? What are the lessons for New Labour?

We have seen that it is difficult to judge the programme a success in terms of the numbers of volunteers recruited. In fact the elements of the programme aimed at the *individual* – the advertising campaign and the telephone helpline – appear to have been the least successful. The new LVDAs did manage to recruit new volunteers (and continue to do so) and interim feedback on the Youth Volunteer Facilitators (one of the last elements of the programme) points to positive results. But overall Make a Difference failed if the criterion for success is seen as an increase in the number of volunteers, at least in the short term.

On another level the achievements look more substantial. One of the key aims of the programme was to develop the infrastructure of volunteering, and the funding of a network of new (and expanded) LVDAs can be seen to have made a significant contribution in this area, although much criticism has been levelled at the 'short-termism' of the policy and the failure to give sufficient attention to the crucial issue of continuation funding.

A more fundamental criticism can perhaps be levelled at the strategic focus within the programme on local placement agencies. While LVDAs clearly have an important role to play in local networking and development, a question mark hangs over their importance in relation to volunteer recruitment. The 1997 National Survey of Volunteering, like the two surveys before it in 1981 and 1991, suggests that volunteer bureaux have only a limited role to play in the recruitment of volunteers, with only 2 per cent of volunteers in 1997 saying they had been introduced through a bureau (Davis Smith, 1998). Make a Difference was very much a scheme aimed at, and taken up by, the specialist volunteer intermediary agencies. This was both a strength and a weakness.

The programme also seems to have made an impact on organisational policy and practice, with respondents to the Institute for Volunteering Research's survey referring to expansion and growth and the development of more professional volunteer practices. It also seems to have had some success in raising the profile of volunteering, at least in the opinion of the volunteer-involving agencies, although whether this permeated through to the public at large is questionable.

The key weakness of Make a Difference was the lack of a regional or local strategy. The LVDA grants programme provided for the development of local volunteering infrastructure bodies, but there was no attempt to replicate the UK Volunteering Strategy at a regional or local level and indeed very little attempt to involve local government in the programme at all. And yet as the 1997 National Survey of Volunteering found, the vast majority of volunteering takes place at a local level in response to local need and as a consequence of a direct one-to-one appeal for assistance. What was clearly missing from Make a Difference was a mechanism for translating national policies at the local level to take into account the reality of how people find out about, and get into, volunteering and to better reflect the regional and local variations in volunteering structures and practices. Any New Labour successor to Make a Difference needs to take this lesson to heart.

Make a Difference was a valiant attempt by government to move beyond the rhetoric of volunteering, to invest in the infrastructure that would underpin its development. It was not a complete success and its failures were due to a combination of insufficient resourcing, lack of strategic thinking, and an inability to translate high strategy into workable solutions on the ground. But there were successes and the foundations were laid on which New Labour, with its Millennium Volunteers scheme and 'Giving Age' initiative, could build in the future.

References

Azeez, W. (1995) 'When there is no more to give', *The Voice*, 19 June 1995, p. 14.

BMRB International (1996) *Evaluation of the Pilot Campaign for Volunteers*, BMRB, London.

Burns, L. (1995) 'No cheap alternative', *Third Force News*, Scottish Council for Voluntary Organisations, June 1995.

Community Development Foundation (CDF) (1997) 'Review of local volunteer agencies', mimeo, National Association of Volunteer Bureaux, Sheffield.

Community Service Volunteers (CSV) (1993) *Volunteers: A Forgotten Resource?*, CSV, London.

Davis Smith, J. (1997) 'Volunteering', in Charities Aid Foundation, *The Non-Profit Sector in the UK*, CAF, West Malling.

Davis Smith, J. (1998) *The 1997 National Survey of Volunteering*, Institute for Volunteering Research, London.

Deakin, N. (1995) 'The perils of partnership: the voluntary sector and the state, 1945–1992', in J. Davis Smith, C. Rochester, and R. Hedley (eds) *An Introduction to the Voluntary Sector*, Routledge, London.

Home Office (1994) *Make a Difference*, Home Office, London.

Howlett, S. and M. Locke (1999) 'Volunteering for Blair: the Third Way', *Voluntary Action*, 1(2): 67–76.

Presland, T. (1993) *Resourcing of Volunteering by Social Services Departments in England*, The Volunteer Centre UK, Berkhamsted.

Russell, L. and D. Scott (1997) *Very Active Citizens? The Impact of Contracts on Volunteers*, University of Manchester, Manchester.

Sheard, J. (1986) *The Politics of Volunteering*, Advance, London.

Sheard, J. (1992) 'Volunteering and society 1960 to 1990', in R. Hedley and J. Davis Smith (eds) *Volunteering and Society: Principles and Practice*, Bedford Square Press, London.

Sheard, J. (1995), 'From Lady Bountiful to active citizen: volunteering and the voluntary sector', in J. Davis Smith, C. Rochester and R. Hedley (eds) *An Introduction to The Voluntary Sector*, Routledge, London.

Sibley, M. (1999) 'Issues in volunteer management: a review', unpublished paper, Home Office, London.

Tarling, R. (1996) *National Volunteering Helpline; A Review*, mimeo, Home Office, London.

Wardell, F. *et al.* (1997) 'Volunteers: making a difference?', *Practice*, 9(2): 20–34.

Webber, H. (1999) 'Building blocks for a new unit', *Third Sector*, 4 February, p. 4.

14

Users: At the Centre or on the Sidelines?

Michael Locke, Paul Robson and Steven Howlett

Introduction

Until the election of Margaret Thatcher's Conservative government in 1979, the idea of 'user involvement' in voluntary organisations was largely rooted in notions of democratic participation. The new government shifted the focus to ideas of consumer preference and demands (Deakin, 1996), fuelled by New Right notions of dismantling the state and enhancing individual freedom.

This produced a 'quasi-market' in community care and other welfare services (Le Grand and Bartlett, 1993), applying market mechanisms and business methods and reducing the role of local government. Following the Griffiths Report (1988), the government separated the roles of 'purchaser' and 'provider' in community care and required local and health authorities to subcontract a large proportion of these services to the 'independent sector', which comprised both private for-profit and voluntary organisations. The product of these measures has been widely characterised as the 'contract culture' (this is discussed more fully in Chapters 4 and 8).

Although the hand of the market was principally exercised through this purchaser–provider relationship, users were a necessary element in the quasi-market. The implementation of the 1989 Children Act and the 1990 National Health Service and Community Care Act required local and health authorities to consult with voluntary organisations and users in planning and decision-making, promoting the user as consumer or customer.

On the whole, community care was received positively by social services department staff as promising a more user-centred practice (Lewis and Glennerster 1996). Although debates about the merits and processes of user involvement were not new, notions of advocacy and empowerment redefined relationships between professionals and users (Monach and Spriggs, 1994). For voluntary organisations, these policies offered the opportunity to engage with the public sector to provide services as part of the mixed economy of welfare (Taylor, Langan and Hoggett, 1995). In the process they were able to increase the scale of their operations and carry through their missions with a greater security of certain funding.

At the same time, users were expressing their frustration with the services they were receiving. They formed pressure groups and associations to make services more responsive to their requirements and to change the basis of welfare provision from paternalistic and philanthropic to democratic, arguing for their right to be regarded as citizens rather than customers (Coote, 1992). The target for this pressure was predominantly statutory organisations, but voluntary organisations came under increased scrutiny (Drake and Owens, 1992). The legitimacy of traditional charities in relation to disabled people was questioned by the disability movement (Campbell and Oliver, 1996; Oliver, 1996). Self-help groups reflected dissatisfaction with official provision (Deakin, 1996).

The combination of these forces meant that a commitment to increasing the involvement of users in welfare organisations was widespread by the mid-1990s (Lindow and Morris, 1995; Morris, 1994; Taylor, 1996). As we ourselves identified, there was a 'tide of change' running in the direction of greater user involvement (Robson, Locke and Dawson, 1997, p. 1).

User involvement

The New Labour government of 1997 did not pull the provision of services back into the public sector, as older Labour governments would have been expected to do, but continued the purchasing of services from voluntary organisations and other independent agencies. However, the new government's view of voluntary organisations was expected to provide a favourable environment for them. For a short phase of policy development before the General Election, the concept of stakeholders, one group of whom would be users, promised to be New Labour's 'big idea' (Hargreaves, 1998; Michael, 1998). Tony Blair's keynote speech to the National Council for Voluntary Organisations (NCVO) conference in January 1999 (Howlett and Locke, 1999) affirmed his intention to encourage voluntary activity, though he praised 'do-gooding' without appearing to recognise that many voluntary organisations have enabled people to help themselves.

The new government also sought a partnership between public and voluntary sectors through the national compact between government and the voluntary sector (Home Office, 1998). The compact set out mutual undertakings, including these by the voluntary and community sector: 'To maintain high standards of governance and conduct and meet reporting and accountability obligations to funders and users', and 'To involve users, wherever possible, in the development and management of activities and services' (p. 8). Less formally, the quest for the 'Third Way' indicated that voluntary organisations would be valued for promoting people's inclusion in civil society (Howlett and Locke, 1999).

Beneath the the continuing 'quasi-market' in welfare provision, it was possible to distinguish some shift in ideologies. New Labour theorists adapted concepts of informed individual choice: in a reflexive and uncertain world individuals would take informed decisions and not have them made for them by experts (Driver and Martell, 1998). Using Le Grand's (1997) metaphors, we can say that whereas the New Right saw professionals or bureaucrats as self-interested 'knaves' and diminished their power over the 'pawns' (users), New Labour sought to encourage the self-interest and self-reliance of 'pawns'. Drawing on the ideas of communitarianism (Etzioni, 1993), it was possible to set the receipt of services in a framework of 'rights and responsibilities' (Driver and Martell, 1998).

The evolving interpretation of charity law established more clearly that it was possible for users to be trustees (that is, members of governing bodies) of charities. It had been widely believed that users as 'beneficiaries' were prevented by charity law from acting as trustees, although the Charity Commission had agreed on a case-by-case basis to constitutions providing for some – usually a minority – of trustees to be users. In the autumn of 1999, however, the Commission clarified its position and declared there was no bar to users being trustees; the essential issue was for trustees to avoid a conflict of interest. At the least this resolved a confusion which had inhibited some formal user involvement in governance but it could be regarded as signalling a more fundamental policy shift in views about user involvement. Thus, the tide in favour of a more central role for users in decision-making in voluntary organisations continued to flow.

Opposing pressures

However, other developments in the environment of voluntary organisations – in particular the tightening of managerial and legal accountability – were working *against* the greater involvement of users.

The processes of contracting with public sector agencies required enhanced professional managerial skills within voluntary organisations, both in bidding for contracts and in managing the delivery of services. Tighter management seemed necessary because the consequences of defaulting on a contract were more serious than defaulting on a grant. The language and techniques of managing contracts were especially undermining to the empowerment of users, while the adoption of more business-like approaches in general (not only contracting) may also have militated against the involvement of users (Taylor and Lewis, 1997). At the same time, charity law was tightened with the 1992 and 1993 Charities Acts which reinforced the duties and liabilities of trustees, and increased the powers of the Charity Commission in the supervision of charities (Harrow and Palmer, 1998).

Of as much impact as the legal changes in themselves was the enhanced awareness of the responsibilities of trustees, following the *On Trust* report from NCVO (Tumim, 1992). Efforts to improve the supervision and accountability of charities were focused on the responsibility of trustees for 'proper administration'. Against this imperative, trustees and senior managers tended to regard the value of having user representatives on the governing body as secondary. Indeed, users' experience could be held to be counter-productive to 'proper administration'.

All of these developments tended to pull in a different direction from user involvement. In some voluntary organisations users and non-expert stakeholders were marginalised (Howlett and Locke, 1997; and see also Chapter 12 in this volume). Deakin (1996, p. 127) offered a provisional conclusion that: 'users have as yet to secure much positive gain from the contract culture . . . it has some potential mostly in terms of efficiency gains providing better quality services for users-as-customers; but any benefits it might have had for users-as-citizens have not yet been realized'.

Whilst purporting to be about user involvement, the introduction of market principles tended to redefine the user as a consumer rather than as a citizen (Lewis and Glennerster, 1996). Users' choice was constrained since selection of providers was done by the staff of local authority social services departments on the basis of whether they could run contracts effectively.

As regards the voluntary organisations which became the new providers, much was expected of them. 'Ultimately, the evidence suggests that the consumer's interests and entitlement will depend on the voluntary organisations maintaining their participatory ethics and practice' (Mocroft and Thomason, 1993, p. 110). Yet many voluntary organisations were in practice less successful in involving users than local authorities appeared to assume (Kumar, 1997).

Implementing user involvement

Many voluntary agencies have sought to increase the involvement of their users in decision-making within the organisation. However, the question of what steps can be taken towards user involvement in the voluntary sector remains a puzzle. In the Centre for Institutional Studies (CIS) at the University of East London, we have undertaken action research to support charities providing community care in the development of user involvement. The project has consisted of:

• exploratory discussions with organisations and with individuals in the user movement, and a survey of senior

managers of voluntary organisations on the issues and problems (carried out in 1993 to 1995 and reported in Robson,
Locke and Dawson, 1997);
- a participatory programme of developing agendas for change
with twelve organisations and their users (undertaken in
1997 and 1998 and reported in Robson, Devenney and Locke,
forthcoming); and
- evaluating these agendas for change with four organisations,
monitoring a wider group of organisations and drawing out
general lessons.

The remainder of this chapter draws on the experience of this
action research in the UK, as well as on studies of voluntary
organisations' governance relationships (Howlett and Locke, 1997,
1998).[1]

Tackling problems

There is no shortage of prescriptive material setting out principles and models for user involvement (Barnes and Walker, 1996;
Beresford and Croft, 1993; CAG Consultants, 1996; Goss and
Miller, 1995; Lindow, 1994; Read and Wallcraft, 1992). Yet, staff,
users and trustees, as individuals and working in various groupings,
have experienced problems translating intentions into action.

Most managers in our survey thought users were more interested in a good-quality service than in management or membership
of the governing body, and we have found in organisations some
confusion as to whether user involvement was a means of gathering feedback about quality of services or an issue of people's
rights and empowerment.

The meaning of user involvement generated much argument
in some organisations we studied, revealing intellectual and practical differences between users and professional staff, even those
with a clear commitment to 'user involvement'. Users expected
more direct involvement in decision-making on a day-to-day basis,
whereas management and trustees expected to use their professional backgrounds to make what they saw as correct decisions
or to conduct 'proper administration'. The challenge from users
provoked a reevaluation of their professionalism, and they often
felt undervalued. Most managers identified operational problems

such as people's lack of know-how in committee procedures. Several thought the condition or status of their users inhibited participation in meetings (citing fatigue, stress, being too emotional, ill-health and illiteracy). However, the problems perceived in some organisations had been overcome in others (Robson, Locke and Dawson, 1997).

Principles and methods

To help organisations clarify their aims for user involvement, we applied the distinction between 'consumerist' and 'democratic' approaches (Robson, Locke and Dawson, 1997), characterising the difference between, on one hand, limited decisions about services in areas defined by the organisation, and, on the other, participation in structures of governance and decisions on strategy. We have also characterised a third approach as 'developmental', where an organisation aims to empower its users within the institutions of local governance and local health and social services, rather than within the organisation itself.

The translation of principles of user involvement into practice and the choice of appropriate methods for a particular organisation at a particular stage of development is a complex challenge requiring considerable commitment of resources at all levels of the organisation – particularly the leadership. We worked collaboratively with organisations and their users to plan agendas for change and select methods appropriate to an organisation's aims, its environment, its characteristics and its capacity for change. Through this process organisations developed individual sets of proposals. Thus, two organisations planned to develop membership schemes which would include users as members with voting rights like other members and hence access to the governing body. By contrast, user involvement in the formal hierarchy of governance was not foreseeable in another organisations: it believed 'it is more honest to say that we are not looking for [partnership with users]'. In another, the focus of developing user involvement was on advocacy and on house committees for residents. Individual managers, staff and users may have had aspirations to involve users in the overall governance and management but this was not on the organisation's agenda. Other organisations undertook a variety of activities including: involving users in monitoring service quality and in recruiting staff; identifying the need for new staff posts to further their plans; organising training for staff, trustees and users; providing support and facilitation; setting up advisory groups and placing users on project committees; and arranging exchange visits with users in other organisations.

Achieving change

The changes towards greater user involvement should not be seen simply as a response by voluntary organisations to social policy. For all the 'tide of change' and the good intentions and commitments within organisations, what actually happens is shaped in any individual voluntary agency by a range of factors.

In understanding how a particular organisation may enhance user involvement we have used Karl Popper's (1994) concept of 'situational analysis' to assist us in analysing the situation in which an organisation is located in terms of institutional and environmental factors and of the individuals and communities concerned; and hence to work alongside the organisation to solve problems and develop a workable programme of implementation. A number of factors emerged as important for individual voluntary organisations:

1. *Policy and funding environment.* Managers in our study frequently pointed to the expectations of funders as the factor that led them to consider user involvement. This was especially so in organisations providing services contracted by health and local authorities. Some managers reported contract funding had encouraged user involvement by making expectations clearer and by requiring users' inputs into planning. On the other hand pressures of time and professional expertise in contracting procedures also have acted as a deterrent.

2. *Organisational features.* The kinds of user involvement and the processes for managing change which are achievable are constrained by an organisation's purposes and values, its history and tradition. A campaigning organisation has a different propensity for involving users than one offering practical support with daily living; a long-established philanthropic

foundation differs from a group originating in self-help. Practical issues, such as pattern of service use and contact with
users (for example, confidential telephone advice versus a
residential facility), or size and geography, also shape what
is likely to be achieved.

3. *Communities.* The 'communities' or 'associations' of users in
different organisations have different implications for how
change can be undertaken. For some organisations, users
are connected into networks or can link up with self-help
associations, which provide political capacity to make the
case for change and support people's organisational capa-
bilities. For others, users are isolated or institutionalised. In
some organisations there are tensions between the involvement of parents who created the organisation and that of
their now adult offspring.

4. *Leadership.* A key factor in organisations which have increased
user involvement has been the identification of individuals
as leaders or 'champions of the change'. In some cases, there
has been a chief executive with a commitment that went
beyond the established stance of the organisation; in others,
an alliance of users and staff has pushed for change; in a
third category, middle managers have seized opportunities
to build a strategy.

5. *Long-term commitment.* The developments towards greater
involvement of users have been shaped also by aspects of
organisations' capacity, their structures and processes, and
their provision of training and support. Sometimes assisted
by external consultancy, organisations have reviewed their
policies and practices and involved users in this process. They
have examined and reformed procedures for meetings and
decision-making, and provided personal support and facilitation for users. They have made opportunities for users, staff
and trustees to meet and work together and have sustained
the involvement of staff and volunteers whilst focusing on
users. Organisations have formulated strategy and kept the
issue central to their agenda and budget. There have been
setbacks when short-term measures were implemented without
long-term strategic planning or finance. In general, organisations that have made progress have had a 'basket' of measures,
not an isolated solution. Some organisations had unrealistic

expectations of change, particularly in the enthusiasm of certain staff to become champions of user involvement where other elements in organisations were not in agreement.

Users have experienced the frustration of waiting for a meaningful voice for years. Progress has been made, though the successful introduction of user involvement in traditionally structured charities has been a long process over, perhaps, a decade or more. It was suggested to us that user involvement should be thought of as a journey, not a destination.

Different futures

The outcome of different change processes – and decisions not to change – has been different degrees of user involvement in different settings. Our work on user involvement has increased our awareness of the differences among voluntary organisations. For a voluntary organisation, its approach to user involvement makes evident its deeper values and its capacity for change as well as its stated policy intentions. The way it deals with the constraints and opportunities of its environment is very telling in terms of who 'owns' the organisations (Robson, 1996). Thus, one organisation has moved from being a traditional and, in some respects, paternalistic charity to having users as the majority of its governing body and its national and regional committees. It has become an organisation 'of' people with the condition it serves; users have a large share in 'owning' it, whereas once it belonged to a professional establishment.

Most of the voluntary organisations with which we have worked have in different measures developed partnership or power-sharing between established leaders (trustees and senior managers) and users. This can involve a protected minority of places for users in formal decision-making bodies or can involve commitment to consultative procedures that feed into formal bodies. In such cases, users may be seen as central in the organisations, though not wholly owning them. Other voluntary organisations may develop as non-profit businesses or social market enterprises, providing services based on business-like methods and focusing on wider accountabilities and customer concern (Knight, 1993).

There have also been more radical developments. Organisations have been taken over by their users, with or without the collaboration of previous leaderships (for example, Hasler, 1997). Self-help groups have been created, which may not only provide direct assistance to their members but also contract with local authorities and health trusts. Indeed, traditional charities may be threatened with losing 'market share' when health and local authorities have turned to smaller community organisations which are closer to the users.

The unresolved question that hangs over this analysis concerns the environment of voluntary organisations and how it will change. Will it encourage or discourage user involvement? Will the policy and funding environment, in particular, encourage differentiation among voluntary organisations? If it does, organisations will be able to develop in distinctive ways and be sustained in their own ecologies – thus offering a diversity of solutions to problems and of opportunities for users and public agencies purchasing services.

Note

1. We are pleased to record our gratitude to the Joseph Rowntree Foundation for funding this research and for helping us formulate our research ideas. We are grateful to the members of our Advisory Groups, and to all the people in the organisations who have taken part in our research. We are very appreciative of the support and criticism from colleagues in the Centre for Institutional Studies, University of East London, and its postgraduate programmes, and in the Institute for Volunteering Research.

The twelve organisations who collaborated on planning agendas for change (1997–98) were: Al-Hasaniya, Arthritis Care, Bath Churches Housing Association, Capability Scotland, Leonard Cheshire Foundation, NICOD, Norwood Ravenswood, National Schizophrenia Fellowship, Ormiston Children and Families Trust, Scope, Seaview Projects, and the Terrence Higgins Trust.

References

Barnes, M. and A. Walker (1996) 'Consumerism versus empowerment: a principled approach to the involvement of older service users', *Policy and Politics*, 24(4): 375–93.

Beresford, P. and S. Croft (1993) *Citizen Involvement: A Practical Guide for Change*, Macmillan, Basingstoke.

CAG Consultants (1996) *A Guide to User Feedback Methods*, London Boroughs Grants Committee, London.

Campbell, J. and M. Oliver (1996) *Disability Politics: Understanding our Past, Changing our Future*, Routledge, London.

Coote, A. (ed.) (1992) *The Welfare of Citizens: Developing New Social Rights,* Institute of Public Policy Research/Rivers Oram Press, London.

Deakin, N. (1996) 'What does contracting do to users?', in D. Billis and M. Harris (eds) *Voluntary Agencies: Challenges of Organisation and Management*, Macmillan, Basingstoke.

Drake, R. and D. Owens (1992) 'Consumer involvement and the voluntary sector in Wales: breakthrough or bandwagon', *Critical Social Policy*, 33: 76–86.

Driver, S. and L. Martell (1998) *New Labour: Politics After Thatcherism*, Polity Press, Cambridge.

Etzioni, A. (1993) *The Spirit of Community: The Reinvention of American Society*, Simon & Schuster, New York.

Goss, S. and C. Miller (1995) *From Margin to Mainstream: Developing User- and Carer-centred Community Care*, Joseph Rowntree Foundation, York.

Griffiths, R. (1988) *Community Care: Agenda for Action*, HMSO, London.

Hargreaves, I. (1998) 'This time, there is an alternative', *New Statesman*, 11 September: 30–2.

Harrow, J. and P. Palmer (1998) 'Reassessing charity trusteeship in Britain? towards Conservatism, not change', *Voluntas*, 9(2): 171–85.

Hasler, F. (1997) *In the Right Hands: Changing Control and Culture in a Disability Organisation*, VOLPROF, The City University, London.

Home Office (1998) *Compact: Getting Right Together,* Home Office, London.

Howlett, S. and M. Locke (1997) 'Governance in the voluntary sector and the reciprocal relationship in the governance of localities', proceedings of the 3rd 'Researching the Voluntary Sector' conference, National Council for Voluntary Organisations, London.

Howlett, S. and M. Locke (1998) 'Trusting in trust', proceedings of the 4th 'Researching the Voluntary Sector' conference, National Council for Voluntary Organisations, London.

Howlett, S. and M. Locke (1999) 'Volunteering for Blair: the Third Way', *Voluntary Action*, 1(2): 67–76.

Knight, B. (1993) *Voluntary Action*, Home Office, London.

Kumar, S. (1997) *Accountability Relationships between Voluntary Sector 'Providers', Local Government 'Purchasers' and Service Users in the Contracting State*, York Publishing Services, York.

Le Grand, J. (1997) 'Knights, knaves or pawns? Human behaviour and social policy', *Journal of Social Policy*, 26(2): 149–69.

Le Grand, J. and W. Bartlett (1993) *Quasi-Markets and Social Policy*, Macmillan, Basingstoke.

Lewis, J. and H. Glennerster (1996) *Implementing the New Community Care*, Open University Press, Buckingham.

Lindow V. (1994) *Self-Help Alternatives to Mental Health Services*, MIND, London.

Lindow, V. and J. Morris (1995) *Service User Involvement: Synthesis of Findings and Experience in the Field of Community Care*, York Publishing Services, York.

Michael, A. (1998) 'This way to the active community', *New Statesman*, 20 February 1998: 20–1.

Mocroft, I. and C. Thomason, (1993) 'The evolution of community care and voluntary organisations', in S. Saxon-Harrold and J. Kendall (eds) *Researching the Voluntary Sector: A National, Local and International Perspective*, Charities Aid Foundation, Tonbridge.

Monach, J. and L. Spriggs (1994) 'The consumer role', in N. Malin (ed.) *Implementing Community Care*, Open University Press, Buckingham.

Morris, J. (1994) *The Shape of Things to Come: User-Led Social Services*, National Institute for Social Work, London.

Oliver, M. (1996) 'User involvement in the voluntary sector – a view from the disability movement', in Commission on the Future of the Voluntary Sector, *Meeting the Challenge of Change: Voluntary Action into the 21st Century: Summary of Evidence and Selected Papers*, National Council for Voluntary Organisations, London.

Popper, K. (1994) *The Myth of the Framework*, Routledge, London.

Read, J. and J. Wallcraft (1992) *Guidelines for Empowering Users of Mental Health Services*, COHSE/MIND, London.

Robson, P. (1996) 'Who owns voluntary organizations?', proceedings of the 2nd 'Researching the Voluntary Sector' conference, National Council for Voluntary Organisations, London.

Robson, P. and M. Locke (1997) 'Accountability and user involvement', in P. Palmer and E. Hoe (eds) *Voluntary Matters: Management and Good Practice in the Voluntary Sector*, Directory of Social Change and The Media Trust, London.

Robson, P., M. Devenney and M. Locke (forthcoming) *Laying the Foundations: A Rough Guide to Increasing Service Participant Involvement*, Policy Press, Bristol.

Robson, P., M. Locke and J. Dawson (1997) *Consumerism or Democracy? User Involvement in the Control of Voluntary Organizations*, Policy Press, Bristol.

Taylor, M. (1996) 'The future of user involvement in the voluntary sector: a contribution to the debate', in Commission on the Future of the Voluntary Sector, *Meeting the Challenge to Change: Voluntary Action into the 21st Century*, National Council for Voluntary Organisations, London.

Taylor, M. and J. Lewis (1997) 'Contracting: what does it do to voluntary and nonprofit organizations?', in Perri 6 and J. Kendall (eds)
The Contract Culture in Public Services, Arena/Avebury, Aldershot.

Taylor, M., J. Langan and P. Hoggett (1995) *Encouraging Diversity:
Voluntary and Private Organisations in Community Care*, School for
Advanced Urban Studies, University of Bristol, Bristol.

Tumim, W. (1992) *On Trust*, National Council for Voluntary Organisations, London.

15

Voluntary Organisations in a Changing Social Policy Environment

Margaret Harris

Introduction

Chapters 1 and 2 of this book outlined the 'seismic shifts' in the social policy landscape of the UK during the last two decades of the twentieth century – including the move from welfare statism to welfare pluralism, the rise of marketisation and the favouring of business management models. What have these shifts meant for the voluntary sector inhabitants of the social policy land-scape, those who have to implement social policy?

- To what extent have they themselves changed in response to their changing environment?
- Have voluntary organisations been forced into change or have they exercised autonomy and choice?
- And have they themselves been able to play a role in the development of social policy?

The contributors to this book, individually and collectively, provide a range of viewpoints on these important questions. They examine how specific aspects of social policy – including social exclusion, contracting, regulation, regeneration and partnership – have been experienced by voluntary sector organisations. They also look at how social policies have affected particular kinds of voluntary organisations – providers of care for older people, grant-making foundations, international development NGOs and non-profit housing agencies. And the final chapters focus on the impact of social policy on key groupings within the voluntary sector – governing bodies, volunteers and users.

Taken together, these varied studies enable us to develop a perspective on the complex linkages between social policy and the voluntary sector at the close of the twentieth century – following a period of major change which rivals the establishment, in the 1940s, of the welfare state itself. This closing chapter, then, reframes the rich material provided by the individual chapter authors in order to address the three key questions outlined above about the implications of social policy change for voluntary organisations. It then moves into a reflexive discussion about the academic field of 'social policy' and how that field has, and has not, been changed itself by the changing role of voluntary organisations in social policy development and delivery. The chapter and the book close with some final reflections on the study and practice of social policy implementation in the era of government/ voluntary sector 'partnerships'.

The impact of social policy change

Deakin suggests in Chapter 2 that the changing role and nature of the state has been the key factor in the changing social policy environment for the voluntary sector in the last two decades of the twentieth century. This change has, in its turn, led to a closer relationship between governmental and third sector organisations – expressed in concepts such as 'partnership', 'compacts' and 'joined-up government', and implemented through mechanisms ranging from consultation in policy development to contracting and 'Best Value' regimes.

But it is a problematic relationship for both parties. The anxieties of governmental agencies about ensuring the accountability of their 'partners' are never far from the surface. They impact on voluntary organisations through tight and complex laws and regulations; through constant pressure on the sector to improve its 'capacity' to deliver services in ways which meet governmental needs; and through requests for consultation and involvement in planning and policy development which can stretch the human resources of smaller and local voluntary agencies to breaking point.

Although the changes in the role of the state and in social policy do not necessarily impact on voluntary sector organisations in a direct or linear fashion, the essays in this book repeatedly point to the conclusion that tighter regulation and the drive to build the capacity (or expertise) of non-governmental organisations are associated with standardisation, formalisation and professionalisation within the voluntary sector. In extreme cases these trends can be seen as 'coercive isomorphism' in which the structures, working practices and even mission preferences of the governmental sector or the business sector are imposed on to the third sector. Research reported here suggests that some voluntary agencies are in effect 'incorporated' into the public or business sectors through the combined effect of competition for funding, tight contracts and close and detailed monitoring.

From one viewpoint this is precisely what is intended – we are witnessing the successful implementation of changing social policies. We have a mixed economy of welfare with non-governmental organisations delivering services on behalf of the state and according to policies developed by politicians and government officials.

Yet this book also shows that tighter regulation and the enhancement of voluntary sector capacity can have contradictory and unanticipated consequences. Volunteers and 'ordinary citizens', who are at the centre of so many governmental expectations, can become marginalised or demoralised; the valued flexibility of voluntary agencies to respond to changing social needs can be compromised; and users' preferences can be sidelined in the drive to demonstrate adherence to the requirements of statutory sector funders. Those same third sector organisations which are held up by politicians as examples of good governance and flexible service delivery are simultaneously subject to policy pressures which erode those very qualities.

In some cases, such as the 'Make a Difference' project described by Davis Smith, it seems that governments attempt to implement broad social policies and new initiatives before giving thought to the implications of implementation, or even to the practicalities of implementation. In other cases, such as the regeneration partnerships described in the chapters by Taylor and by Osborne and Ross, there seems to be a gap between the rhetoric of politicians and their commitment in practice. The

talk is the talk of valuing the voluntary sector for its own qualities and in its own right but the walk is the walk of governmental
instrumentalism – a view of the third sector as just one instrument amongst many through which governments can attain their
social policy goals.

The closer relationship between governmental and voluntary
organisations is reflected in funding which flows from the former
to the latter in increasing amounts and within increasingly complex agreements. But continuity of government funding is often
uncertain and confined to specific projects, leaving voluntary
agencies with problems about maintaining core funding, developing long-term plans and retaining their central mission. In
chapter after chapter the metaphor about the payers of pipers
calling the tunes is salient. The tension between voluntary sector
receipt of governmental funding and maintenance of organisational autonomy is probably not resolvable but the effort to
maintain some kind of equilibrium is clearly an enduring challenge of the new 'partnerships' – at least for the voluntary sector
partners.

Although these challenges for voluntary agencies – accountability demands, tight regulation, capacity-building, funding
uncertainties – emerge clearly from the chapters in this book as
general trends, it is also clear that changes in social policy do
not impact evenly throughout the voluntary sector. The evidence
here confirms that it is the small, local voluntary agencies which
generally struggle most to respond to the turbulence of the new
policy environment (Alexander, 1999). Since social policy is largely
still implemented at the local level in the UK, these local voluntary agencies are at the front line of social policy implementation.
But they are also generally those with the least spare capacity in
terms of human and financial resources. Multiple regulations,
monitoring requirements and performance measures, which can
be absorbed with relative ease into the working practices of
medium and large voluntary agencies, can be major organisational burdens to smaller ones. The boards of local voluntary
agencies struggle to get to grips with complex contracts and regulations and their paid staff are challenged to find sufficient time
to engage in the 'networking' which is becoming a prerequisite
of successful funding applications and advocacy.

Social policy change also impacts differently on voluntary agencies according to the field in which they are working. In some fields, such as social housing, there has been a remarkable proliferation of social policy streams and regulations in recent years whereas voluntary agencies in other fields, such as grant-making, have had to cope with rather less complex environments. Again, voluntary agencies in different fields may move in and out of the social policy spotlight as government interests and priorities change. Thus those which can contribute to urban and rural 'regeneration' have attracted both governmental and academic interest in the late 1990s whereas those providing social housing or residential and community care were more to the fore in the late 1980s and early 1990s.

Choices for voluntary organisations?

So voluntary organisations are changing. But are they changing by choice? Are they making explicit and conscious decisions or are they merely 'sliding into change' (Billis, 1993b) under the combined pressures of their policy and organisational environments? And what is the cumulative impact of these changes on the voluntary sector as a whole?

The chapters in this book provide numerous examples of the dilemmas faced by voluntary organisations in an environment in which social policy has not only changed rapidly and radically, but where those very social policy changes have also included rising expectations on the voluntary sector to deliver welfare services. Many of the dilemmas involve trade-offs between responding positively to social policy trends and losing their distinctive and valued organisational features, including their independence.

Thus one dilemma for voluntary agencies is about whether to opt for organisational growth; to seek funding for new projects from governmental and National Lottery sources; to participate in European and government-sponsored programmes such as those concerned with regeneration; and consciously to 'build capacity'. The trend in business management thinking during the last two decades of the twentieth century has been to elevate organisational growth to the status of a prerequisite of survival – an idea which has impacted on the voluntary sector too. Yet for voluntary agencies, especially the smaller ones, organisational growth is likely to be associated with loss of informality, flexibility and responsiveness to individual needs. It is also likely to be associated with standardisation of services, professionalisation and replacement of volunteers by paid staff.

Another dilemma concerns the extent to which it is appropriate to negotiate, debate with or challenge the approaches of potential and actual governmental funders. Tightly drawn contracts and close regulation and monitoring can restrict the ability of voluntary organisations to develop their own responses to social needs, demoralise paid staff and volunteers, and absorb disproportionate amounts of management time. Participation in government programmes and new projects can deflect voluntary agencies from their core missions and receipt of governmental funding can inhibit voluntary agencies from expressing viewpoints different from those of their funders. Voluntary agencies can find it increasingly difficult to make choices about whose needs get priority and how those needs are met. Yet perhaps all of these constitute a price worth paying for organisational survival and growth, for increasing the number and range of welfare services provided and for the opportunity to be an insider in policy formulation?

A third dilemma concerns the simultaneous pressures on voluntary agencies to both collaborate and compete. Marketisation has meant that many voluntary agencies are implicitly or explicitly in competition with one another and with providers in other sectors, both to obtain governmental funding and to get their views and specialist niches understood by policy-makers. Yet competing goes against deeply held cooperative values of many voluntary organisations. Moreover, the pressures on voluntary agencies to compete with one another are in contradiction to other social policy pressures on voluntary agencies to collaborate – in order to provide a single voice in policy-making and in order to ensure that services are efficiently delivered (Harris *et al.*, 1999).

In general, the contributors to this book find voluntary agencies uncertain about their ability, or right, to dissent from dominant pressures to conform with governmental funding requirements and governmental perspectives on the role of voluntary agencies in social welfare provision. They may well recognise the dilemmas described here but when faced with a choice, they tend to opt for the immediate rewards of organisational continuity and growth – which are associated with conformity to governmental agendas and expectations.

The opportunities for entrepreneurial voluntary agencies to grow through closer cooperation with governmental agencies are likely to continue to increase in the immediate future. Over the last two decades of the twentieth century the voluntary sector has taken on the delivery of numerous services which statutory agencies want to shed – because they are seen as too expensive or too controversial – as well as numerous services which statutory agencies have been forced to shed such as residential and domiciliary care for elderly people. And there is every indication that the New Labour government will be prepared to transfer even more services from statutory authorities in the future, especially if, like some local authority schools, they are seen to be 'failing'. Thus the question for the sector now is how much further it will go down the path of conformity with governmental expectations.

For individual voluntary agencies the chapters by Kendall and Knapp and by Mullins and Riseborough provide a warning. From being an 'agent' of government in the delivery of welfare it is but a short step to becoming a 'governmental service provider'. From there it may be an even shorter step to being classified as a 'local public spending body' – subject to the full panoply of public accountability and probity procedures just like any other governmental agency. For those voluntary agencies sliding into change, they need to be aware of just how long and slippery the slope of change may be and how traumatic the arrival at the destination. Short-term organisational growth may be achieved at the expense of long-term survival as an independent third sector organisation.

Even if these changes are regarded as advantageous by and for individual voluntary *agencies*, the question of what they are doing to the voluntary *sector* as a whole must now be faced. In fact, this question emerges from this book as a major public and social policy issue in its own right. For this may well be a case in which the cumulative impact of the pursuit of individual voluntary *agency* advantage is to the detriment of the survival of a distinctive voluntary *sector* in welfare. If the third sector has no distinctive organisational features, no separate voice or voices, no alternative responses to social need, no different ways of doing its work, what will be the rationale for its inclusion within a mixed economy of welfare in the future? As Deakin shows, it is becoming possible to envisage a future in which the partners of choice for governmental funders will be in the private commercial sector rather than the voluntary sector.

Voluntary sector voices in social policy

Generally, then, the contributors to this book are sceptical about the ability of voluntary agencies to resist the pressure to respond in a cooperative fashion to governmental expectations – whatever the longer-term organisational cost. They also show how formidable are the obstacles to effective and active participation in social policy debate and formulation. The barriers noted here include asymmetry in the distribution of power between governmental and voluntary agencies, the breakdown of trust between them, the tendency of governmental agencies to frame major policies *before* consultation with the voluntary sector and the inclination of public sector officials to see voluntary agencies as organisational mirror images of themselves. Some types of voluntary agencies, as both Billis and Lewis show, are consistently marginalised by policy-makers. In any case, voluntary agencies often do not have the necessary financial and human resources to participate in the social policy process, even when the opportunities are available. Engaging in the politics of policy formulation requires not only time but also knowledge about the way governmental institutions work as well as sophisticated lobbying and negotiating skills.

All the same, the chapters of this book do provide positive evidence of the ability of voluntary agencies to influence their social policy environment if they are sufficiently determined and self-confident. Deakin, for example, finds a growing realisation amongst both voluntary and governmental agencies of the benefits associated with mutual respect rather than domination by one party and Rochester detects a gradual acceptance that small community organisations are different from the big agencies of either the voluntary or governmental sectors. Lewis finds overseas aid agencies influencing central government development policies in what he calls a 'reverse agenda' and Mullins and

Riseborough note a similar effect in the field of housing policy. Locke and his colleagues show that voluntary agencies can be in the forefront of demonstrating how to involve service users.

Several authors indicate some of the ways in which this kind of voluntary sector participation in social policy formulation can be achieved: for example, by responding selectively to new policy currents (Billis); by building on the promises underlying 'compacts' (Deakin); and by filling gaps in policy ideas in new areas such as regeneration (Osborne and Ross). Mullins and Riseborough show how voluntary agencies can use 'policy networks' to position themselves strategically in the policy process.

Thus a picture emerges of a voluntary sector which has the *potential* to be a more proactive partner in the social policy formulation process. There are already some role models and indications of possible routes. But there are also obstacles. Overcoming these will necessitate not only more self-confidence within the voluntary sector, but also some investment in voluntary sector infrastructure including the kinds of development agencies referred to in the Osborne and Ross chapter. Enhanced infrastructure for the sector will ensure that the diverse voices and experiences of the sector are expressed effectively – but in ways which also reflect their richness and variety. It will also facilitate voluntary sector involvement with the devolved authorities, regional agencies and European institutions which are set to become increasingly significant players in UK social policy in the twenty-first century.

Voluntary organisations and the study of social policy

As explained in Chapter 1, this book draws on the proceedings of the 20th anniversary celebration of the Centre for Voluntary Organisation at the London School of Economics – a specialist unit for the study of voluntary organisations based within the UK's oldest university Department of Social Policy (although that was not its original name). It is appropriate, therefore, to conclude with some reflections about the future of specialist voluntary sector studies and the link between those studies and the study of social policy generally. For in spite of the seismic shifts in social policy which have thrust the voluntary sector into the light and given it an expanded role in welfare provision, there are still surprisingly few social policy academics in the UK who have chosen to focus their research on voluntary organisations.

In some cases the lack of interest is ideologically based: those concerned regret the passing of the welfare state era and are reluctant to face the reality of welfare pluralism and its implications for the social policy academic field – the need to understand the working not only of the governmental sector but also of the commercial, informal and voluntary sectors (Offer, 1999). Others are intimidated by the complexity of welfare pluralism and marketisation and seek to minimise the variables they need to consider in their research by 'screening' out the various non-governmental sectors in welfare, including the voluntary sector.

Yet others are just not interested in the institutions in and through which social policy is delivered. Their lack of interest in the voluntary sector is part of a broader inclination to focus their attention on the grand questions of policy *development* and policy *outcomes* rather than on the messy practicalities of the mediating organisations through which social policy *implementation* is achieved.

There are also academics who *have* acknowledged the fact that the voluntary sector is now an important player in the social policy field but whose acknowledgement is grudging. They study the voluntary sector but instead of seeing it as a distinct player and contributor to welfare provision, they have reinvented it as just one more instrument amongst many through which governmental agencies can deliver their chosen policy goals. The 'public services' are reconceptualised as *including* voluntary organisations – at least in so far as they are in receipt of governmental funding and are delivering services which are for 'public benefit'.

Although it is rarely explicit, this too is an ideologically driven viewpoint. It assumes that *governmental* policies are always synonymous with the common good. And it sees the outcomes of social policy as far more important than the organisational means and processes through which it is delivered. Thus by implication this viewpoint marginalises means and process values such as civil association, individual dignity and worth, participation, choice, empowerment, equality of access, philanthropy, voluntarism and altruism. It plays down the tendency of even apparently benign governments to feel uncomfortable with diversity and their tendency to colonise and control 'civil society' (Williams, 1999). Ultimately, it raises the spectre of the attrition of democracy by default – as academics describe uncritically the erosion of voluntary sector boundaries, encourage partnerships and 'joined up' relationships between the governmental and voluntary sectors however unequal these turn out to be, or merely neglect to argue the case for a distinct and distinctive voluntary sector with its own voices and contributions to make to policy formulation and practice.

The chapters in this volume collectively constitute a powerful critique of both the rejectors and the grudging accepters of the importance of the voluntary sector in social policy studies. They demonstrate that delivery and implementation of social policy are now dependent on the contributions of the voluntary sector in numerous and complex ways. More important, they also suggest that successful implementation of governmental policies is most likely to be achieved by acknowledging and nurturing the distinctive features and contributions of voluntary agencies.

The empirical findings confirm earlier theoretical propositions that the historical and organisational roots of voluntary agencies are different from those of governmental agencies and for-profit businesses; that they have distinctive organisational features and that they experience changes in their policy environments in ways which are different from statutory or commercial organisations (Billis, 1993a; Harris, 1998; Lewis, 1999; Wagner, 1999). Yet there remains a marked reluctance amongst politicians and government officials to encompass this perspective in practice. In general, they continue to conceptualise the voluntary sector within bureaucratic or business sector frameworks (Milofsky, 1999). They castigate voluntary organisations for being 'amateurish', for taking too long to reach decisions, or for failing to be 'entrepreneurial'. Or they wonder why voluntary agencies cannot produce one single voice on key social policy issues.

These frustrations are reminiscent of Professor Higgins in *My Fair Lady* asking 'Why can't a woman be more like a man?' They stem from a logical and intellectual fallacy about the nature of the voluntary sector: one that sees the voluntary sector as a poor imitation of another sector, rather than as a sector with its own distinctive and intrinsically valuable features. Lohmann demonstrated the flaws in this approach some time ago when he criticised the tendency for the voluntary sector to be defined in terms of what it is not, rather than what it is:

> Classifying lettuce as a mammal produces approximately the same effect. Lettuce is a non-fur-bearing, non-milk-producing, non-child-bearing, and non-warm-blooded nonanimal. Further, as a mammal, lettuce is highly ineffective, being sedentary and not warm-blooded. All other mammals are much faster! Lettuce is also remarkably nonagile and fails to protect its young. On the whole, lettuce is a miserable excuse for a mammal! (Lohmann, 1987, p. 369)

Social policy scholars now need to move beyond this fallacious framework. They need to recognise – to use some examples from this volume – that local voluntary agencies are not amateurish versions of social services departments; that local development agencies are not necessarily intended to provide one common voice for the local voluntary sector; that volunteers do not aspire to work as paid employees do; that voluntary sector residential care provision does not need to mirror the provision of profit-making companies; and that the task of voluntary sector governance differs in fundamental ways from that of corporate governance.

Voluntary organisations and social policy implementation

The emphasis on government/voluntary sector 'partnerships' and on citizen participation in the policies of New Labour (Giddens, 1998; Straw, 1999) underlines the need for students of social policy not only to recognise the crucial role of the voluntary sector in welfare provision but also to understand its distinctive organisational features and specialist potential and limitations. As between two individuals, successful 'partnerships' between governmental and voluntary agencies are founded on mutual respect, assumptions about complementarity of contribution, and respect for distinctive qualities and difference in general – not on a constant effort by one party to change the other into a new kind of creature. The contributors to this book have each in their own way demonstrated how this can be achieved. And in doing so they are following deep and well-trod furrows in the field of social policy studies.

One such furrow is the tradition which sees policy-making and policy implementation not as two separate threads but as part of a policy *process* (Sabatier, 1999). In this tradition the study of social and public policy is conceptualised as a seamless web: the making and evaluation of policy have to be considered *alongside* the organisations, institutions and systems through which policy is implemented and welfare services are delivered (Beyer *et al.*, 1983; Schlager, 1999). This tradition also recognises that implementation is in practice an integral part of policy development (Dunsire, 1973; Fudge and Barrett, 1981).

The second (adjacent) furrow reflects elements of the 'social administration' tradition within the social policy field. Although open to criticism for its prescriptive and atheoretical tendencies (Pinker, 1993; Wilding, 1983), one of the social administration tradition's enduring legacies has been the recognition that micro analyses of face-to-face interactions and macro analyses of large-scale systems need to proceed hand in hand and are complementary (Hall *et al.*, 1978; Lewis and Glennerster, 1996; Titmuss, 1970). Interactions in a micro context affect larger social processes and macro systems influence the more confined settings of individual organisations. As social policy changes, it causes changes to occur in the organisations through which it is mediated. And these organisational changes, in their turn, can call into question the assumptions on which the original social policies were based.

Thus, the social administration tradition pays close attention to practical problems of policy implementation (Billis, 1984; Glennerster, 1988; Lewis, 1994), a point made clearly by David Donnison in his inaugural address at the London School of Economics:

We are concerned with an ill-defined but recognizable territory: the development of collective action for the advancement of social welfare. Our job is to identify and clarify problems within this territory, to throw light upon them – drawing light from any discipline that appears to be relevant – and to contribute when we can to the solution of these problems. (Donnison, 1973, p. 36)

Responding in a scholarly fashion to practical problems of policy implementation was the key guiding principle of the Centre for Voluntary Organisation at its inception and that principle is reflected twenty years later in many of the contributions to this volume.

While following these long-standing traditions in social policy scholarship – theories of policy process and attention to practical problems of implementation – the contributors to this book have also risen to the challenge of responding to the changing realities of social policy at the beginning of the twenty-first century. They recognise the need to move beyond analyses of governmental activities and governmental organisations; to return in fact to the earliest days of social policy scholarship which assumed the importance of non-state welfare provision for individuals in need. And in carrying out their analyses they are prepared to move, as necessary, outside of the mainstream disciplines of sociology, political science and economics in their search for conceptual tools and better explanatory theory. The influence of management sciences and organisational behaviour concepts are particularly evident in this collection.

Thus this book is at one and the same time a reflection of long-standing traditions of academic social policy studies *and also* a pioneering contribution to the field. It should establish unequivocally the crucial role of voluntary organisations in both the formulation and implementation of social policy.

References

Alexander, J. (1999) 'The impact of devolution on nonprofits: a multiphase study of social service organizations', *Nonprofit Management and Leadership*, 10(1): 57–70.

Beyer, J.M., J.M. Stevens and H.M. Trice (1983) 'The implementing organization: exploring the black box in research in public policy', in R.H. Hall and R.E. Quinn (eds) *Organizational Theory and Public Policy*, Sage, London.

Billis, D. (1984) *Welfare Bureaucracies: Their Design and Change in Response to Social Problems*, Heinemann, London.

Billis, D. (1993a) *Organising Public and Voluntary Agencies*, Routledge, London.

Billis, D. (1993b) 'Sliding into change: the future of the voluntary sector', in *the Mixed Organisation of Welfare*, CVO Working Paper 14, London School of Economics, London.

Donnison, D. (1973) 'The development of social administration', in W.D. Birrell, P.A.R. Hillyard, A.S. Murrie and D.J.D. Roche (eds) *Social Administration: Readings in Applied Social Science*, Penguin, Middlesex.

Dunsire, A. (1973) *Administration: The Word and the Science*, Martin Robertson, London.

Fudge, C. and S. Barrett (1981) 'Reconstructing the field of analysis', in S. Barrett and C. Fudge (eds) *Policy and Action: Essays on the Implementation of Public Policy*, Methuen, London.

Giddens, A. (1998) *The Third Way*, Polity Press, Cambridge.

Glennerster, H. (1988) 'Requiem for the Social Administration Association', *Journal of Social Policy*, 17(1): 83–4.

Hall, P., H. Land, R. Parker and A. Webb (1978) *Change, Choice and Conflict in Social Policy*, Heinemann, London.

Harris, M. (1998) *Organizing God's Work: Challenges for Churches and Synagogues*, Macmillan, London.

Harris, M., J. Harris, R. Hutchison and C. Rochester (1999) 'Mergers, collaborations and alliances: drivers of change in the UK voluntary sector', paper presented to the Annual Meeting of ARNOVA (Association for Research on Nonprofit Organisations and Voluntary Action), Washington, DC.

Lewis, J. (1994) 'Voluntary organisations in new partnerships with local authorities: the anatomy of a contract', *Social Policy and Administration*, 28(3): 206–20.

Lewis, J. (1999) 'Reviewing the relationship between the voluntary sector and the state in Britain in the 1990s', *Voluntas*, 10(3): 255–70.

Lewis, J. and H. Glennerster (1996) *Implementing the New Community Care*, Open University Press, Buckingham.

Lohmann, R. (1987) 'And lettuce is nonanimal: toward a positive economics of voluntary action', *Nonprofit and Voluntary Sector Quarterly*, 18(4): 367–83.

Milofsky, C. (1999) *Smallville: Nonprofit Organizations and Community*, Department of Sociology and Anthropology, Bucknell University, Pennsylvania.

Offer, J. (1999) 'Idealist thought, social policy and the rediscovery of informal care', *British Journal of Sociology*, 50(3): 467–88.

Pinker, R. (1993) 'Social policy in the post-Titmuss era', in R. Page and J. Baldock (eds) *Social Policy Review 5*, Social Policy Association, Canterbury.

Sabatier, P. (1999) 'The need for better theories', in P. Sabatier (ed.) *Theories of the Policy Process*, Westview Press, Oxford.

Schlager, E. (1999) 'A comparison of frameworks, theories and models of the policy process', in P. Sabatier (ed.) *Theories of the Policy Process*, Westview Press, Oxford.

Straw, J. (1999) 'Citizens, corporations, parties and government: rights and responsibilities in the new democracy', *The Constitution Unit Annual Lecture*, University College, London.

Titmuss, R. (1970) *Commitment to Welfare*, George, Allen & Unwin, London.

Wagner, A. (1999) 'Reframing "social origins theory": the structural transformation of the public sphere', paper presented to the Annual Meeting of ARNOVA (Association for Research on Nonprofit Organizations and Voluntary Action), Washington, DC.

Wilding, P. (1983) 'The evolution of social administration', in P. Bean and S. McPherson (eds) *Approaches to Welfare*, Routledge & Kegan Paul, London.

Williams, F. (1999) 'Good-enough principles for welfare', *Journal of Social Policy*, 28(4): 667–88.

Index